HOW THE LEOPARD CHANGED ITS SPOTS

Evolutionary Values for an Age in Crisis

Julian Gresser

HOW THE LEOPARD CHANGED ITS SPOTS

Evolutionary Values for an Age in Crisis

Julian Gresser

Published by

Evolutionary Values Press

Early Reviews

This magisterial book made me "stop-look-go". It promotes desirable ingenuity rather than innovation. It weaves together wiser, overlapping futures. Gresser is a world expert in the "hard" humanities. The hard humanities is an attempt to redefine and focus classical wisdom to solve social problems in a complex system of 8 billion humans. Gresser applies Einstein's dictum by offering a new way to think about planetary challenges. He has changed my thinking, favorably, and often, in the half century I have known him. *Roger Malina, PhD, Professor of Art and Technology, Professor of Physics, University of Texas, Houston; Executive Director Emeritus, Leonardo*

Thank you for this valedictory address to your life, and to life itself. The 'evolutionary values' you explore and articulate so masterfully, is a kind of Dharma of its own accord. It's also—I sense—a love poem to your wise teachers of all faiths, the opportunities that have befallen and engaged you and to your beloved Angela (all part of your Sangha!). Those of us—your family heritage and friends- can only count the leopard spots, even as they continuously change. *Randall Weingarten, MD Adjunct Clinical Professor, Psychiatry and Behavioral Sciences, Stanford Medical School*

Your beautiful and fascinating book is so beautifully written, thoughtful and inspiring, and we're taking our time to digest and fully appreciate the wisdom and peacefulness which pervades the book. *Doug Wood, Founder and Director Americans for Responsible Technology*

With the world undergoing massive social, political and climate changes, Julian Gresser's book provides an invaluable guide to the personal changes in our mindsets and hearts that we need to make to meet the challenges of the 21st century. Grounded in decades of deep study and professional practice, he explores Evolutionary Values as the lodestone to creating positive paths out of the dystopias plaguing us today. Both philosophical and practical, his Big Heart Intelligence (BHI) and Connectome (BHC) methodologies provide concrete ways to create sustainable "Gaiapolis" cities and towns as open, loving and healthy grassroots communities. What is our future? It begins within each of us evolving rapidly to meet the challenges of our times. *Sheridan Tatsuno, city planner, author of Technopolis Strategy (1986) and Gaiapolis Strategy (2022)*

Dedication

For Angela, my love

Table of Contents

Handel Overture[1]

Author's Preface

I believe it is an act of kindness for a writer to alert readers in advance if something unusual is about to happen. An author must not presume that readers will embrace naturally and be equally thrilled by a subject simply because the author is. I offer here a short explanation of some challenges in writing this story of my professional life and also a framework for the reader to have better control of the tiller while navigating this book.

My purpose is to express a *cry of heart* over what is happening around us in the world, and to offer a diagnosis and a practical pathway that will help us to shift and to survive. The reader may detect a sense of urgency in the manuscript. It appears to me that our world is rapidly falling apart and yet paradoxically coming together at the same time, at accelerating speed. I believe we still have time to shape our destiny.

My principal challenge has been that I am seeking to align and balance two very different modes of interacting with ourselves and the world. The first is the Path of Heart, Wisdom, and Ethics; the second is the Path of Mind, Logic, and Practical Action. In our current global society these two modes do not dwell easily together.

Another challenge has been that my subject is alive. I always assumed that a book is a concrete "thing," a noun. But the writing of it has caused me to realize that a book can also be unfolding and emergent, and somewhat magical. Events in the "outside" web of the world seemed to appear unbidden, exactly at the moment I was writing about them.

If this book were only about discovering magic in ordinary "reality," my task would have been relatively easy. The book would be whimsical and elusive. But I am also trying to open a serious conversation with a broad group of readers who are deeply concerned about the current state of the world and the future of our planet. These readers are searching for fresh ideas, principles, innovations, and value-based practices that can lead us to a beneficial shift.

The book suggests that an ability to bring Heart, Mind, and Hand together will open a path through a web of shadows in which we now find ourselves. In the Chinese and Japanese languages this idea is embodied in the character for *"integrity,"* conceived in these cultures as our line of connection with the Tao, the natural and harmonious order of the universe. As our world today is falling deeply out of integrity, the steady cultivation of integrity, and the Evolutionary Values underlying it, offer a viable alternative to collective madness. This theme is developed in the chapters on Wisdom in Business, community empowerment, and our legal team's challenges to the Satellite Experiment.

When writing about Heart—and here I am referring to an energy field surrounding the physical heart—it is very difficult to do so in a linear or logical sequence. The Heart appears to live in a different realm of imagination, dreams, and emotions, and also of values such as vision, compassion, and beauty. The Heart is also a marvelous integrator of diverse, seemingly unrelated domains of knowledge, and contains a deep reservoir of wisdom. It is difficult to describe the Heart in ordinary prose, as the moment we seek to do this, the experience starts to wither, as if by the telling of it. Therefore, I decided early on to give the reader a direct personal experience of the Way of Heart rather than an intellectual understanding of it. There is an interesting parallel here with the recommended practice of working with Zen *koans:* If you try to "solve" a *koan* by logic, your goose is cooked. I suggest readers approach the section on "Essentials" in this same non-linear fashion—simply listen to your Heart, and then when the spirit moves you, drop into any chapter or page that seems to tug at you—by chance.

A related challenge has been that my subject is so alive that everything appears to flow in and around it. One indication of flow is the phenomenon of remarkable coincidences, synchronicities, and serendipities that have appeared as faithful familiars on my journey. Past, present, and future have all intermingled with the writing of the book. They can reveal at any moment how to flow, adapt, and even evolve. What is latent can rapidly become possible, and that even seemingly impossible things can actually happen. Each of us is a leopard, each of us, when the opening presents itself, can transform and change our spots. For this reason the book carries a message of hope.

One secret of flow is to learn how to "open" the Heart, or more specifically as I describe, the energy field around the Heart. The book offers a simple practice, "Just Click!" that activates this energy field which is Love. With a little practice, we begin to see new and unobserved connections everywhere, and not only in our own "inner" reality, but also with the "external" world. The marvel of it is when I connect my own Heart's energy field of Love to anything that happens in the moment, the moment reciprocates with the energy of Love. I invite the reader to test and to verify this proposition for yourself.

I made a decision early on to give the reader a personal experience of the above, drawing upon the beauty and wisdom of Eastern and Western classics, and in a style of writing that approaches stream of consciousness. As I proceeded, the book acquired a life and personality of its own. It seemed to have its own independent opinion on how it wanted to be written. You can imagine this is not so easy for a lawyer whose profession attempts to control everything.

In response, I coined the term "intertidal thinking" some years ago and have come to see the term is more felicitous than I imagined. The intertidal zone of the seashore is biologically rich, and its richness is enhanced by the ocean. The ocean is a metaphor for the great unconscious that is within us in our daily lives. But there are also risks in opening boundaries in this way. This is where the cultivation of Evolutionary Values becomes vital. They steady us on the journey by cultivating wisdom, gravitas, courage, and so on. Chance favors us when we set the sails and turn the wheel in this way.

A final comment on why I decided to include over fifty pages of endnotes. I thought some readers might find it entertaining at the very moment of reading a particular section to pause and enjoy Toscanini conducting Mozart's Jupiter Symphony, or to watch the martial artist George Xu demonstrating his *gongfu,* or to read Beryl Markham's remarkable commentary on silence, and so on. I hope some readers will want to explore more deeply these branches and will find the endnotes in this way useful. Many references are listed as hyperlinks on our website **JustClick.Earth,** and will be continuously updated with new materials from our online Evolutionary Conversations. And to address the conceivable concern of some readers that most of the book was fabricated in smoky imagination, I have sought to provide a solid body of scholarly references behind it.

BEGINNINGS

Prologue

We are just visitors here
To this time, this place
We are just passing through
Our purpose here is to observe, to grow, to love
Then we go home
—Aboriginal Proverb

Small time, but in that small most greatly lived.
—Shakespeare *Henry V*, Epilogue

Albert Einstein once observed "We cannot solve our problems with the same thinking we used when we created them." For our present age of accelerating and compounding crises, this book will show that not only new thinking but also new values—Evolutionary Values—are critical for our collective survival. By Evolutionary Values I mean those values that can help us to adapt successfully during the great spiraling transition in which our planet is now engaged—toward a kinder, more peaceful, and abundant life for everyone. Evolutionary Values build upon ancient values embraced by virtually all societies throughout time, but here are refined and transformed to address the whirlwind of technological changes in the early twenty-first century.

This book views the concept of Evolutionary Values not solely as static, but rather as a fluid process of inquiry. It offers a simple way for the reader to explore and directly to experience for him or herself the possibility of an expanded reality, which itself expresses and embodies these Evolutionary Values. And the process is emergent, empirical, replicable, and verifiable. Fundamentally, it offers a message of hope. Notwithstanding the chaos around us, we still possess—individually and collectively—the ultimate choice to survive or not. We are the makers of our own destinies.

Our planet is in the vise of centralized forces and shadowy agendas that undermine our long-cherished personal liberties, even privacy and the security of our homes, and enable them to be systematically taken from us without our even realizing it. Nature itself is being turned into a commodity before our eyes, and even the Heavens and the Oceans, which our remote ancestors gazed upon in wonder and reverence, are fast coming under the control of the world's military forces, a few commercial companies, and the inordinately wealthy and powerful people who own and run them.

When we look through a different lens and probe more deeply, every global concern or conflict today raises a question of values and choices, although the issues are rarely presented specifically—if at all—in these terms. For example: Does Russia have a right to invade Ukraine and initiate a nuclear war? What constraints, if any, must be imposed upon those who are rushing to exploit the Heavens and believe it is a free good?[2] Should corporate profits, and the interests of shareholders and investors, take priority over public and environmental health or personal privacy? What are the rights of children, the disabled, minorities, or economically disadvantaged persons in the face of a Wireless Juggernaut that is rapidly blanketing communities everywhere, without their informed consent, with radiation-emitting products? Must "military security"—however vaguely defined—always trump other concerns, under all circumstances?

What are balanced and responsible pathways for the development and deployment of frontier technologies—for example, artificial intelligence or genetic engineering, so these technologies and products best serve consumers and the rest of humanity, not mainly producers, shareholders, and investors? How can scientists, indeed science itself, maintain "independence" and "objectivity" when scientific inquiry is riddled with biases; when scientific uncertainty has historically been used as a cudgel in the service of the powerful against the most vulnerable and defenseless in our communities?[3]

Recognizing that science by its very nature is uncertain and investigative, who should bear the burden of proof of the harms inflicted by these new products and technologies, and by what principle, by which values, should the public, not the perpetrators, pay the social and environmental costs of conducting their businesses? What do we sacrifice when honesty, truthfulness, and integrity give way to cynical falsehoods, misrepresentations, and distortions which themselves have become lucrative commodities? Boiled down to their essences, these and a host of similar concerns present difficult questions of values and choices. But why does it even matter?

It matters because we will not survive much longer as a species and as a planet if we continue in this way.[4] If we had world enough and time, we might ponder these questions at leisure, as philosophers or poets do. But we may not have that luxury. In fact, we already appear to be disintegrating emotionally and physically from within as we desperately grapple unsuccessfully with battalions of everyday stresses.

In neurological terms, as a response to these stressors we are constantly in "fight or flight" overdrive, where our sympathetic nervous system is continuously being overstimulated and our parasympathetic nervous system is constantly engaged in calming us down. This widespread neurological and biologic overheating translates into biochemical stress reactions that are expressed in behavioral changes, including a reduced tolerance for uncertainty and ambiguity, a limited capacity for critical thinking, abandonment of civil discourse, decline in curiosity, social and political polarization and imbalance, helplessness, hopelessness, random violence (even against great works of art),[5] and suicide.

These maladaptive and self-destructive behaviors are further reinforced by business models, in particular involving cell phones, social media, and the Internet, that are designed around, depend upon, and directly profit from widespread public reliance on and addiction to these products and services. Thus, a negative feedback loop is generated that rewards commercial companies for promoting the most counter-adaptive behaviors to the public, while these same companies are increasingly shielded by legislatures and courts, traditionally the last protectors of civil rights and liberties.

None of this is particularly new, and yet the situation is different today because of our increasing ability to destroy the planet at will.[6] When there is no easy off-ramp, or effective means to stabilize our tightly coupled systems[7], it is very easy for a single event—a remote, seemingly innocuous, inconspicuous occurrence—to trigger a virtually unstoppable cascade of destruction. The fight or flight response, and the values this behavior reinforces, is very maladapted to the complex challenges of the twenty-first century. A downshift in values, however, need not be a neurological imperative. There are various accounts confirming that desperate circumstances actually create opportunities for altruistic action, a theme we explore in later chapters.[8]

My purpose in writing this book is to open a far-ranging conversation around these issues. I am not a physicist, biologist, social scientist, physician, political philosopher, or even any longer an academic. But after exploring these and many other fields in my seventy-nine years, I believe I can draw on two deep wells of life experience to contribute some useful insights that may be of interest to the reader. First, as an international, environmental, and public interest lawyer, advocate, professional negotiator, and government advisor I have worked for over fifty years at the soft underbelly of society, contending with the Shadow, Shadow Players, and the Shadow Game

(Chapter 2). All the public controversies I describe in this book present complex questions of values and ethical choices, while at the same time suggesting paths to wiser, more balanced solutions.

Many readers may not be familiar with these issues—such as the unfolding public and environmental catastrophe produced by the proliferation in residential communities, schools, and workplaces of products that emit dangerous levels of non-ionizing radiation (NIR);[9] or the enmeshing of the entire planet—the earth, skies, and oceans—in a wireless web, supported by low-orbiting, non-geostationary satellites communicating with earth and base stations[10] and devices submerged beneath the oceans. This is understandable. We are not meant to know the harmful effects of all of this radiation, which is in reality a global experiment without any prior careful assessment of the risks. There is currently a blackout by the mainstream media that limits public awareness and debate.[11] The media blackout is just beginning to breach.[12]

The second source is my own explorer's life journey. This book describes some of the curious adventures and some remarkable people I have encountered along the way. It includes stories and parables, as well as accounts of grand masters of law, Zen, Chinese qigong, and the martial arts, whom I have been fortunate to learn from and in many instances train with, and the discoveries I have made by their inspiration. I have been especially influenced by the beauty and wisdom of the classics, both Western and Eastern, and so have also included many references to works of literature, music, and art.

Throughout my life I have tried to integrate these insights. Thus my autobiography and professional work are deeply entwined. My professional life tests the mettle of my philosophical and spiritual discoveries. Often the stakes in these matters are extremely high. There is little room for equivocation. Conversely, I do believe I am a better lawyer and advocate by what I have learned from exploring many fields.

In writing this book I have looked back on my life's journey, and there in the labyrinth I have discovered a golden thread that for me lends insight into how, at the threshold of old age, I find in many respects that I am more open, less rigid, and growing younger. For me, the golden thread to my own personal transformation lies in seven core values that I cultivate, as if I am their loving gardener.

These values are:

o   Unconditional Love

o   Beauty

o   Wisdom

o   Vitality and Resilience

o   Compassionate Connection with all living beings

o   Gratitude and Paying Forward

o   Humor

I make a giant conjecture in this book—a leap of faith—and therefore will state it plainly: that the values that are enabling me to navigate more effectively and with greater balance in the stormy seas of my own life may be of broader use and interest; and, in their way, strengthen our collective capacity to adapt and to evolve as a species to the planetary challenges before us.

A growing body of commentary from writers in many fields points in a similar philosophical direction.[13] In the last third of this book I take the additional step of offering practical ways for communities of all kinds to pilot test these ideas and to innovate. I do not see a beneficial shift coming from present leadership, either corporate or governmental. So far, the top is far too compromised. The fundamental changes will begin, in my view, through local "Communities of Light", empowered by immediately available, new frontier technologies. For example, in my work as a lawyer I am collaborating closely with experts in some of these new technical fields, and have seen how innovations such as optical fiber supplied to homes and workplaces and supporting intelligent micro-grids can empower local communities to reclaim ownership, control, and financing of their basic energy, power, and communications infrastructure.

Communities of Light—or what I call "Big Heart Connectomes (BHCs)"—also create a kind of economic paradox. In BHCs a great number of people have an opportunity to discover and actively to engage in their "soul's work"--not what they are forced to do by economic necessity—and to be paid fairly for their contributions. At the same time their customers and other participants, including corporations and nonprofit entities, can advance their missions, generate stakeholder value, enlarge market share, and enhance competitive advantage by creating shared community value.[14]

But are such utopian visions even possible, here on this earth? When I described this book the other day to one of the benefactors of our Broadband International Legal Action Network (BBILAN[15]), he replied, "Sounds lovely, but your vision will never happen. You don't stand a chance against the forces of greed, self-interest, and corruption. They are vastly too powerful. I'm supporting you because I believe in you and this work. But frankly, it is already over. I do what I can while I'm on this earth, but frankly, I'm done. I'm never coming back."

And yet, there are real reasons for hope:

o   As calamities proliferate, we may have no other choice but to adapt and evolve.

- The alternative to our present worldview, which is predicated on scarcity, competition and conflict, is a world of peace, abundance, and joy.

- Time is compressing and accelerating. Significant societal changes that would have taken generations now can happen in a matter of months. The same mass communication technologies—social media, Internet, cell phones—that have fostered maladaptive addictive behaviors, can instead be deployed to accelerate beneficial, life-affirming evolutionary change, and not over decades, but in a few years.

- Future generations will observe, learn from, and build upon what we do here, and our efforts will not be wasted.

- And, as described in Chapter 3—Just Click!—you needn't wait. You can experience what I conceive of as Evolutionary Values in an instant, right now, and, if you wish, repeat the experience as often as you like.

It is all possible. To paraphrase the First Psalm:

> And we shall be like a tree planted by the rivers of water, that bringeth forth fruit in its season; its leaf also shall not wither; and whatsoever we do, shall prosper.

Chapter 1: My Journey

*The most beautiful thing we can experience is the
mysterious. It is the source of all true art and science.*
—Albert Einstein

What was that?
—Voltaire's last words—attributed

When I was a child, we spent our summers in Gloucester, Massachusetts, a seaside fishing town dating from the Pilgrims, pungent with the fragrance of history, fish, and Queen Ann's Lace.[16] I am told that the grandparents of today's right whales would surface and watch the witch trials extending from Salem to these same shores. During my childhood there was an ancient relic known as the Moorlands Hotel (since burned down) perched by the Bass Rocks, where we would spend our summer holidays. I have the memory of waiting in my little bed at nighttime for the headlights of an occasional car approaching silently along the Scenic Drive, and how the light and I and the roar of the waves against the rocks would merge as I fell asleep. In the morning one of those elegant old station wagons framed with wood would stop at the Moorlands to take us kids to the beach, and there I would stroll in search of pretty pebbles, which I would collect and run to show my parents. I didn't know who placed these pebbles there, but I fancied I was party to an extraordinary secret.

In a flash, seventy-five years have passed, and I am still on the lookout for curiosities. But these days they take the form of discoveries and inventions and hold their own secrets.

The central idea—the core discovery and the experience I wish to explore with you in these pages—is that each singular moment is an unfolding miracle. For me the present moment is a place of refuge—of beauty, happiness, vitality, and gratefulness. This moment appears in a flash. We can enter whenever we choose. There is a gate but no barrier. I experience the moment as a garden alive with extraordinary happenings. I am witnessing them as a floating stream—people, trees, rocks, ideas, events, clips of stories — suddenly appearing, vibrating like a hummingbird, then flowing on. I have discovered that the key to this wondrous garden is the energy field of the Heart, which is Love.

Entering this energy field of Love and connecting Love to whatever presents itself seems, as if magically, to endow that thing, that person, that thought with life. Then, I have discovered, it immediately gives back, and I feel more alive inside. At first I thought of this garden as a separate, alternative reality to my daily, expected, one might say consensus reality. But in recent years I am coming to realize that they are one and the same. And another extraordinary thing: we can choose to enter this garden, whenever we want. We possess the means— each of us—to change our lives, our destinies in a moment, in the twinkling of an eye. Three pivotal experiences, which I describe below, have led me to this realization.

Case # 1—Snake or Delusion? (*Makyo*)

On a sultry summer's day in Kamakura, Japan during the 1980s just after my teacher, Yamada Koun Roshi[17], confirmed my *kensho* (in the Zen tradition this is the first taste of realization—passing a first gate), I returned to my cushion to resume my practice. Everything was still; twenty or so other students were in deep meditation; not a leaf moved. I happened to look out toward the entrance to the Zendo. There coiled at the entry was a large yellow snake. I was amazed that no one noticed it. I got up quietly to investigate, but the snake had vanished. I went into the kitchen, and the cook came out to see—no snake. To this day I don't know whether this was simply a real snake—there are snakes in Kamakura. But why there? Why at that very moment? Or perhaps as Yamada Roshi later remarked it was a *makyo*—a sudden apparition that often appears as the student is approaching an important way station of discovery. To this day, I don't know whether the snake was real or a figment of my imagination. I am caught in this liminal world between one reality and another. Zen masters tend to dismiss *makyo* as unnecessary distractions on the student's journey into deeper realms.

Brief Coda—What Is Real? What Is Not Real?

In the summer of 2021 when I was organizing a Discovery Expedition[18] on Coincidence, Synchronicity, and Serendipity (CSS), including some of my most interesting friends, I approached an old Harvard chum who is today one of the world's preeminent mathematicians to see if he might be interested in joining our Corps of Discovery. "No way," he immediately replied. "I am interested to know," I continued undaunted. "Because it's not real," he stated with assurance, "no way to measure, no way to replicate." The next day I contacted another close friend, a psychologist, one of the core members of an earlier expedition on "discovery engineering." He said, "Funny you are asking me this now. I was just discussing CSS with my daughter last night, and I said to her, 'You know what really strikes me as interesting is how real CSS encounters appear!'"

So, what is real? What is not real? Might it be possible that some things can appear to be both real and not real at the same time? What is this CSS encounter telling us?

Case # 2—My First Encounter with Brother David Steindl-Rast

In early spring 2017, I was riding my bike on Cabrillo Boulevard in Santa Barbara, and had been musing for nearly an hour with deep gratitude about Brother David Steindl-Rast's wonderful teaching—*Stop Look Go*[19]—which I was planning to include in my new book and webinars. Precisely—I mean precisely and simultaneously—as I was cycling home just by Santa Barbara Wharf (a bridge, perhaps itself a metaphor), I observed an elderly man and his young companion. Ordinarily, I would have simply passed by. But something told me to look more closely. And lo!—the elderly gentlemen appeared to be Brother David Steindl-Rast. I dismounted, and said to him, "I can't believe this, are you Brother David!? How is this possible? You are a monk, and you live in a monastery in Austria, not in Santa Barbara. What are you doing here? I was just thinking of you! You have materialized!"

"Why, yes, I am," he replied in his deep, melodious voice (with just a slight hint of an Austrian accent), smiling and bemused, as if nothing remarkable was happening. "Please let me introduce my young friend. He is Cesar Chavez's grandson," he said kindly.

"But what are you doing **here?**" I insisted. "I am a great admirer of your work, In fact, I was completely engrossed for the last half hour in your wonderful teaching, *Stop Look Go.*"

"Well, I'm here only for the day. I've been interviewed by Oprah Winfrey," he observed casually.

Our conversation then flowed easily toward many topics of shared interest. As we are both lovers of music, Brother David recommended his favorite Hayden Symphony #22. It was if we were old friends meeting after many years apart. Brother David invited me to visit his monastery in Austria, and I gladly accepted. The following year out of the blue I received a birthday greeting from him. To this day I treasure Brother David and honor him in my heart.

Case # 3—Grand Epiphany—No Lifeguard on Duty

It has taken me 79 years to rediscover something I likely knew all along, but forgot. Perhaps we forget so that we can enjoy relearning the really important lessons in life. My grand epiphany began casually. The day before, my dear friend and former law partner Anthony Slingsby, an English solicitor now retired in Portugal, remarked, "You know, we lawyers are trained to try to control everything." (By the way, I had discovered many years before, over dinner with him in a London pub, that Anthony and I had been born in the same year, the same month, and the same day, possibly at almost the same hour, without either of us knowing this curious fact —despite some 10 years of practicing law together.) The next day I joined Dr. Bernard Beitman's online *Coincidence Café*, where the theme of the month was "CSS and Humor." One CSS explorer in a wheelchair was describing his humorous encounters with spirits, who appeared to him as real as any of us who had joined the Zoom call. Another participant noted that laughing Buddhas

(*Hotei*) are merry and amused at how we humans are so preoccupied with trying to control everything.

At this exact moment, I was about to open my mouth and opine on laughing Buddhas when I was literally cut off in mid-sentence. The lights went out! Untimely ripped from the Zoom meeting by MacDuff's invisible hand. At first, I was perplexed—no chance for the other members to hear my important ideas, as if they mattered! But almost **instantly**, I experienced an epiphany. An inner voice said, "Wait! It's OK to be cut off. You never know. You can be cut off at any moment, the lights can go off, and, you know—that's OK! The key is to live now, right now, and you have a choice: You pick. Alive or dead?"

Like a stone striking bamboo[20]—a sudden flash; the great irony, the marvelous freedom to know that we can die at every second and that's OK, to be OK with our own death, the dance of it, the exhilaration of it! To be alive! Now!

I passed the day in glorious gratitude for this luminous realization. Connections flowed out of nowhere, in multitudes. Cycling along Cabrillo Boulevard, I looked up at a pure eggshell blue sky, slashed in two by a single, brilliant white cloud. I passed a silent sign on the beach. It read, "No lifeguard on duty." That's it! "No lifeguard on duty; no need to protect, no need to fear."[21] I cycled on.

Origins

Because this book is organized around a central discovery, Love and its ramifications, and a series of related inventions, it may be useful to take a brief look at its origins. First of all, I am grateful to my parents. Among their greatest gifts was introducing me to the classics. One of my earliest memories is my father playing Bach's *Well Tempered Clavier*[22] on the piano after dinner. Even today, any time I wish, I can return to this childhood memory and feel Bach's creation flowing like lifeblood through my veins. My mother was a prodigy who with the aid of her tutor translated Homer at the age of eight. She was widely read, and after graduating from Radcliffe won a coveted scholarship to study archeology in Greece. My parents loved Africa, and years after my father died my mother would return every summer to the Shelly Beach Hotel in Mombasa, Kenya. Once when she was in her eighties and returning to Europe, her plane was forced to land in the Libyan desert, where the passengers sat in the sweltering heat and were not permitted to deplane for five days. She treated the event as an inconvenience. Such was my zany, courageous, extraordinary mother.

Since my earliest years my life has been entwined with Japan, where my grandfather, Julius Kahn, owned several steel factories before World War II. (He is also recognized as the principal inventor of pre-stressed and reinforced concrete[23], which was the foundation of the Old Imperial Hotel, considered in those days to be earthquake-proof.) I have always felt a close connection with my grandfather even though he died in 1942, a year before I was born. "He would have loved you," my mother often told me, "your minds are similar." On my desk I have a picture of my grandfather (shaking hands in Illustration #1) at the Fujiya Hotel in Miyanoshita, Japan, surrounded by what appears to be the American consul, his staff, and a giant sumo wrestler. I have tried unsuccessfully over the years to contact my grandfather's spirit using some of the techniques I describe in this book. However, in an odd way our life's streams have touched, as so much of my present and past work has involved inventions and Japan.[24]

Illustration 1

My main sport in high school and college was judo—the "gentle way"—and I have long imagined myself a samurai, perhaps in some past life. When I first visited Japan at the age of thirteen and looked out of the bus window as we traveled from the Old Haneda Airport into Tokyo, I saw ladies in *yukata* heading toward the public baths—and had the odd sensation on that sultry July evening of having lived that scene before. Like the character in the film trilogy Life of Miyamoto Musahi[25] portrayed by Toshiro Mifune, I have fancied myself a samurai trodding the dusty roads of life, protecting poor villagers, righting wrongs—then continuing on with a shrug, or as the saying goes in Japanese, *"kaze wo kata de kiru"*—literally cutting the wind with the shoulder.

Youthful Exuberance

My first passion as a young lawyer was environmental law. After a year of drudgery with an international law firm, I resigned and joined the Center for Law and Social Policy in Washington and the Center for Law in the Public Interest in Los Angeles. It was 1971-72, the heyday of Ralph Nader, the environmental movement, and the UN Stockholm Conference on the Human Environment. I had my first vision.

Japan Center for Human Environment Problems

I was working on a case involving the pollution of the Southern California Bight, where I discovered mounting evidence of fish floating to the surface with lesions, bulging eyes, the collapse of the kelp beds, and proliferation of sea urchins—all sure signs of environmental degradation. In materials published for the Stockholm Conference I read about how the Japanese citizens movement[26] (*jumin undo*) began with the protest of victims of Minamata disease (mercury poisoning), *ittai-ittai* ("it hurts!, it hurts!) disease (cadmium poisoning), and Yokkaiichi air pollution[27] (sulfur oxides and nitrogen oxides-induced asthma, bronchitis, and emphysema). It was clear to me that both Japan and the U.S. faced common scientific, political, and legal issues. I suddenly thought: why not establish an international collaborative network to share data, innovations, and legal solutions to these common challenges?

I decided to write to the two principal Japanese thought leaders on environmental law and policy: Dr. Shigeto Tsuru, an economist and president of Hitotsubashi University, and Dr. Ichiro Kato, president of Tokyo University and a law scholar. I asked for their assistance in establishing a Japan Center for Human Environmental Problems (JCHEP).[28] To my great surprise and delight, I soon received letters from them enthusiastically encouraging me to visit Japan, and I did so immediately. After meeting with both university presidents and many other environmental experts, I presented my proposal to the heads of the leading environmental and nature protection organizations, was interviewed by the national press, and was invited by the U.S. Embassy to lecture on my idea throughout Japan. Thus was born JCHEP, which engaged in many worthy projects over the next thirty years, including publishing a journal under its name.

I was lucky. My timing was perfect, and my luck continued. During my master's degree program at Harvard I had studied with Professor Jerome A. Cohen, a preeminent scholar of Chinese law. Professor Cohen became my mentor and helped me to secure a grant from the Ford Foundation to teach an academic year course on environmental law as a Visiting Professor at Doshisha University in Kyoto. With his continuing friendship and generous support I obtained a position as an Associate Professor at the University of Hawaii, then gained tenure and promotion to full professor, which was followed by an invitation from Professor Cohen to share the Mitsubishi Visiting Professorship at Harvard Law School in 1976-77 with two distinguished Japanese legal scholars, Professor Koichiro Fujikura (Doshisha University) and Professor Akio Morishima (Nagoya University). It was during the spring semester that I was engaged as legal counsel by an international consortium of environmental organizations concerned about a U.S.-Japanese government/industrial consortium planning to construct a massive superport in Palau, Micronesia.

Palau Superport

The idea of the Superport project was to bypass the Malacca Straits by building a shorter route for trans-shipment of oil to Japan through the Lombok Straights. As an energy strategy, the Palau Superport made some sense. Japan's historic Achilles heel has been reliable access to oil— the *casus belli* of World War II, when the U.S. cut off Japan's oil pipeline. However, from an environmental perspective the Superport would precipitate an environmental catastrophe. Palau was a paradise of coral reefs supporting more endangered species than any other marine sanctuary in the world. The Superport was to be constructed directly on the reefs. Moreover, Palau was also an international protectorate of the UN, and the U.S. and Japan were members of the UN Security Council. Reactions from the leaders of Palau were mixed. Some chiefs favored the Superport, which they viewed as a source of much-needed jobs. Other leaders were opposed, not only on environmental grounds, but also because they recognized that Palau as a nation would soon become subservient to powerful Japanese and U.S. industrial interests. There was also some evidence that the promoters of the project were bribing some of the chiefs, while the CIA, the Nixon Administration, and Japan's powerful Ministry of International Trade and Industry (MITI) all strongly favored the Superport.

One day I received a call from my friends at the National Resources Defense Council (NRDC), Jacob Scheer and Tom Stoel, requesting my assistance on the case. A large number of international organizations, including Friends of the Earth (which I subsequently represented at the Third UN Law of the Sea Conference in Caracas, Venezuela in 1973), the Sierra Club, and other prominent environmental groups joined the coalition. But what could practically be done? The key decision makers were in Japan, and Japan had a very different culture, language, and legal system.

Together we came up with the bold idea of submitting an international citizens' petition to the Japanese Diet[29] (Parliament). Our strategy was to appeal to the key Japanese bureaucrats and political leaders, urging them to recognize that Japan along with the U.S. were members of the UN Security Council, and as such they had a fiduciary duty to uphold an international public trust to protect the people of Palau and safeguard its coral reefs. In April 1977 I flew to Japan to present the petition, which I had prepared as a legal brief to the Japanese Diet. A link to the text of my petition is contained in the footnote, excerpted from my treatise *Environmental Law in Japan* (MIT Press, 1981).[30]

Two fortunate things then happened. The first was a tip from my friend, Hiroyuki Ishi[31], who was the senior science writer at the Asahi News and the founder of the Japanese Association for Nature Protection.[32] Ishi told me that the Petition Office in the Diet was going to reject my appeal on the grounds that foreigners had no legal right to petition the Diet. What a break! Often the best thing you can hand a lawyer is a procedural obstacle set up to block dealing with a substantive matter, in this case, fundamental human and environmental rights. The second break was my friendship with Rex Coleman, an expert on Japanese tax law, whom I had met at Harvard Law School. Rex just happened to be in Japan at that time, and together we pored over the U.S.-Japan Treaty on Friendship and Commerce and the Japanese Petition Law. Nowhere was there any explicit denial of foreigners' rights to petition. In fact, the Petition Law clearly states that "any person can petition ….." I had my leverage.

The day of my hearing arrived. I met a functionary at the Petition Office. Ishi showed up with photographers from the Asahi News. I will recall the scene in the present tense, as if it is happening again right before my eyes. We are on prime-time television. I present my case in Japanese. The officer pauses, shakes his head, sucks in air, and proceeds to tell me that he is very sorry that I have traveled all the way to Japan, but the Diet Office cannot accept my petition. The reason: the petitioners are mainly foreigners. I pull out the Petition Law and read him the relevant section. He continues to puff on his cigarette. The meeting ends with the officer telling me he will take my petition under consideration. In Japanese there is a wonderful phrase to describe his assurance: "*maimuki ni kento shimasu*". Literally, this means, "We will adopt a forward-looking attitude." In reality, everyone in Japan understands this to mean, "Sorry, mate, don't count on it." The Japanese language preserves that subtle ambiguity, keeping all options open.

I understood this. I thanked him courteously for his time. It was apparent that I would have to reach out to the heads of the leading political parties in the Diet. Here again, Ishi's assistance and the contacts at Asahi were invaluable. Even though Asahi was a left-leaning newspaper, the petition was being covered by the full spectrum of mainstream media. In fact, Ishi in his exuberance nominated me as Asahi's "man of the day (hito–)" and the award was announced in the newspaper the next day— my brief moment of national celebrity.

I quickly realized that to build on this momentum, I must try not to align or be identified with any specific political party. Rather, I must take advantage of the fact that I am a foreigner, representing many international environmental organizations, and adopt what is referred to today as a "trans-partisan" position. In my meetings with leaders of the majority Liberal Democratic Party, the Democratic Socialist Party, the Socialist Party, the Komeito, and the Japan Communist Party, I emphasized that the issues at stake transcended politics, and that here was a unique opportunity to come together for a higher humanitarian and environmental purpose. I was received cordially. I had prepared and delivered my presentation entirely in Japanese, which may have impressed the Diet members.

Having completed my work, I returned home to Cambridge in time to teach my Harvard Law School class. A few weeks later the Japanese government announced it was withdrawing from the Palau Superport project.

When I reflect fifty years later on this youthful adventure, I recognize that I was a useful instrument within a larger context. Most importantly, the cause itself was compelling. The future of Palau, an impoverished island nation, and its international environmental heritage hung in the balance. The procedural obstruction was a gift. The Petition Office could have accepted the petition and then quietly ignored or denied it. There is a colorful term in Japanese for this standard bureaucratic tactic— *mokusatsu*— to kill by silence. Also, the case made good media copy: a young maverick attorney with a prestigious title, Mitsubishi Visiting Professor, debating technical matters of Japanese law in Japanese on prime-time television. The theater of it captured the public imagination. Lastly, in the 1970s Japanese society was impressed by the special status and prestige of Harvard University, and in particular, Harvard Law School. I strongly doubt that if I embarked on such a mission today anyone would bother to listen.

Westinghouse Nuclear Reactor

My string of lucky breaks continued, but the next time in a way I could not possibly foresee. Several years later I applied for and was awarded a Council on Foreign Relations (CFR) fellowship and was assigned to Richard Holbrooke[33], then Assistant Secretary of State and Chief of the East Asia Bureau. The purpose of the prestigious CFR fellowship was to expose promising academics for a year to the inside workings of our government. I proposed to work on international environmental law and policy with a special emphasis on Asia.

A week after my arrival I was in touch with my friends at NRDC, who brought to my attention the imminent approval by the State Department of a nuclear reactor, manufactured by Westinghouse that was proposed to be located in the Philippines. As we investigated the case, we discovered that the proposed site was at the very center of an earthquake zone highly prone to tsunami. The National Geological Survey called the project "the most dangerous in the developing world." I wrote my first memorandum and presented it to Holbrooke. "You simply cannot sign off on this project," I said confidently. "It's going to blow up. At the very least there ought to be an environmental impact assessment under NEPA (National Environmental Policy Act.)"

Returning to my office, I encountered the Deputy Chief of Mission (DCM), a distinguished, graying foreign service officer. Very suave, very cool. "You know, Julian, you're new here. I'm not sure that you know the name of the game. I'll give you a piece of advice. It's CYA." "I'm not sure I understand," I said. "Do you mean CIA?" I really thought he was talking about the involvement of the CIA, which was likely in the Westinghouse project. "No, CYA," he smiled in an avuncular way. I finally got it. How stupid! (I later came to understand that this is also why most documents in the State Department are written in the passive voice, so that no one can be held responsible.)

That afternoon returning to my office in the State Department I discovered all my belongings in a shopping cart by the elevator— not an auspicious way to begin a year-long fellowship. I returned with the cart to my office and had another encounter with the DCM. It was clear the State Department didn't know what to do with me.

Japan Industrial Policy Group

The next morning I was told to report to Herb Cochran at the Japan Desk. Herb was in charge of U.S.-Japanese trade and industrial relations. He was a smart, experienced, no-bullshit, dedicated foreign officer, and he came right to the point. "We have a much more important project for you to spend your time on: what do we do about Japan's strategic industrial policy, especially favoring the 64K DRAM?" I didn't have a clue what he was talking about. "We are assigning a young foreign service officer, Andrew Osterman, to work with you," he continued. I do believe that at the time my new assignment was probably the lowest-priority (lowest-risk) project the DCM and Holbrooke could have possibly come up with. It was a perfect example of the mushroom treatment, the venerable State Department way of handling outside "advisors" like me by keeping them in the dark with lots of manure on them. In fact, the assignment turned out to be of the highest national importance and opened an entirely new vista for me that continues to influence my professional life to this day.

Osterman soon proved a brilliant foil—in his words, he rode "shotgun." He had an unusual mix of an insider's savvy with a terrific sense of humor. He knew the characters of all the principal players in the State Department, including the ones "who you only realize they have stabbed you in the back after the knife has been removed."

We (Cochran, Osterman, and I) quickly realized that in light of the Japanese challenge and the U.S. demand for semiconductors, our national trade laws were entirely inadequate, and the country needed an effective industrial policy, based on a more sophisticated understanding of national security. In those days the term "national security"—at least as used by the U.S. government—meant only defense or military security and did not include economic security. Cochran's concern was that Japanese government agencies, in particular MITI, were implementing "beggar-thy-neighbor" neo-mercantilist[34] practices to favor Japanese companies at the expense of U.S. companies. With this strategic leverage, the Japanese government and industry in concert could exert an extraordinary influence over U.S. industrial infrastructure and productivity by coming to dominate other closely "linked" industries, such as computers, robotics, and telecommunications—all of which depend on semiconductors.

In those days, the term "economic security" itself was rarely mentioned. For example, early on in the project our team met with a distinguished Harvard economics professor, who asked what to us was an extraordinary and revealing question: "Why does it matter if we lose the semiconductor industry, if the U.S. continues to maintain competitive advantage in the shoe industry?" A great question for a seminar at the Harvard Business School; but a dangerous line of thinking for anyone making national policy, because it failed to account for the unique leverage of some technologies, such as semiconductors, on the overall economy.

Osterman and I got to work. It was imperative that we recruit the smartest, most talented, and most experienced people in the U.S. government, the semiconductor industry, and academia to form a task force. We baptized the initiative "The Japan Industrial Policy Group (JIPG)", and our mission was to produce, in the eight remaining months of my tenure at the State Department, a coherent national policy for the semiconductor industry. We succeeded beyond our expectations. We enlisted the most experienced and thoughtful participants from eight Congressional committees, every major U.S. government agency, and the top specialists at Harvard, UC Berkeley, the Brookings Institution, the Council on Foreign Relations, and other think tanks. Most importantly, we had the strong support of the presidents of the leading semiconductor companies and

U.S. Semiconductor Industry Association. We used a "Single Negotiation Text"[35] process to raise awareness of the challenge and to shape an effective solution.

The result was the first, and perhaps last, coherent industrial policy framework to offer a qualitative, and to some extent quantitative, way to assess the "strategic economic leverage" of a specific technology or industry. Our report was published by the House Ways and Means Committee under the title "*High Technology and Japanese Industrial Policy*[36]." I then returned to Harvard Law School and MIT, where I was invited to lead a two-year research project based on the work of the JIPG. During this period I wrote a book, *Partners in Prosperity—Strategic Industries for the U.S. and Japan,* which proposed a productive way for the U.S. and Japan to increase the public benefits of next-generation semiconductor technologies by combining collaboration and competition (co-opetition) in their development. One important bi-product of these years was the semiconductor industry consortium, Sematech[37].

Today, the concepts of economic security and strategic technologies and industries are very much in play, although the focus has shifted to critical national infrastructure. Other countries, in particular China, have adopted "neo-mercantilist" industrial policies imitating the Japanese model of the 1980s, except for the crucial difference that Chinese policies today combine strategic military and defense strategies along with a long-term economic plan. The core idea of strategic leverage is fundamental to China's ambitions to dominate artificial intelligence and to control the global supply of rare earth metals, which are the basis for thousands of strategic military and economic applications. Recent U.S. administrations, however, have been unwilling to learn from history, and have failed to convene a China Industrial Policy Group on the lines of the JIPG. In the present hyper-polarized political environment, there may be little room for mavericks. My friend Andy

Osterman died suddenly in 2017, and his obituary provides a snapshot[38] of this remarkable and talented person.

With the hindsight of many years, I do believe it was very much to Richard Holbrooke's credit that he permitted such a wild-eyed and open-ended industrial collaborative to operate under his watch in the East Asia Bureau. In turf-conscious Washington, the project might be expected to have originated in the Commerce Department or the Office of the Special Trade Representative (both agencies were represented in the JIPG). I had an affectionate and excellent working relationship with Richard Holbrooke.[39] When Senator Robert Byrd visited China, Holbrooke invited me to come along and watch brain surgery using acupuncture for anesthesia at one of Beijing's leading hospitals. Holbrooke was later nominated by President Clinton to be U.S. Ambassador to the UN. He died suddenly in 2010.

Fast Forward

Almost forty years later, after many vicissitudes and crisscrossing of life paths, I find myself once again engaged in addressing industrial policy challenges, but now as a veteran lawyer and negotiator taking on cases that involve some of the great issues of the age—the commercial exploitation and despoliation of Outer Space and the Oceans, the continuous exposure of local communities and workplaces to non-ionizing radiation (NIR)[40] from fourth- and fifth-generation ("5-G") wireless technology, the sacrifice of national treasures like Lake Tahoe, the widespread appropriation, packaging, and sale of private personal information to manipulate and addict consumers.

My goal in every one of these cases as a lawyer and advocate is to be a voice for sanity and balance, in the face of a corporate and governmental juggernaut that ruthlessly rolls on, heedless of law and mindless of the suffering it inflicts. The odds of our stopping this monstrous global assault are small, but there is a chance to redirect its energies so that they are less destructive to people and the planet. Our veteran legal team and our clients, mainly grassroots and national organizations, are part of a great awakening to the injustices being perpetrated by powerful corporations and their captive government agencies that are, at least in theory, supposed to protect their citizens. With each modest victory, each hill taken, the playing field becomes a bit more even. We are only at the beginning.

I am grateful to have a chance to play in this arena, to be one of a few lawyers given an opportunity to make a difference. On a personal level I am also deeply grateful to have the chance to draw together the many threads in the tapestry of my life and to tell my story while I still have the wit and energy to do so. For despite my advancing chronological age, I do believe—and feel in my bones—that a part of me is steadily growing younger.

As I look back on my life, I can detect a distinct line of demarcation at the age of forty. Before forty, I spent my life acquiring advanced professional skills, teaching at great universities, serving as an advisor to governments and international organizations, dabbling in entrepreneurial ventures, and writing academic articles and books. In my leisure I practiced the *oboe d'amore* and chess and read the classics.

My greatest good fortune has been to marry Angela, my constant companion, my best friend, and my soul's joy. Angela is my external conscience.

I can tell you truly that until forty I actually believed that I was immortal. As chess has always been a part of my family (my mother was nine times U.S. women's chess champion), I fancied myself the knight in Ingmar Bergman's *Seventh Seal*[41], returning from the Crusades and meeting Death on a beach, where Death challenges the knight to a game of chess: If the knight wins, Death will let him go. I believed such things then.

Life has disabused me of such beliefs. I now have the data, as they say, to show that something was crazily wrong with my model. My father, mother, brother, and many of my closest friends are all dead. When I'm glum, I am always amused by a family joke. My grandfather would begin dinner with the observation, "Leonardo da Vinci is dead; Shakespeare is dead, Mozart is dead; and I'm not feeling so well myself."

At the age of forty, I opened a law office in Tokyo in a place called the "Tiger's Gate" (Toranomon)[42], while at the same time beginning the serious practice of Zen under a great master teacher, Yamada Koun[43]. Corporate deals during the week, the *koan*[44] "Mu" (無)—vast nothing—in the city of Kamakura during the weekends. In Kamakura, I learned how to do nothing very well. From this serious Zen practice I came upon some core insights that have inspired my life, and I would like now to provide a first taste of these discoveries, because they underlie the proposals in the last part of this book.

Milestones

o I have discovered that the solution to Mu already exists inside us, that the personal "self" and Mu are one and the same. There is no distance.

o Since law school I had been interested in the process of discovery and particularly intrigued by the word *discover*, whose Latin origins provide a hint: the root is *discooperīre* means to "uncover." While in Japan I organized a Discoverers Society with Japanese psychologists, entrepreneurs, and an academic historian of "macro-engineering." The core premise was this: if the discovery already exists, but we fail to see it (because it is somehow embedded below the surface of consciousness), a collaborative of imaginative minds schooled in different disciplines might well increase the chances of uncovering it. We explored this premise in several interesting meetings. But then I returned to the U.S.

○ Soon after I came upon Dr. Elmer and Alyce Green's *Beyond Biofeedback*,[45] and was deeply intrigued. I contacted Elmer, visited Topeka, Kansas, and thus began a 25 year friendship and collaboration with him. Together with Elmer's close associates at the Menninger Institute in Topeka, and a Japanese entrepreneur, we founded a company, Discovery Engineering International. Using our brainwave biofeedback system, which Elmer and his colleagues had developed based on their research with yogis in India and with a Native American shaman, we taught business and government officials how to gain access to "higher consciousness" by freely entering a state of "creative reverie." It was a remarkable idea described in his book, *Beyond Biofeedback*.[46] The book's core premise is that biofeedback training merely scratches the surface, because the entire universe is a feedback process. As a result of this venture, I discovered a rich and ongoing dialogue between my own "inner" and "outer" worlds that is a recurrent theme in this book.

○ During this period, I conceived the idea of taking foreign companies public on the Japanese stock market. In close collaboration with Jim Schrager[47], the acting CEO of Getz Brothers (Jim has since become a specialist in corporate strategy and is a clinical professor at the University of Chicago Booth School of Business), we succeeded in transforming Getz's $8 million after-tax Japanese branch into a $1 billion+ company in just three years. After negotiating this landmark capital markets transaction, we established a consulting company to help other foreign companies with operations in Japan achieve similar success.

We were amazed to find that not one foreign company was interested in hiring us. We discovered that prospective clients were willing to sacrifice points from their IPO for the boardroom assurance of a gold star investment banking firm like Goldman Sachs. Goldman Sachs provided instant board room credibility, which was far more important than hiring our maverick startup team.

And yet again, Fortune's Wheel turned in my favor. My disbelief and frustration led me to become interested in the art of negotiation, and one day I was introduced to a former U.S. Air Force fighter pilot, Jim Camp, who had developed his own quirky "system" of negotiation (2002,[48] 2007[49]). In turn, I introduced Jim to the world of Japanese negotiations.

o After thousands of hours of experience in randori (a Japanese judo term[50] for vigorous practice) with some of the most resourceful Japanese business negotiators, I wrote a book, *Piloting Through Chaos—Wise Leadership/Effective Negotiation for the 21st Century*[51] (2013), which introduces my own negotiation system. My key insight was the fundamental principle of **integrity**—the state of being whole, connected, and dynamically alive. In Chinese culture "integrity" or "Te" (pronounced "de") holds the thread that connects us to the Tao (Chinese) or Cosmos (Greek), the natural, organizing principle of the universe. Integrity is written in the Chinese and Japanese languages by combining the characters for "eye" (intelligence) with "hand" (action) and "heart" (compassion). In my book I show that 'integrity' is a fundamental skill that can be cultivated with practice.

o This empirical finding led directly to *The Artful Navigator*, a software app that offers a practical way to encode the "wisdom genome" of the great actors of history and literature and transform them into our personal mentors.

The core idea is: Wisdom is a skill. We can learn to become wiser with practice.

o I spent several years thereafter exploring and developing best practices for successful strategic alliances, including alliance mediation. I combined these insights with my earlier work on creative problem solving in an article I published in 2000, *Inventing for Humanity—A Collaborative Strategy for Global Survival*[52]. Here again the core premise was, and is, that solutions to most of the wicked problems[53] facing the world are within our grasp; we simply fail to see them, because we fear to step out of our comfortable ways of thinking and engaging with one another.[54] As I explain later, I have recently come to believe that brain/mind power is insufficient. It must be guided by a fundamental upshift in societal values and priorities, which in turn can be guided and inspired by the energy field around the Heart, which is Love.

o During this period I wrote a sequel, *The Explorers Mind,*[55] which contained several related inventions, among these an Explorers Wheel that enables the adventurer to connect and apply diverse domains of knowledge to a central core theme through a process I call "intertidal thinking."[56] The book you are reading is a living example of intertidal thinking. *The Explorer's Mind* was, I believe, one of the world's first smart books —that is, books using QR codes and AI that also enabled the book to learn about, and along with its readers and to adapt to their interests.[57] This invention innocently preceded our present shadowy world of surveillance, where private data is daily being converted without the informed consent of its owners for corporate profit and competitive advantage.

o On March 11, 2011 the Fukushima Daiichi nuclear accident[58] occurred. Afterwards I wrote a series of blogs[59] proposing a new way to predict earthquakes, which in those days were considered by the National Geological Service to be inherently unpredictable. Also, in collaboration with my MIT colleague Professor Ernst Frankel, a leading expert on systems engineering, and my old mentor Professor Jerome A. Cohen, I published an Open Letter[60] in the South China Morning News to Japanese Prime Minister Abe proposing a practical solution for controlling the ongoing radioactive discharges into the surrounding ocean from the Fukushima plant. The Japanese government never responded, but the core approach might still be viable, as the plant continues to discharge toxic waste.

o   The next remarkable encounter on my journey was with the *qigong* grandmaster and martial artist Li Junfeng.[61] I pay deep tribute here to Master Li, who has pioneered an energetic practice focused on the Heart and Love called *Sheng Zhen*.[62] My several years of training with Master Li inspired me to develop with my close colleague of many years, William Moulton, a new field we call "Big Heart Intelligence (BHI)." BHI expands upon the principle of integrity I explored in depth in *Piloting Through Chaos*, and is described in another book entitled, *Laughing Heart—A Field Guide to Exuberant Vitality for All Ages –10 Essential Moves.*[63]

o   My present work all derives from, and continues to expound upon, the core insights of Big Heart Intelligence.[64] One important offshoot is the principle of *Integral Resilience*[65] and the accompanying app *5 Minutes to Resilience*[66] which shows how individuals, organizations, and communities can cultivate this core life competency.

o   All of which brings me today to my lifelong interest in Coincidence, Synchronicity, and Serendipity (CSS). CSS has been for me a constant companion, and the book you are reading weaves together some of the most startling threads in the tapestry of my journey. I do believe and hope to show how CSS events, along with Heart and Love, can play a critical redeeming role at this pivotal point in our planet's history.

These are urgent times. As Tennyson wrote, an old order is passing, giving rise to the new. We have a chance, each in our own way, to bring together the diverse strands of our professional, intellectual, and personal lives to contribute to a new and more compassionate world. We are acutely out of sync with the natural world, and today, as never before during my lifetime, the grinning specter has an aggressive nuclear face.[67]

There are seeds of positive change scattered everywhere that can flower despite our present dangers and calamities. We must resolutely seek out and nourish these seeds. Yet in our seeking, we have a constant companion. It is called the Shadow to which we now turn.

Chapter 2: Shadow

And be these juggling fiends no more believed,
That palter with us in a double sense,
That keep the word of promise to our ear
And break it to our hope.
—Shakespeare, *Macbeth*, Act 5, Scene 8

"Father, forgive them, for they know not what they do."
—Luke 23:34

"It is only through shadows that we come to know the
light."
—St. Catherine of Siena

As I write this chapter, following Vladimir Putin's orders over a million people are being driven into despair, penury, and homelessness by the invasion of Ukraine. This is Putin's Shadow at work, and may likely involve other actors' shadows in this complex and tragic situation.[68] Another of the myriad small examples of the Shadow at work: One of my clients is an elderly man with advanced multiple myeloma. His life depends on undergoing an experimental trial with a new FDA-approved drug, because he is being exposed daily to non-ionizing radiation (NIR) emitted from a small cell tower, soon to be amplified by a monstrous macro cell tower that has been installed on a hill above his property. Yet in denying our plea for a reasonable accommodation under the Americans with Disabilities Act, counsel to the telecom company argued in a Zoom meeting, effectively, if we save your client's life, we will be obliged to save many other lives (repeated in court papers). Again, the Shadow in play.[69] According to Luke 23:34, Jesus' last words on the cross, responding to those calling for his crucifixion, were, "Father, forgive them, for they do not know what they do."

This "not knowing what we do" is the domain of Shadow. In the realm of the human psyche, it can be compared to the dark energy which, physicists tell us, constitutes approximately 70% of all energy in the Universe. In this book, I define Shadow as the domain of our subconscious "negative" drives, conceits, fears, rages, and obsessions, but also as a vast, yet unexplored source of kindness, compassion, beauty, abundance, charity, warmth, and love. Later I will describe what I have discovered about engaging with the Shadow's energy and power in a personal and practical way.

Tightly Coupled Systems

I first learned about tightly coupled systems from reading Yale sociologist Charles Perrow's *Normal Accidents: Living with High-Risk Technologies*.[70] A nuclear power plant is an example of a tightly coupled system in that all the parts, routines, and programs are tightly integrated into one system and are dependent upon each other. Well-designed, tightly coupled systems build in redundancy, so that in case of failure or accidents that are to be expected (in Perrow's terms, "normal" accidents), catastrophes can be anticipated and prevented.

Because of the increasing complexity of modern technology, today most human-made systems are tightly coupled, entwined, and closely integrated, and therefore become very dangerous when they fail. The two nuclear power plants captured by the Russian Army[71] are tightly coupled and principal elements of Ukraine's energy infrastructure. Critical national telecommunications infrastructure in the U.S. is being built out at an accelerating pace to be dependent on wireless technology, products, software, and protocols.

The commercialization and exploitation of Outer Space is increasingly being integrated with terrestrial and oceanic infrastructure through the Internet of Things (IoT) and the Internet of the Oceans (IoO). All biological systems are tightly coupled. The world's financial and economic systems are tightly coupled. Supply chains and logistical systems are tightly coupled. Our own psyche, and the collective psyche of all of humankind, is itself a tightly coupled system, and is being manipulated by a constant stream of mis- and disinformation to influence and to control our behavior by the unauthorized use and sale without our consent of our most personal and private information. Each of these systems and subsystems is today becoming increasingly tightly coupled, interdependent, and vulnerable to accident or direct assault, with consequences that can engulf our planet.

Tightly coupled systems present several formidable challenges, especially from the perspective of the Shadow. First, breakdowns are common, indeed "normal." Second, the risk of breakdown increases significantly when the system is exposed to constant stress. The more tightly coupled a system is, the less resilient it is to perturbations, and therefore the more likely it is to collapse. Third, a breakdown in any part of a subsystem can rapidly be transferred to other parts of the system in the tightly coupled network. Fourth, the accident can cascade, compound, and gain destructive force, like a hurricane or a tidal wave. Fifth, in far from equilibrium conditions, a small perturbation or stressor can trigger or trip a continuous stream of increasingly incoherent, unbalanced effects, leading to systemic collapse. When human intentions, driven by the Shadow, are introduced into this scenario, the consequences can be catastrophic over decades. A single action by a fanatic—the assassination of Gandhi in 1948—irrevocably altered the course of India, with ripples continuing to the present day.

With Russia's invasion of Ukraine the world may be fast approaching a Shadow tipping point, where a sudden shock to one subsystem—military, financial, economic, health, cyber—rapidly compromises the resilience and security of all the others. In a world of tightly coupled systems currently under massive and intensifying stress, the chances of catastrophe triggered by a random event, a mistake, an impulsive action, or a cascade of crazy actions based on mis- or disinformation or simply on mad delusion, increase exponentially.

What are our individual chances to escape unscathed when the collective psyche runs amok? If nations cannot cope with the Shadow, what possible chance has a single individual? Yet here is a paradox. We actually have leverage in our personal and business transactions. The most basic first step is to become aware of the Shadow. The signs and signals are everywhere; they are screaming at us, but we are asleep. Often we awake only when it is too late. Here are three personal examples of success and failure in meeting the Shadow.

Going Behind the Mask

As a professional negotiator, one learns to sense and anticipate the Shadow and to intervene in practical ways. The Shadow can become our ally. I call this skill *"Going Behind the Mask."*[72]

o **Rats everywhere.** We were planning a tripartite joint venture in Japan to introduce Western techniques of creative problem solving. Several weeks before leaving for Japan we began to encounter rats— rats scurrying down allies, rats scampering over walls, dead rats in the street, rats suddenly appearing in improbable places. I noticed but didn't know what to make of this strange phenomenon. After the first day of welcome ceremonies in Japan, we got down to business. Almost immediately our other American partner made a preemptive power move, demanding primary ownership and control of the venture which we had all nourished as equal partners for months. "He always does this," his American colleague observed. "He can't seem to help himself." The negotiations fizzled, and trust was irrevocably impaired. He was my friend, but he couldn't control his Shadow—and the rats were harbingers of the kind of behavior we were about to encounter.

But now something curious has happened. He has suddenly reappeared in my life, contacting me in connection about a new venture he has started in Santa Barbara; and we have taken up where we left off—friends, as if 40 years and the breach of trust in Japan scarcely matters any more.

o **Omori.** The Japanese partner in our venture was Omori. I had always known him as a man of great integrity, a spiritual man, founder and president of a small entrepreneurial media company, an adventurer, who would take time off to travel to the North Pole to witness the aurora borealis. He was an esteemed client who had also become my friend and partner. We were therefore all shocked when we discovered that he had registered the Japanese company we established, along with its intellectual property, in his company's name. How could this be? Of all people, Omori?

That evening our American team—myself, a clinical psychologist, and an engineer—were sitting around our brainwave biofeedback machines in our "salon" in Tokyo when one of our members made the obvious suggestion, "Why don't we use our own discovery engineering technology and find out?" So we harnessed ourselves to our EEG biofeedback monitors and dropped into the "creative reverie" state, the liminal state between sleep and wakefulness that we learn through biofeedback training to access at will. The tell-tale sign that we have entered a creative reverie is the sudden appearance of hypnagogic images that seem so real, one can hardly differentiate them from normal "reality." (See Chapter 9.)

After a few minutes of quietly waiting in reverie (patience is important…it usually takes a few minutes to "go online" with one's Unconscious), Omori's face suddenly appeared before me in my mind's eye, as if all the world were a stage and this was his moment. It was a familiar face. I looked up at his cathedral forehead framing two piercing, deep-set, compassionate eyes. "Yes," I said, "that is Omori." I visually scanned his face: strong samurai nose, high cheek bones, all suggesting to me nobility of character and fierceness of purpose. Then, as I continued my reverie, the terrain began to change, as I scrolled down his face. I arrived at the jaw, but there something was very different. I had not noticed it before, over the many months I had spent with Omori: the jaw was savage, large, pugnacious, and feral. It could tear whatever it encountered to pieces. And then in a flash I saw the answer to the riddle about Omori's behavior. He was both saint and carnivore! But because I and our team of psychology "experts" so needed to view him in a way that reinforced our vision and hope for the venture, we had filtered out the other signals that had been staring us in the face all along.

Once we understood that the conflict in Omori's character encrypted into his face was irreconcilable, we realized the venture was doomed.[73] As the Greek philosopher, Heraklites[74] observed, "Character is destiny." We could never hope to change Omori. The American team returned home, and the venture on which we had pinned our high hopes, foundered. In a sense the Shadow prevailed. But in another, our team's becoming aware of the Shadow at the threshold of the business venture, helped us to avoid a likely disaster later on.

o **Typhoon.** Our team at Discovery Engineering International was hired by a prominent Midwest foundation interested in supporting frontier research in human consciousness. Our assignment was to demonstrate our EEG biofeedback system by training the president and other members of the board of directors. The basic protocol was for each participant to harness up to the machines, learn to enter creative reverie, and then to record our images, which would be discussed afterwards. There was to be no prior disclosure of the images.

The images that appeared were remarkably similar: a wolf's head, swamps, quicksand, someone drowning, a typhoon brewing. In many instances, two or more participants reported the same image. The board did not know what to make of this odd collective phenomenon.

In our final report we simply reported back to the participants their own images and suggested that the members of the board be on the alert for trouble, even upheaval, at the foundation. Our admonition was ignored. But a few months later exactly the events that the shadowy images foretold occurred. There was a palace coup, the president and his personally selected board were fired, and a new board appointed.

I will return to this case in chapter 9, as it raises interesting questions about the synchronicity of present, past, and future events.

Rape of the Heavens

The exploration and exploitation of Outer Space is perhaps the grandest arena to view how humanity's technological virtuosity and the Shadow are connected and running amok. At present, the Federal Communications Commission has received over 100,000 frequency license applications for satellites and millions of earth stations. The FCC is issuing these licenses without any systematic assessment of the risks, including space debris, collisions, cyberattacks (our experts tell us that a satellite can be cyber-captured and weaponized in thirty seconds), interference with astronomical research, and a wide swath of environmental impacts. These risks are starkly outlined in the Healthy Heavens Trust Citizens Petition to the FCC of March 11, 2021, endorsing an International Declaration calling for comprehensive programmatic risk assessment.[75] The Petition pointed out how these risks amplify one another, with the increasing possibility that even a minor perturbation in one area could trigger a cascade of damage in others. Among these risks, one of the most significant is the possibility of conflict with China. There appears to be no off-ramp or even effective international dialogue to prevent a war between China and the U.S. in Outer Space.

The Healthy Heavens Trust Initiative asserts that we cannot allow decisions of this magnitude to be made behind closed doors by powerful satellite company executives and their compliant regulators. The international public has a fundamental human right to be accurately informed about such technological experiments and their likely consequences. Without any legal or political check on the Shadow, Outer Space along with the oceans (which are currently being colonized in the new "Ocean of Things") will be irretrievably altered and lost as the common heritage of humanity and our living planet.

This is an unfolding tragedy that I discuss in Chapter 15 of this book, especially the efforts of our legal team at BBILAN[76] (Balanced Broadband International Legal Action Network) to forestall it.

Learning from the Shadow

What do these stories tell us? First, the Shadow is ubiquitous, and our psyches are entangled, in individual transactions and on a grand planetary scale. Second, with social media, the Internet of Things (IoT), and artificial intelligence (AI), it is becoming increasingly difficult to distinguish what is "real" from what is contrived. We are living and working in a world based on other powerful people's agendas. Third, as the case of the Midwest foundation suggests, the fruits of the past and the seeds of the future all reside in the present. Fourth, perhaps surprisingly, we have far greater sway over how we respond to the Shadow, both external and internal, than we suppose. We may not be able to control the Shadow, but we can become aware of it, and that is a powerful first step.

Lastly, the Shadow contains within itself not only negative and destructive tendencies, but also an infinite and unrealized potential for beauty, wisdom, kindness, and love that we are all heir to. Leonardo da Vinci perfected the use of shadow, which he called *sfumato*, into the highest art form in the Mona Lisa and other paintings. I find in my own attempts at artistic expression that the Shadow can sometimes appear by chance, unintended, for example in this dream-like image of a *Dragon Guarding the Source*.[77]

Illustration 2

The Shadow's power and beauty reside within each of us, just below the surface of our personal awareness. The Shadow is also a vital source of our creativity. We have no cause to fear the Shadow, if we can learn to accept and work with it.

The ancients may have believed that character is destiny, but I have found that we have to a surprising extent free will and personal choice. A leopard can indeed change its spots.

ESSENTIALS

Chapter 3: Just Click!

*One day Chang Sha went for a ramble in the
mountains. When he returned and reached the gate, the
head monk inquired, "Where are you coming from,
Master?*
Sha said, "from wandering in the mountains."
The head monk continued, "Where did you go?"
*Sha replied, "First, I pursued the fragrant grasses, then I
returned following the falling flowers."*
—*Blue Cliff Record* (Hekiganroku), Case 36

Soon after I arrived in Tokyo in 1984 to open the Pacific Law Group I contacted Yamada Koun Roshi, through an introduction from my Zen teacher in Hawaii, Robert Aiken.[78] The Roshi promptly invited me to visit him in Kamakura. His home was a 20-minute walk from the train station and not too distant from the famous statue of the Great Sitting Buddha.[79] From our very first encounter, Yamada Roshi and his wonderful wife, Dr. Myoen Yamada ("Okusama") glowed with warmth and kindness toward me, as if we were old friends.

As we were drinking coffee, the Roshi smiled and suddenly inquired, "Can you show me the taste of this coffee? Don't describe it with words, show me!" What an odd Zen question, I thought, and stumbled around, stabbing at answers. And so began our friendship, which lasted another five years until his death at age 83.

Everything in the universe seemed to focus at that moment on that singular question. We worked together on *koans* over those years, whenever I visited Japan to train at the San-un zendo. A *koan* is a Zen case or story that guides the student toward discovering the essential.[80] You don't "solve" a *koan* as you would an intellectual puzzle. You simply hang out with it, and if you are patient, often the *koan*, at its own pace and time, will approach you, something like zoologist Dian Fossey's experience with the mountain gorillas.

Chang Sha's story in the headnote is one of my favorite *koans*. I spent the first forty years of my life chasing after fragrant grasses—this passion, that entrepreneurial venture; now, during my second forty years, I am following the falling flowers, until one day I will be one of them.

As part of their training, Yamada Roshi introduced to his students—via dharma talks (*teisho*) and direct encounters (*dokusan*)—what he described as the "Source". Although not a mathematician, the Roshi was interested in capturing precisely and succinctly, as a mathematic expression, the essence of his own discoveries distilled from a life of Zen practice. The ratio below expresses his most important insight:

$$1 \equiv \frac{\alpha}{\textcircled{\infty}}$$

The denominator is depicted as a circle containing the symbol for infinity. Yamada Roshi often referred to the "essential world" of Zen in this way, each moment—boundless and infinite. The numerator is depicted as "alpha." In other words, the essential world suddenly reveals itself in this very moment, then vanishes, giving way to the next. The art of Zen, which is the art of life, points directly to the experience of what is happening in this moment—right here, right now.

Illustrations # 3 & 4 below depict an octopus and a monkey contemplating the Source and having this experience of simply being in the moment. I view the octopus and monkey[81] (honoring Hasegawa Tōhaku) as benevolent familiars, available to guide us on the path.

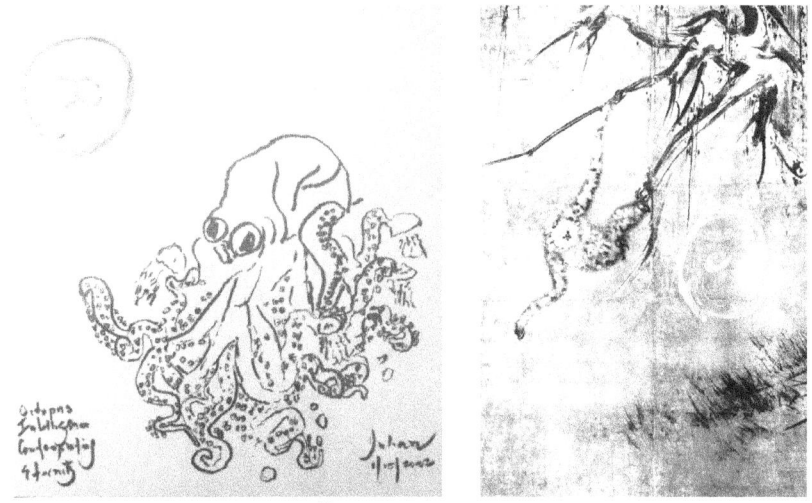

Illustrations 3 & 4

Just Click!—A Simple Practice

A simple practice can change your life in an instant. It is possible. Try this.

First, Just Click your fingers. I recommend clicking (or snapping) both fingers simultaneously, which may promote the brain's hemispheric coherence.[82] As you practice, you may want to formulate your own mnemonic device that enables you instantly to enter this state.[83]

Refuge. For me, this is a place of refuge.[84] In this moment, the troubles and turmoil of the outside world slip away and vanish, and the inner becomes alive.[85]

Quieting the Heart.[86] Next, I quiet the energy field around the Heart. My teacher, *qigong* grandmaster Li Junfeng, observes, "The Heart is the governor of the Mind. When the Heart is quiet, the Mind also becomes peaceful." In *Paradise Lost* John Milton writes, "The mind is its own place, and in itself can make a heaven of hell, a hell of heaven." Quieting the Heart offers in an instant a way to transit out of hell.

Here is an image that helps me to quiet the Heart. I simply merge with the stillness, the light of the moon over the lake.

I have come to learn and directly to experience that the Heart is a powerful transmitter and receiver of Love, and another vital life energy, which is called "*Qi*" in the Chinese language and "*Ki*" in Japanese.

Opening the Heart.[87] I bring awareness to "open" this Heart energy field of Love and Qi which surrounds the physical heart, and direct the field back to my heart. This produces an eddy of vital energy around my physical heart. There is no tension between a tranquil mind and an open Heart. They complement one another.

Dialoguing with the Heart. Often the physical heart responds, and thus begins a dialogue with the energetic Heart.

Connecting the Heart Energy to External and Inner Fields.[88] Next, I observe what is happening right before me in the external or inner worlds. I take note of whatever presents itself, or seems at that moment to tug at my awareness, saying, however gently, "How about me?" It can be a hummingbird, a leaf, a cloud, an idea, an emotion, or simply silence.[89] For this practice, it really doesn't matter. What matters is whatever appears at this moment in my life, as if for the very first time. I experience this moment in innocence. Then I connect the Heart energy field to this sudden manifestation of the essential world, with Love...and often it reciprocates. I find even a rock can reciprocate with Love. The deeper I connect, the more powerfully what is appearing, responds.[90]

It is an ancient discovery embraced by many indigenous people. Henry Crow Dog speaks:

> The earth is a living thing. Mountains speak, trees sing, lakes can think, pebbles have a soul, rocks have power.

Similarly in Shakespeare's *As You Like It* (Act II, Scene I):

> And this our life, exempt from public haunt,
> Finds tongues in trees, books in the running brooks,
> Sermons in stones, and good in everything.

Happiness. For me, this dynamic exchange of Love with each moment is a state of Happiness, even bliss. I am reminded once again that what is most essential is to love our life.

Vitality and Resilience. After experiencing all of the above, I feel my life force, resilience, and creative powers gathering.

Gratitude. I am deeply grateful for this chance encounter, which is available to me, whenever I choose, each day, each moment, ever new.[91]

Paying Forward. I do not hoard the joy it has brought me, but rather pass it on.[92]

Chapter 4: Love

Take away these hearts of stone and give us hearts of flesh; take away this 'murdherin' hate and give us thy own Eternal Love.
—Sean O'Casey, *Juno and the Paycock*

But if the while I think on thee, dear friend,
All losses are restor'd, and sorrows end.
—Shakespeare Sonnet 80

Though I speak with the tongues of men and of angels, and have not charity, I am become as sounding brass, or a tinkling cymbal.
—1 Corinthians 13:1, *King James Bible*

Kindness is the language which the deaf can hear and the blind can see.
—Mark Twain

Most people view Love as an emotion. Professor Barbara Fredrickson of the University of North Carolina has extensively researched the subject and has written a book, *Love 2.0*, based on this premise. I suggest that in addition to its emotional valence, however, Love is an especially powerful energy field that is concentrated around the Heart.

The simple practice I described in Chapter 3 enables us instantly to cultivate this dynamic energy field of Love; first by quieting and then opening, the energy field of the Heart, which is Love and Qi; thereafter, connecting these sources of powerful energy to everything, both within and outside of ourself.[93] All of creation is alive—hummingbirds, flowers, and spiders. Ostensibly inanimate things can also receive and return Love— rocks, bridges, sounds and their echoes, the moon, and the sun; and, hard as it may be to believe, mechanic devices or computer systems like the Internet! They are all, at least potentially, transceivers of this extraordinary, subtle, as-yet unmeasured form of energy.

When we imbue each living moment with the Heart's energy, when we intentionally connect with Love to what is happening before our eyes and other senses, I have discovered that something extraordinary happens. A feedback loop is created— everything gives back Love, and the bounty is compounded. The miracle, which defies the conventional laws of diminishing marginal returns,[94] is that the more Love is given away, the more it increases. The abundance of Love turns the conventional economics of scarcity on its head.

I have discovered that there is a simple and direct relationship between Love and resilience. The more fully we engage in giving and receiving Love unconditionally, the greater our personal resilience; and the more powerfully it is transmitted and empowers others. I call this the "Resilience Multiplier Effect."

Our distant ancestors, and the ancient Greeks, and indigenous peoples throughout time have understood this secret. They made gods of the Sun, the Moon, the Sky, the Winds, and the Tides; and they connected with the natural world through Love and reverence.

The Whole World is Medicine[95]

There is a wonderful *koan* by Yunmen—"The whole world is medicine." (*Blue Cliff Record,* Case 87) For me, Love and Beauty have profound healing properties, as they work at the deep heart's core. Thus, every moment can be a source of nourishment when imbued with unconditional Love.

Self-Care

Vitality, which I discuss in Chapter 6, begins with self-care, and the root of self-care is Love. Here is one of my favorite *koans,* Case 94 from the *Book of Equanimity* (*Shoyoroku* in Japanese):

> Tôzan was unwell. A monk asked, "Your Reverence is unwell. Is there anyone who does not become ill?" Tôzan said, "There is."
> The monk continued, "Does the one who does not get ill take care of Your Reverence?" Tôzan said, "'The old monk' is properly taking care of that one."
> The monk queried, "How about when 'your Reverence' takes care of that one?" Tôzan replied, "[The old monk] does not see that there is illness."

How does one discover "that one?" There is no pat answer. The *koan* is an invitation and points the way. It is a personal journey. This book chronicles my personal experience: to open the heart of Love is to discover that one. Each of us is the old monk.

Enhanced Placebo

The placebo effect generally refers to a beneficial outcome, caused by a pharmacological treatment, that is not attributable to the properties of the drug itself. This effect occurs if, for example, individuals taking pills with no active pharmacological agent have improved health outcomes compared with those taking no pills. There is an increasing body of research[96] pointing to the mind and creative imagination as producing a placebo effect. A recent Harvard study[97] confirms that placebos work on symptoms modulated by the brain, such as the perception of pain. "Placebos may make you feel better, but they will not cure you," states Professor Ted Kaptchuk of the Harvard-affiliated Beth Israel Deaconess Medical Center. "They have been shown to be most effective for conditions like pain management, stress-related insomnia, and cancer treatment side effects like fatigue and nausea."

I hypothesize that Love, in particular unconditional Love, which allows this uniquely powerful energy field surrounding the Heart to flow without interruption, will enhance the placebo effect. There is some scientific research that supports this conjecture. A recent study[98] confirms that oxytocin,[99] a hormone that fosters bonding and feelings of trust, may enhance the placebo effect. There are also a number of scientific studies on the power of prayer in healing.[100]

As I write this section, I am putting my idea to the test. A few weeks ago, on August 25, 2022, I underwent full ankle replacement surgery and as I write this section am now confined to a wheelchair and walker. I have a sixty-year history of trauma involving my right ankle, beginning with a bad sprain at seventeen when I caught my baseball shoe's spike in a fence, frequent injuries in judo, and over one hundred subluxations and dislocations. According to my surgeon, a leading ankle specialist, my prognosis is good, but at my age no one can know for sure what the outcome will be.

My protocol is simple. First, I acknowledge the suffering my ankle has undergone over many years. It occurs to me that my ankle must feel orphaned; no one has cared, no one has really listened for sixty years. Like Cosette in Victor Hugo's *Les Miserables,* my ankle has been an abused drudge consigned to the most menial of tasks. When I connect my Heart Love energy to my ankle, this sense of unattended grievance is the first message I get from my ankle. But now it is telling me much more. When I go into "creative reverie," which I explain in Chapter 9, my ankle is happy and grateful, especially when I talk to it, actually see and feel the ankle taking cautious first steps; and then, slowly, strong, powerful, and healthy steps, supporting my running swift as the wind, as it once did when I was young. I perceive a light emanating from my ankle, and I have the sense it is sending Love back to me. I check in with my ankle several times a day, but I am careful not to intrude. I like to think of myself in this regard as a respectful and caring friend. As I adopt this attitude, I begin to sense that the ankle, while part of me, has its own personality, its own journey; and I listen to it and respect it.

However, I do not focus solely on the ankle. I am actively cultivating my life force, in Japanese *"joriki"* [101] (定力) —the power, strength, or ability to remain stable, undisturbed, balanced, and focused, with equanimity, in the midst of the vicissitudes of life. *Joriki* builds from zazen practice. I connect my Heart Love energy field to the entire universe, and receive its Love in return. I understand that not only my ankle has been injured, and then traumatized by the surgery, but my entire body as well. Thus, I have a larger healing strategy to restore and to rebuild my body's integral resilience on every level, viewing the challenge of my ankle as an opportunity.

I don't have a clue if any of this will hasten my healing.[102] I suspect it will.[103] But I know enough about these processes, as I explain in later chapters, to get out of the way. Wise farmers do not dig up the ground to check on the seedlings they have just planted.

Week Nine Update

I can now walk easily, without a cast, boot, or cane. I am told by the therapist that this speed of recovery is a near record for a full ankle replacement, or arthroplasty, performed on someone who is approaching eighty. I give great credit to my surgeon. Surely my accelerated recovery is a tribute to his art and skill, especially as I was informed by a local orthopedic surgeon that my operation was too risky to perform. I like to believe that my protocol of connecting the Heart energy of love in a dialogue with the ankle has also helped, and has connected this same energy with the healing powers of the natural world. When the ankle swells, I feel the swelling melting upward toward the knee. The ankle is alive! Then, too, the fact that my surgeon has taken the time, despite being very busy, to respond kindly to my various questions and concerns has also played a part. It matters for patients to know that their physician actually cares. I am humbly and gratefully amazed at the results.[104]

Loving Our Life

When I practice Just Click! I enter a sanctuary, shielded from the turmoil of the world, and am reminded to love my life. It is not that I completely forget this admonition in the midst of my day-to-day activities, but often the realization of just how brief, delicate, and precious each moment is, recedes from consciousness, like an actor exiting the stage.

I have discovered that I can reexperience loving my life not only in the living moment but also through memories—thousands and thousands of them—that I can reanimate by illuminating them with the light of Love. One such special memory that often returns to me is of an inn at Matsuyama, a city on the island of Shikoku by the shore of Japan's Inland Sea. It is a beautiful summer's evening and the sun is slowly sinking to rest in the water. I am sitting on a veranda with my friends, Dr. Daijo Hashimoto, and his childhood playmate, a Japanese mixture of a sumo wrestler and Falstaff, whom we both affectionately refer to as "Takachan" (his last name is Nakajima). The fishermen are gathering their nets and hauling their boats across the beach—"yoosh! yoran soran, yoi dokoisho!"—they cry.[105] The conditions are ideal. It will be a bountiful catch.

From a neighboring *okiya* (geisha house) the sound of a plucked *samisen*[106] and a song, *Soran Bushi,*[107] of the fishermen float in the air, joined by bursts of laughter as the drinking guests disport themselves with the *geisha.* This song brings me back to years before, when I first arrived in Japan as a young law student. In those days, I played my recorder and oboe at *Oiwake Minyo Sakaba,* a people's pub in a section of Tokyo known as *Uguisudani,* "the Nightingale Valley," where *Soran Bushi* was very popular among the guests. My Japanese is strong, and as the evening and the drafts of beer gather steam, Daijo, Takachan, and I share our thoughts about a broad range of topics—personal, philosophical, and ribald. It all seemed second nature to me. I loved the feeling of dropping the robes of one identity and becoming part of an entirely different world, not only of contemporary Japan but also its past.

When I conjure this memory, especially when I animate it with the Heart's energy of Love, it becomes as alive to me as if I were there now; fifty-five years vanish in a second. I will return to this insight in Chapter 7.

It seems to me that our past can be as alive as our present. Our memories reach out to us, merging in the present with our projections of the future, and Love can shape this process.

One of the most intriguing ways Love is revealed to us is through Coincidence, Synchronicity, and Serendipity (CSS), which I discuss in Chapter 9. Unexpected, extraordinary things happen, which religious traditions identify as miracles. I suggest that CSS events present opportunities to rediscover that we are intimately connected with the enduring power and energy of Love. Given the widespread trauma in the world today, that in itself is a miracle.

Chapter 5: Beauty

Beloved Pan, and all ye other gods who haunt this place,
Grant me the beauty of the inward spirit
And may the outer and inner be as one.
—Fifth century BC, *Prayer of Socrates*, translated by
Gisela Kahn Gresser

"If I should say to this moment, 'Stay a while, you are so
beautiful.'" (Verweile doch, du bist so schön.)
—Goethe, *Faust* Part I

Legends say that hummingbirds float free of time,
carrying our hopes for love, joy and celebration.
Hummingbirds open our eyes to the wonder of the world
and inspire us to open our hearts to loved ones and
friends. Like a hummingbird, we aspire to hover and to
savor each moment as it passes, embrace all that life has
to offer and to celebrate the joy of everyday. The
hummingbird's delicate grace reminds us that life is rich,
beauty is everywhere, every personal connection has
meaning and that laughter is life's sweetest creation.
—Papyrus Greeting Card

The most beautiful expression of Just Click! I know is Saint Francis's Simple Prayer:[108]

> Lord, make me an instrument of your peace.
> where there is hatred, let me bring love.
> where there is offense, let me bring pardon.
> where there is discord, let me bring union.
> where there is error, let me bring truth.
> where there is doubt, let me bring faith.
> where there is despair, let me bring hope.
> where there is darkness, let me bring your light.
> where there is sadness, let me bring joy.
>
> O Master, let me not seek as much
> to be consoled as to console,
> to be understood as to understand,
> to be loved as to love,
>
> For it is in giving that one receives,
> it is in self-forgetting that one finds,
> it is in pardoning that one is pardoned,
> it is in dying that one is raised to eternal life.
> Amen.

The historic Giovanni di Pietro di Bernadone was a Catholic monk who lived in the thirteenth century in the Italian hill town of Assisi. After his death the Church sanctified him as Saint Francis,[109] recognizing his piety and original innocence. His poetry shines across eight centuries, illuminating the entire world. For me, not a religious person, the *Simple Prayer* becomes even more powerful when we understand "Master" and "Lord" to be none other than our own true self.

The experience of Beauty interrupts our endless cycle of busyness and connects us for a moment to the Eternal. Our souls thirst for Beauty, and yet we often fail to sense this yearning, even when Beauty stands right before us, pleading to be acknowledged. A *koan* from the *Blue Cliff Record* points to this failure to recognize Beauty: "People these days see this flower as in a dream."

And yet like Love, Beauty is everywhere, and to be found in the simplest of things. Victor Hugo wrote of his hero Jean Valjean in *Les Miserables*:

> A garden to walk in and an immensity to dream
> in. What more could he ask? A few flowers at his
> feet and above him the stars.

The goal is to be open to discovering Beauty in the most unremarkable and unexpected places. There is a wonderful poem in the *Zenrinkushu*:[110]

> I visited and returned; it was nothing special.
> Mount Ro veiled in misty rain; the Sekko River at
> high tide.

When we discover the extraordinary in nothing special, the arc of Beauty easily expands to include everything we encounter.

References:

The following links offer for me what the late pianist Glenn Gould found in the works of J. S. Bach's Brandenburg Concerto no. 5, "The joyous essence of being."

Discovering Beauty[111]
Softly Sweet in Lydian Measures[112]
Art Thou Troubled?[113]

Connecting to Nature

Jungian psychologist James Hillman called it "notitia," careful attention that is sustained, patient, observing, and subtly attuned to the images, metaphors, and signals from Nature.[114] The botanist Stephen Harrod Buhner, in *Plant Intelligence and the Imaginal Realm*, calls it "The Golden Thread," citing Basho, Blake, Goethe, and Fukuoka. The Golden Thread is the subtle energy abiding in all creations. It connects and leads us, as Blake writes, to "Heaven's Gate." The wave that carries us there is Love, simply "being with" what is. Because Nature is beautiful and bountiful, it is easy to catch The Golden Thread. It is everywhere. Just watch, wait, and notice. When we do, not knowing becomes a gate to intimacy and empathy.

References:

Connecting with Nature[115]
Secret Teachings of Plants[116]
Plant Intelligence and the Imaginal Realm[117]

Forgetting Oneself

On a sultry summer day in Kamakura, I met with Yamada Roshi in *dokusan*—a private, one-on-one interview. At that moment a cat was making its marvelous acrobatic way along the top of a wall. In admiration, I asked in all seriousness, "Sensei, how can I become that cat?" "Forget yourself," Yamada Roshi replied kindly. What a secret to become anything! Just forget yourself. Almost 40 years later, I am still exploring that deceptively simple "just."

Compassion: A Blind Man's Story

For me Love, Compassion, and Beauty are inextricably linked. Here is a Zen story retold by Paul Reps, in *Zen Flesh Zen Bones*, which I have slightly revised to distill its essence.

After the Zen master Bankei passed away, pilgrims visited his temple and would question a blind man who continued to seek alms outside the temple.

> Tell us of Master Bankei," they would ask, "you must have encountered him." "Because I am blind," he replied, "I cannot see a person's face, so I must judge a person by the sound of his or her voice. Ordinarily, when I hear someone congratulate another on happiness or success, I also hear a secret tone of envy. When condolence is expressed for the misfortune of another, I detect relief that this misfortune did not fall upon them. But Bankei was different. When he learned of the happiness of another, I heard only happiness in his voice. And when another told him of sadness or misfortune, I could hear only sadness in his response.

Gratefulness

The Benedictine monk Brother David Steindl-Rast, whom I mentioned in the Preface, summarized all that I have learned in almost forty years of Zen practice in three words: *Stop! Look! Go!*[118] In any moment, Stop what you are doing. Look at what is happening. Then, Go with the flow. You don't ask for this moment—it is given to you. This day, this moment, will never come again. They are a gift. By loving our life in this way, gratefulness comes easily.

But there is an interesting hitch. In his essay on *Compensation*[119], Emerson presents this challenge:

> In the order of nature, we cannot render benefits to those from whom we receive them, or only seldom. But the benefit we receive must be rendered again, line for line, deed for deed, cent for cent, to somebody. Beware of too much good staying in your hand. It will fast corrupt and worm worms. Pay it away quickly in some sort.

Why does hoarding too much good "worm worms?"[120] Because hoarding blocks the flow of our creative energies, our life force. The next chapter explores what can happen when we release our coiling vital powers.

Coda on Beauty

Seamus Heaney, *Postscript:*

And some time make the time to drive out west
Into County Clare, along the Flaggy Shore,
In September or October, when the wind
And the light are working off each other
So that the ocean on one side is wild
With foam and glitter, and inland among stones
The surface of a slate-grey lake is lit
By the earthed lightning of a flock of swans,
Their feathers roughed and ruffling, white on white,
Their fully grown headstrong-looking heads
Tucked or cresting or busy underwater.
Useless to think you'll park and capture it

More thoroughly. You are neither here nor there,
A hurry through which known and strange things pass
As big soft buffetings come at the car sideways
And catch the heart off guard and blow it open.

Seamus Heaney on writing "*Postscript*": a "sidelong glimpse
of something flying past" —*The Irish Times*[121]

And then there is this reply by his countryman William
Butler Yeats, now dead these 88 years. You can hear his living
voice in "*The Lake Isle of Innisfree*" by visiting the link provided
in the Endnote.[122]

Chapter 6: Vitality

O' for a Muse of fire, that would ascend
The brightest heaven of invention
—Shakespeare, *Henry V*, Prologue

A monk asks, "This physical body perishes and
decays. What is the hard, fast, imperishable
body of reality?"
The teacher responds: "Mountain flowers bloom
like brocade. The valley streams brim deep
indigo."
—*The Blue Cliff Record*, Case 82

Be like water my friend.
—Bruce Lee

In my salad days, when I was green in judgment,[123] I would leave the aikido dojo in Tokyo after hard training and believe that if I were hit by a bus, it would be too bad for the bus. "I was so much older then, I'm younger than that now," as Dylan rhapsodizes.[124] I did not understand in those days how to balance youthful exuberance with wisdom.

In this chapter I want to explore more deeply how Love and Qi together are the wellsprings of Vitality and Creativity, and in Chapters 7-9 how they also hold keys to Wisdom and Synchronicity.

To be clear, when I refer to "Vitality" I have in mind three powerful sources of energy: 1) Conventional physical energy as understood in the West, such as physical light or energy from biological reactions; 2) Qi, a subtle form of energy (also known as "Ki" in Japanese). (Interestingly, Qi is written in both languages with the character of rice, a staple of nourishment in East Asia, bubbling in a caldron); and 3) Love, as described in Chapter 4. All three are wellsprings of Vitality, an extraordinary reservoir we can draw on to undertake positive and creative work in the world.

Thus, every moment can be a source of nourishment when imbued with Love. As expressed in Yumen's great *koan*: "The whole world is medicine."

Finding Your Power[125]

I once asked my qigong teacher, Master Li Junfeng, head coach of the Chinese Women's Wushu (Kung Fu) Olympic Team who, I am told, guided the team to over a hundred gold medals:

> "Where is the source of power?"
> "Relax," he replied.
> "But how to relax?" I continued.
> "Loose," he smiled, "like a snake, no bones."

During the 1990s I trained in San Francisco's Golden Gate Park with gong fu Master George Xu.[126] Master Xu would invite his own teachers from China to visit San Francisco and instruct his students. On one occasion he invited Grandmaster Yueh Xiao Lung, a diminutive elderly Chinese teacher, who George (who had himself trained the Chinese Red Guards) was terrified of. "Don't go near him," he warned. "His power is formidable." As I learned, one secret of Grandmaster Yueh's power was that he was able to relax his muscles and tendons, so that his individual Qi connected to the energy and power (Qi) of the Earth. When he struck, it was no longer Master Yueh striking you. It was the Earth's Qi transmuted through Grandmaster Yueh. Master Xu instructed us, "Relax, yes; but not tofu!"

Here is another George Xu story:

> Master Xu had just returned from a visit to his home city, Shanghai, where on the Bund[127] he encountered a lady surrounded by a crowd, demonstrating her extraordinary Qi power. "I can kill you even from a distance," she bragged. George, who was observing her carefully, challenged, "OK, kill me. Let me see you do it!" The lady qigong 'master' demurred. "Not here, some other time."
>
> "George, that was pretty ballsy of you. What if she really delivered?" I asked.
>
> "Look, I'm a martial artist. I must be prepared to die at any moment," George replied, and then added, almost as an afterthought, "Anyway, I wanted the taste of it!"

I like this remarkable answer: He wanted to taste her power, to experience the real taste of being alive without fear. My friend the master calligrapher/painter Kazuaki Tanahashi calls this getting in touch with our "inner wildness." I try to express this freed energy in my own Zenga (a Zen style of calligraphy and painting), illustrated in earlier chapters.

Creative Imagination

One route to finding your power is through creative imagination. Here is a favorite story of mine, largely borrowed from the artist, poet, and author Paul Reps:

> "In the early days of the Meiji era there lived a well-known wrestler called O-nami, which means Great Waves. O-nami was immensely strong and knew the art of wrestling. In his private bouts he defeated even his teacher, but in public he was so bashful that his own pupils threw him.
>
> O-nami felt he should go to a Zen master for help. Hakuju, a wandering teacher, was residing in a little temple nearby, so O-nami went to see him and told him of his trouble. Great Waves is your name,' the teacher advised, 'so stay in this temple tonight. Imagine that you are those billows. You are no longer a wrestler who is afraid. You are those huge waves sweeping everything before them, swallowing all in their path. Do this and you will be the greatest wrestler in the land.'
>
> The teacher retired. O-nami sat in meditation trying to imagine himself as waves. He thought of many different things. Then gradually he turned more and more to the feelings of the waves. As the night advanced the waves became larger and larger. They swept away the flowers in their vases. Even the Buddha in the shrine was inundated.

Before dawn the temple was nothing but the ebb
and flow of an immense sea.

In the morning the teacher found O-nami
meditating, a faint smile on his face. He patted the
wrestler's shoulder. 'Now nothing can disturb
you.' he said. 'You are the waves. You will sweep
everything before you.' The same day O-nami
entered the wrestling contests and won. After
that, no one in Japan was able to defeat him."
(From Paul Reps and Nyogen Senzaki, *Zen Flesh,
Zen Bones,* 1957).

The reader may enjoy pondering this story while listening to
The Many Great Waves of Kanagawa[128] on the Laughing Heart
website.[129]

Harvesting Creative Genius in Music[130]

Since ancient times many cultures have recognized that certain
frequencies of sound, embodied in chants, sutras, and mantras,
have special healing effects, or can enable us to enter states of
empowerment and expanded awareness. The Greek
philosopher Pythagoras, for example, was among the first to
perceive the close connection between the "harmony of the
spheres," mathematics, and healing. The energy field of the
Heart is fine-tuned to receive and transmit the special qualities
of sound.

I have had the sense for many years—especially when
listening to the works of J. S. Bach, Mozart, Beethoven, and
Handel—that their musical genius was flowing directly into my
cells, like a magical herb, transforming everything it touches.
Perhaps you too have had this experience?

For example, what if it is possible to "step down" the
Promethean creative energy encoded in Mozart's Jupiter

Symphony[131] (scroll to link of Arturo Toscanini conducting) and transmute it to nourish and support our efforts to do good work in the world? The key is simply to connect the energy field of the Heart, which is Love, to the symphony and let the flow take you where it will. Just like the Many Great Waves of Kanagawa.[132]

Note: If you have enjoyed the experiment with the *Jupiter*, try tapping into the mad energy of Beethoven's Kreutzer Sonata.[133]

Alive Inside[134]

In Greek mythology Mnemosyne[135], the goddess of memory, daughter of Uranus (Heaven) and Gaea (Earth), was the mother of the nine Muses, one of whom, Euterpe[136], was the patron of music and lyric poetry. Hence, music and memory are deeply linked as archetypes in the collective Western consciousness.

In an extraordinary documentary, *Alive Inside*, social worker Dan Cohen describes his work in bringing light and life to patients in nursing homes and old age centers. "The power of music," Cohen explains, "only becomes understandable when we understand their isolation." Over 1,600,000 patients in these facilities in the US today are isolated, unreachable, despairing, hopeless, discarded, and forgotten. Says Dr. Eric Thomas, a gerontologist, who eloquently co-narrates the video, "We haven't done anything medically speaking to touch the heart and soul of the patient." Too often, it is more convenient to treat patients as machines and dose them with pharmaceuticals.

But Dan Cohen and Dr. Thomas are doing something radically different. As the famous neurologist Dr. Oliver Sacks[137] explains, "Music is the quickening art." The patients they engage with are presented with an iPod and asked this simple question: "Do you like music?" And all the patients, for a moment, light up. Then, when their favorite music is played on an iPod, they come to life, instantly. One patient, Mary Lou, has been lost in Alzheimer's for many years, but now, the narrator explains, "she thinks she is perfect again! She's flowing through life." "Music," he says, "gives us something we hunger for deeply, which we have possessed for thousands of years, our very brains are wired for. Music awakens in us our most profound safety."

Dr. Sacks and Dr. Thomas also provide some important insights on what is happening from a neurological perspective:

o   Music is inseparable from emotions and feelings.

o   Music affects and activates many parts of the brain, in some cases those dedicated to other functions and purposes, such as motion.

o   Music has the power to activate regions of the brain more than any other stimulus.

o   The parts of the brain activated by music are relatively unaffected by Alzheimer's and other forms of dementia.

o   Even before birth a fetus learns how to sing by listening to the mother's spoken words.

o   "It is surprising that a little music can evoke so much joy."

o   After twenty days a single cell jolts to life, followed by other cells all beating in unison, that become the human heart.

o   Music is as quintessentially human as language.

o   Music creates spontaneity (CSS).

o   Old age is viewed as a broken-down version of our former selves, instead of the next exciting stage in life's journey.

o   Music touches our sense of empathy. It is very painful for an isolated elderly person to have no one to receive these gifts of joy.

o   There is life after adulthood. We are made to age and learn, and to pass on what we have learned to others.

o Medicine dims the light. "These people need to engage in the world around them." (quote from video)

o The present health care system is actually blocking these patients' opportunities to reach out and become human again.

o The gift of a single headset can change the lives of 1.6 million people in nursing homes in the US.

Expanding the Inquiry

Alive Inside offers an immediate and compassionate solution to a major societal problem affecting more than a million and a half patients in nursing homes. *Alive Inside* also raises another set of intriguing questions:

o If music can animate the living dead lost in dementia, what about the rest of us?

o What if music can unlock distant memories for people of all ages?

o What happens when we connect the energy field of Love around the Heart to what we are hearing when listening to music? Will the energy of Love attract other memories?

o What happens when we connect the Heart's energy field of Love to memories, even without the aid of music?

o What happens when we explore this process within a community?

o What is the relationship between music, love, memory, and neuroplasticity?[138]

For me, music activates Kazuaki Tanahashi's "inner wildness." It is fascinating to observe the memories that start to constellate if I pay close attention while I listen to music. When

I quiet my Heart and then connect Love to these memories, something quite marvelous starts to happen: the memories come alive, and expand and multiply on their own. I can even take a heart-snapshot of this process, which enhances my ability to recall the experience at will, together with the cluster of memories it has evoked. Moreover, these memories acquire their own personality, especially when inspired by the energy of Love. I am reminded of this passage in Goethe's *Faust*:

> I nothing had, and yet enough for youth,
> Joy in Illusion, ardent thirst for Truth.
> Give unrestrained, the old emotion,
> The bliss that touched the verge of pain,
> The strength of Hate, Love's deep devotion,
> O, give me back my youth again!
> —Goethe, *Faust,* Part I

Even without music, when I engage the power of Love, the memories return. I am young again.

In exploring the subject of memory it is important to set a baseline. A good starting point is the research of the German psychologist Hermann Ebbinghaus[139] on the "forgetting curve." In 2015 a research team successfully reproduced his findings and concluded that his methods and theories still largely held true: even healthy people will forget as much as seventy percent of what they experience within only a few days!

Despite their conclusions, however, there are other reports[140] that underscore the positive interrelationships of Heart, the energy of Love, neuroplasticity, and healing in enhancing memory. There is also growing interest in the role of communities in supporting these processes.[141]

One study[142] from the Auditory Neuroscience Laboratory, Department of Communication Sciences and Disorders, Northwestern University reports:

Children from disadvantaged backgrounds often face impoverished auditory environments, such as greater exposure to ambient noise and fewer opportunities to participate in complex language interactions during development. These circumstances increase their risk for academic failure and dropout. Given the academic and neural benefits associated with musicianship, music training may be one method for providing auditory enrichment to children from disadvantaged backgrounds. We followed a group of primary-school students from gang reduction zones in Los Angeles, CA, USA for 2 years as they participated in Harmony Project. By providing free community music instruction for disadvantaged children, Harmony Project promotes the healthy development of children as learners, the development of children as ambassadors of peace and understanding, and the development of stronger communities. Children who were more engaged in the music program—as defined by better attendance and classroom participation—developed stronger brain encoding of speech after 2 years than their less-engaged peers in the program.

The Explorers Wheel[143]

Some years ago I conceived the idea of an Explorers Wheel, which is described in detail in my book *Piloting Through Chaos—The Explorers Mind*.[144] My earliest passion was to become an explorer, and this invention is its reflection. Unlike many inventors, I was not trying to solve a specific problem. The

Explorers Wheel simply appeared in my life as an expression of artistic exuberance.[145]

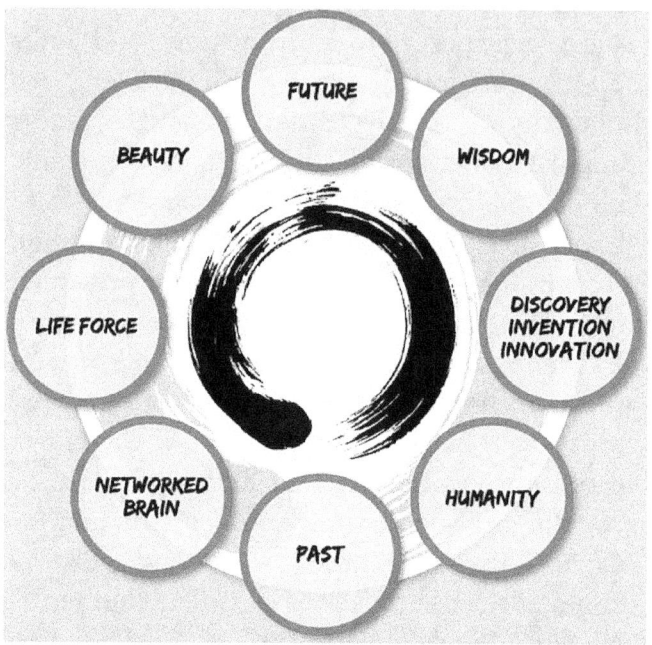

Diagram 1

The first thing you might notice is that the Wheel is arranged in eight "moons" around a central space or *enso*. I have a special feeling for the number 8, as I have always been an admirer of the octopus (see image in Chapter 3 of *Octopus Intelligence Contemplating the Source*[146]), and I like to think of the Explorers Wheel as an invitation to cultivate octopus intelligence[147]. It has been suggested that each octopus tentacle is a brain with its own special and independent intelligence. Like these tentacles, each moon in the Explorers Wheel has its own special dignity and also invites a dialogue with every other moon, separately and together. I call this process "intertidal thinking."[148] The intertidal zone is the area of the seashore where the ocean meets the land, as the tides flow in and out, and is generally recognized by marine biologists to be a place of great fertility. I believe the same is true for the intertidal zone where the Conscious meets the Unconscious (and Higher Conscious) Mind.

I invite you to begin the Explorers Wheel process by posing a central Discovery Question to the *enso*. Then spin the Wheel in your Mind and wait for a signal from any of the moons. Listen attentively. I find that if I am patient, I will often feel a tug, as if one or several of the moons is trying to tell me something. Sometimes the signal is very soft and subtle. I start to explore and soon find myself in dialogue with yet another moon. I begin to see the connection between these moons and my central Discovery Question.

These days as I am keenly interested in practically applying Big Heart Intelligence (BHI) whenever I have a chance to do so. I am experimenting with placing BHI at the center of the *enso* and noting what happens when each moon is imbued and enhanced with the Love of the Heart. For example, when I enter the moon of the Past, old memories, stories, and resentments I have carried with me for years seem to soften and to lose their grip. I understand better why in the Zen tradition tea houses play an important role for sojourners as way stations. While relaxing and enjoying a cup of tea, we let go of the weight of the many stories that we have carried in our minds for so many years.[149]

The Unconscious Mind has its own traps. I am also finding that by lightening up and really letting go of self-limiting thoughts and feelings, a floodgate of blocked creative energies and life force opens. I am experimenting with inserting the *koan Mu* inside the *enso*. In Japanese Zen practice *Mu* (*Wu* in Chinese) refers to vast and infinite spaciousness/nothingness. It is entertaining to explore each moon—Wisdom, Beauty, Life Force, Past, Future, and so forth—through the direct experience of *Mu*. And just as I am exploring the creative emptiness of *Mu*,

I open Paul Reps' *Zen Flesh, Zen Bones* and am greeted by this story, which I have shortened here:

A fourteenth-century Zen master, Bassui,[150] wrote the following letter to one of his disciples, who was about to die:

> The essence of your mind is not born, so it will never die. It is not emptiness which is mere void. It is neither color nor form. It enjoys no pleasures and suffers no pains. I know you are very ill. Like a good Zen student, you are facing that sickness squarely. You may not know exactly who is suffering, but question yourself in this way: what is the essence of this mind? Think only of this. You will need no more. Covet nothing. Your end which is endless is like a snowflake dissolving in pure air.

Resilience

> I have no parents. I make heaven and earth my parents.
> I have no home. I make awareness my home.
> I have no life or death. I make breath tides my life and death.
> I have no divine power. I make integrity my divine power.
> I have no means. I make understanding my means.
> I have no body. I make endurance my body.
> I have no eyes. I make the lightning flash my eyes.
> I have no ears. I make sensibility my ears.
> I have no limbs. I make promptness my limbs.
> I have no strategy. I make unshadowed-by-thought my strategy.

I have no designs. I make opportunity my design.
I have no miracles. I make right action my
miracles.
I have no principles. I make adaptability my
principle.
I have no tactics. I make emptiness/fullness my
tactics.
I have no friends. I make you, mind, my friend(s).
I have no enemy. I make carelessness my enemy.
I have no armor. I make compassion my armor.
I have no castle. I make heaven/earth my castle.
I have no sword. I make absence of self my sword.
—Fourteenth-century anonymous Samurai

Advanced Practice—Discovering Life Force

I want to introduce here an advanced practice that simultaneously builds vitality (life force), connectedness, and resilience. I return for a moment to the discoveries relating to my own healing process for my ankle which I discussed in Chapter 4. As noted, I view this process as strategic and holistic, engaging not only the operated ankle but also my entire body. My protocol contains these essential elements:

o Zhongtian Movement[151]—as explained by Qigong Grandmaster Li Junfeng in this video (up to 1:40), the Zhongtian Movement establishes the basic connection between ourselves and the universe.

o **A Simple Smile.** This straightforward practice in itself has wondrous healing properties.

o **Quieting the Heart**—see Chapter 3, Just Click!

o **Opening the Heart Energy Field of Love and Qi**—see Chapter 3, Just Click!

○ **Sending out Heart Energy** (see image of Hotei, one of seven happy deities, below). I send the Heart Energy of Love and Qi everywhere, and it is returned.

○ **Receiving Universal Energy.** The dialogue begins as in the above image of Hotei. I open the important Qi receptors, including the crown of the head (*baihui*), palms *(laogong)*, the center of my feet (bubbling spring, or *yongquan*), core solar plexus *(dantian)*, and, of course, heart energy field. I store overflowing vital energy in the *dantian*, one inch below and behind the navel.

○ **Connecting to Nature.** I especially connect with the wondrous energy of nature—a tree, a bird, the sky. The vital energy of nature is freely available to us anywhere, everywhere, anytime.

○ **Connecting to the Healing Life Force.** I simply enjoy connecting to my life force in this way, and find that when I do, life force can become a constant companion.

- o **Closing**—Zhongtian Movement performed in gratefulness.

Reference: *Laughing Heart—10 Essential Moves*[152]

A Simple Smile[153]
Finding Your Power[154]
Connecting to Nature[155]

Vitality and Resilience complement each other, although they are not the same. Vitality powers Resilience and Resilience nourishes Vitality. At seventy-nine I am less vital than I was at nineteen, when I practiced judo at the Kodokan in Tokyo. But I am not certain that I am any less resilient.

I am delighted that I can find support for this "aging paradox" in formal studies by researchers at NASA[156] and other scientists. With aging we gain gravitas, steadiness, and perspective that enables us to flow through turbulence. These qualities are also closely associated with Wisdom.

I have discovered a pattern in Resilience that I call "Adversity's Spiraling and Creative Wave Form,"[157] which is depicted in Diagram 2. *(see next page)*

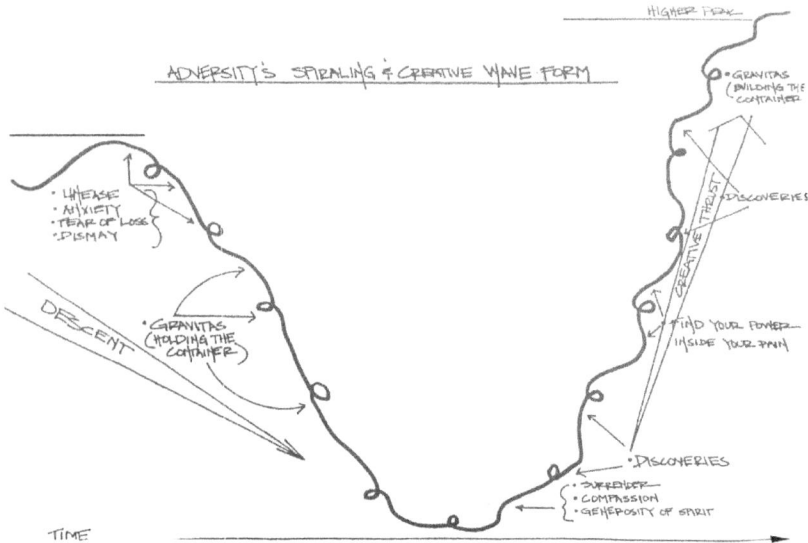

Life expresses itself in many colors and wavelike surges. The art of possessing a Laughing Heart is to work with what is. In this way every moment in the wave becomes an opening and a gate. Here is how the Laughing Heart approach can be applied to especially challenging circumstances.

The above diagram "Adversity's Spiraling and Creative Waves" traces the hero's and heroine's journey as described in countless myths, legends, and classics of literature—which is also our personal journey. At the upper left an event occurs. It may be just a slight shift that we interpret as a movement "downward," the beginning of a descent into difficulties, darkness, and despair. This gives rise to a vague sense of unease, an amorphous fear. Then something distinctly untoward happens, and we see a pattern developing. We call this "bad luck" or "adversity." Often the pattern continues to unfold and the spiral intensifies. As Shakespeare writes in *Hamlet,* "Sorrows come not as single spies but in battalions."

We descend further. Our journey into the dark wood becomes more treacherous. We try to find firm ground, but we falter, and soon we are approaching a place of despair. In *King Lear* (Act IV Scene 1) Shakespeare warns in the words of Edgar his son: "The worst is not so long as we can say, 'This is the worst.'" At this final place without a name, all that remains is a choice: to surrender and submit; or affirmatively to accept what the world appears to be offering us with generosity of heart and with compassion for ourselves and others. And then, in the midst of these desperate straits, I have found often there suddenly comes a moment of grace, a tender mercy in the form of a subtle shift—a kind act, a gentle word--a quiet glimmer of insight. If we can pay attention to the signal, the light will uplift us.

Then, unexpectedly, there is an opening, a loosening in the fabric that binds us. We begin, inexplicably, to sense our power, and we find our power inside our pain. Now we are on a creative upswing. More discoveries ensue; they come in flocks, like butterflies. Our creative energies uncoil and thrust us forward and upward. We emerge, gloriously, from the darkness, and arrive at a new, higher peak of life force and power. We are **ALIVE!** There can be no doubt of it, and our vessel is sturdier for the trials we have endured. Like ancient mariners in a stormy sea, we have held the tiller firm and found an opening through the waves. We have "Created Our Own Luck."[158]

Here are stories of three remarkable and dear friends who succeeded in working with Adversity's Spiraling and Creative Waves:

Grand Master Li Junfeng Lost in the Gobi Desert.[159] How resourceful Master Li survived for many days in the Gobi Desert without food or water.

The Tales of Dr. Harry Brown.[160] How Dr. Harry Brown, the founder of Surgical Eye Expeditions International (SEE International[161]) survived early struggles and adventures that led to his founding SEE International, which has restored sight to over 460,000 blind patients in economically disadvantaged countries around the world.

The Heroism of the Nass Family.[162] How the Nass family sheltered Jewish families during the Nazi occupation of Brussels in World War II, when at any moment they could have been executed.

All three stories illustrate the interplay of Vitality, Resilience, and Survival, and also Synchronicity, as discussed in Chapter 9. But there is another evolutionary value to cultivate, Wisdom, which I have often found is nourished by vitality in interesting ways.

Chapter 7: Wisdom in Daily Life

Happy is the person who finds wisdom,
And gains understanding;
For her proceeds are better than the profits of silver,
And her gain than fine gold.
She is more precious than rubies,
And all the things you may desire cannot compare with
her.
—*Proverbs* 3:13-15, King James Version

Thou shouldst not have been old till thou hadst been
wise.
—Shakespeare, *King Lear*, Fool's comment in Act, 1
Scene 5

Not knowing is most intimate.
—*Book of Equanimity*, Case 20

Vitality, Creativity, Resilience, Joy, Happiness—all have a connection with Wisdom, but they are not the same. Wisdom nourishes and is nourished by these and other evolutionary virtues, but it is distinct. In my work on *systemic integrity,* which I view as intimately tied to Wisdom, I have learned that Wisdom is a universal virtue treasured throughout history in all cultures and societies, ancient and modern, industrialized and indigenous. Sadly, in most "advanced" industrialized and commercialized societies greed and the pursuit of profit appear to have supplanted wisdom as a primary cultural value.

Through my work as a professional negotiator I have discovered that Wisdom is also a cultivatable skill. We can learn to become wise, or at least to grow wiser. This insight motivated me to create an app, *The Artful Navigator,* to harness the power of computers in a "Logos Network" (in Greek the "*Logos*" is equivalent to the *Tao,* an ordering principle of the Universe) that would enable individual users, organizations, indeed whole communities to discover their "Wisdom Genome" and help members learn to tap their innate potential to become wiser. The app transformed the great figures of history and literature into guides and mentors. I began by designing a Wisdom profile highlighting some of the key characteristics of a wise negotiator.

Using the concept of "integrity," which I defined as a dynamic balance between Mind, Heart, and Hand as the essential resource of a successful negotiator, and based on what I had learned from dealing with some of the most skillful and resourceful negotiators in the world, I produced a simple checklist, the Player Integrity Profile(s) (PIPS), which is illustrated below. Each component is discussed in my book *Piloting Through Chaos–The Explorers Mind. (see next page)*

PLAYER INTEGRITY PROFILE (PIPS)

Critical Factors	Low	Moderate	High
Matching (No Mismatching)			
Containment			
Trainability			
No Need, Non-Attachment			
The Pain/Need Ratio			
No Assumptions			
No Expectations			
Embraces "No"			
Controls Arrogance, Vanity & Greed			
Sense of Ease/Time to Spare			
Listens			
Ability to Attend			
Focus			
Nurtures			
Gravitas			
Thoroughly Awake & Present			
Sees the Work As It Is			
PIPS Total Score			

Diagram 3

I then studied the classics of Western and Eastern cultures, beginning with the Old and New Testaments, Shakespeare, and the *I Ching*. I selected passages that seemed to best express each specific attribute of my integrity/wisdom framework. Now, I had a practical way to transform Shakespeare and the *I Ching* into my personalized guides on every important life decision or challenge. For me, Shakespeare is as alive as my right hand.

One example: In all my current work as a professional negotiator, *No Assumptions* and *No Expectations* is an essential principle or "move." I consult my app The Artful Navigator (TAN), scroll through the index to Shakespeare, and there under the heading No Assumptions/No Expectations I come upon this remarkable quotation:

Be these juggling fiends no more believed, that palter with us in a double sense. That keep the word of l promise to our ear and break it to our hope.

The quote is from a critical moment in Shakespeare's *Macbeth*. Macbeth has discovered that his hubris, ambition, and arrogance have caused him to be blinded by the false assumption that Birnam Wood could never possibly advance and breach his castle walls at Dunsinane—notwithstanding what the three "weird sisters" (witches) had foretold. Yet, at this pivotal moment, where victory and defeat hang in the balance, Birnam Wood does start to move, because his enemy has cut down the trees and is using them as camouflage.

In the play, the "juggling fiends" are three witches, who very well may be projections of Macbeth's own Shadow. The language is beautiful, albeit archaic; but the core message— Challenge Your Assumptions and Expectations—is as applicable today in the early 21ˢᵗ century as it was in Elizabethan England. Beware the inner voice that urges us to ignore what is actually happening in our life! This is a central challenge of our times.

Hexagram 39[163] in the Chinese Wisdom classic the *I Ching or Book of Changes* has always been a particular favorite of mine. It addresses *Obstruction* and advises:

Difficulties or obstructions throw us back on ourselves. While the inferior person seeks to place the blame on others, bewailing fate, the superior person seeks to find the source of the error within, and through this introspection the external obstacles become an occasion for inner enrichment and education.

In other words, obstacles create opportunities to refine our character. Reflecting a similar perspective, the Greek philosopher Heraclites observed: "Character is destiny." I find it extraordinary how the difficulties and blockages in life can open fresh opportunities to change course and influence our personal destiny. This ability to discover the opening in the haze of an unbreachable obstacle is the very essence of personal resilience.

It is unnecessary to master every category in PIPS to become wiser; focusing on any element will begin the process. I have found that "Trainability," or the ability to inquire and rapidly learn from experience, is among the important markers of Wisdom. My colleague Ben jokingly characterizes its opposite, obdurate stubbornness, as "Often wrong, never in doubt."

Trainability does not apply only to momentary transactions. I find it valuable to look back over the course of my life and to ask myself: "What were the great fiascos? What were the dysfunctional behaviors that have weighed me down or constrained my creative energies?" As noted earlier, holding on to troubling memories or old resentments is high on my list. Especially as I age, I find that letting these go is very liberating.

Equanimity—When Present Reality Suddenly Breaks Through

Here is a story that illustrates an important aspect of Wisdom. I am at my desk in Santa Barbara. I am up against a deadline to file a Third Amended Complaint in litigation to save Lake Tahoe from being overrun with ever more cell towers emitting NIR that is already harming its residents. We must file in a few hours. I am also in the midst of writing this chapter on Wisdom.

Suddenly I get a call from Angela, my wife, who is in her mid-70s. She is in the hospital after having tripped and fallen. She has broken her arm and has a complex compound fracture. What do I do? Ben says to me on one of our regular Zoom calls,

"There's nothing you can do right now; she'll be fine. She's getting good care at the hospital. That's the data. Let's finish the Complaint." I can hear the pain and bewilderment in Angela's voice as she talks to me on the phone. Tears well up. I must help her, but I also must focus on the task at hand. I can't leave Ben in the lurch, as he is on a Zoom call from New Zealand. But my mind is not at ease. Suddenly Angela's myriad kindnesses and the abiding love that she has shown me over 40 years flash before me. It still hasn't dawned on me that I might—I will—someday lose her. But now? I begin to panic. What happened to the years of martial arts and Zen practice? All that training, and still my mind is not at rest in this situation.

Later that day, I had even greater cause for anguish. At around 2:00 a.m., hours after her release, Angela was in such pain as the nerve block medication wore off that we had to rush her to Santa Barbara's Cottage Hospital's Emergency Unit. We waited for three interminable hours while she writhed in unbearable pain and doctors and nurses struggled to find a way to alleviate her suffering, but to no avail. I could hardly bear it.

I have reflected during the weeks that have followed on the relationship of Wisdom to this issue of equanimity in the midst of pain. Here is an important *koan* that can provide some solace when we are lonely.

Gateless Gate Case 10 Alone and Poor

> A monk named Seizei asked of Master Sozan:
> "I am solitary and poor. Will you give him support?"
> Sozan asked:
> "Venerable Seizei?"
> "Yes, Master," replied Seizei.
> Sozan observed:

"You have already drunk three cups of fine Hakka wine, and still you say you have not moistened your lips."

And another famous *koan* pointing to the path of equanimity.

Mumonkan - Case 41: Bodhidharma Puts the Mind at Rest

The great patriarch Bodhidharma sat facing the wall. The second patriarch (Shenguang[164], later called Huike[165]) approached him and said, "Your disciple's mind is not yet at peace. I beg you, Master, give it rest."
Bodhidharma said, "Bring your mind to me and I will give it rest."
The second patriarch replied, "I have searched for the mind, but have never been able to find it."
Bodhidharma said, "I have finished putting it to rest for you."

What do these two *koans* together tell us? That the world of vast spaciousness and infinity is immediately available, right at this very moment, if we will only realize it![166] This state of "No mind" (in Japanese martial arts, *mushin*), which is beyond thoughts, beliefs, and emotions, is a place of refuge and nourishment.[167]

Everyday Equanimity

Aitken Roshi[168] once remarked to me, "You can't do zazen in a tin factory." But I am not so sure. You don't have to be a Zen master to find equanimity in any situation. A few weeks ago Angela, who has zero Zen training, went to her physical therapist, an energy worker, for treatment of her injured elbow. A few minutes into the procedure the tree cutters began, which disturbed both of them. And this was followed by chip cutting, which, if you've ever experienced it, sounds worse than a tin factory. Angela faced a choice: leave, or reconcile herself to the situation? She chose acceptance. The first minute or so was tough, she said, but soon she settled down into the sounds themselves. "Each sound had a distinct cadence, and I began to notice the spaces in between the sounds. I found the experience fascinating, and ultimately the noise didn't matter at all."

Any place or situation can be our *dojo*.

Authenticity—The Passing of Yamada Koun Roshi

Authenticity is a less noticed but nonetheless important element of Wisdom.

In her essay *"Barua a Soldani"* ("letter from a King"), describing a letter of thanks she received from Danish King Christian X, the great writer of tales about Africa, Isak Dinesen, recounts how she made a present to the King of the skin of a lion she had killed, and how even in death the lion maintained his proud authenticity, "every inch a lion."[169]

At the height of my friendship with Yamada Roshi, he suddenly became ill. He was 82. I had hardly noticed his advancing age, as he was such a living engaged presence for me. When I visited him in the hospital in Tokyo he was alone—no attending nurses, no devoted students. He smiled kindly, and said enthusiastically, "I am discovering so much about the world of *Mu*. When I am released from the hospital, I'll show you." That was the last time we met. He died some months later at his home in Kamakura, when I was back in California.

During my next visit to Kamakura I asked Mrs. Yamada, who was a medical doctor, to tell me about how he died. "It was very simple and beautiful," she said. "I sat by his side, and he was lying on the tatami. He breathed deeply in and out. At first, strongly, but then a little weaker, then weaker still. Soon I could not quite detect whether he was breathing at all. Then, he was gone. Perfectly peaceful. It was like a feather catching a gentle breeze. It was the Roshi's great *teisho.*"[170] She smiled and nodded her head to affirm this point.[171]

Double-Bladed Sword

In the Zen tradition, the practice itself is viewed as a double-bladed sword. One blade cuts down delusions for a Mind that is not yet at rest. The other blade opens the Mind to the miracle before our very eyes. The samurai tradition strongly embraced the first blade; it was well-suited to warriors who faced death at any moment.

Here are several stories that illustrate this perspective. In his important book *Zen and the Ways*, which describes the Kamakura School of samurai Zen, Trevor Leggett, (whom I met at twenty on the evening of my first visit to the Kodokan Judo Institute in Tokyo in 1963), describes a fascinating encounter between Hojo Tokimune[172] and the Zen master Bukko.[173] Tokimune was then eighteen and had become the regent of Japan, holding absolute power. But he was experiencing fears and anxiety and had entered Zen practice to rid himself of them. Here is Leggett's account:

> Tokimune: "Of all the ills of life, fear is the worst. How can I be free of it?"
> Bukko: "You must shut off the place where it comes from."
> Tokimune: "Where does fear come from?"
> Bukko: "It comes from Tokimune."
> Tokimune: "Tokimune hates fear so much. How can you say it comes from Tokimune?"

Bukko: "Try and see. Abandon Tokimune, and come back tomorrow; your courage will be as great as the whole world."

Tokimune: "How do I abandon Tokimune?"

Bukko: "You must simply cut off all thinking."

Tokimune: "What is the way to cut off all thinking?"

Bukko: "Plunge into meditation and wait for the body and mind to become serene."

Tokimune: "My duties in this world leave me little time. What can I do?"

Bukko: "Going and sitting, staying and rising, whatever you have to do, that is the best place of practice (dojo). That is the best place to learn meditation."

And here is another story in the same spirit.

From Trevor Leggett—The Tiger's Cave

When a rebel army swept into a town in Korea, all the monks of the Zen temple fled except for the Abbot. The general came into the temple and was annoyed that the Abbot did not receive him with respect. "Don't you know," he shouted "that you are looking at a man who can run you through without blinking?"

"And you," replied the Abbott," are looking at a man who can be run through without blinking." The general stared at him, made a bow, and retired.

Pure samurai, in its highest most dramatic sense. But is there a shadow to non-attachment? What aspects of non-attachment are well-suited to cutting through, to not believing the plethora of disabling false narratives circulating in our times? And what aspects are dysfunctional and will not serve us (in other words, are non-evolutionary) in navigating through and adapting effectively to the chaos of our times?

The Shadow of Non-Attachment

I have had a memorable personal encounter with the samurai mindset. I relate this event because it powerfully grounds the main point. By telling it, I mean no disrespect to the present managers of the zendo in Kamakura, as I feel only deep gratitude and affection for all that I learned there.

After Yamada Roshi passed away, according to Robert Aitken Roshi some of the managers of the zendo in Kamakura decided to require all Western teachers to undergo recertification in order to test the depth of their "enlightenment." The testing *koan* was:

> Your child has just run out in front of a car and has been killed. Present this case.[174]

Aitken Roshi, who was also my teacher and friend, approached me as a professional negotiator to challenge the board's decision to single out Western teachers, beginning with him. He was also indignant at the supposed "answer" to the testing question.

A cry of grief and horror was not acceptable. No, that was not it at all.

The correct answer is "**the child does not exist!**"[175]

We prepared a Discovery Question for Aitken Roshi's meeting with the certification committee, although I do not know that Aitken Roshi, who has since passed on, ever got to ask it:

How long will the Great Tree survive, if we tear
away the Heart of Compassion that nourishes it?

I cite these negotiations with the Kamakura zendo managers
because they raise for me deep questions about what place, if
any, feelings and emotions have when pursuing equanimity and
Wisdom? In Case 89 of the *Blue Cliff Record*, entitled "The
Hands and Eyes of the Boddhisatva of Great Compassion," there
is this remarkable instruction:

> You must cut off emotional defilements and
> conceptual thinking, become clean and naked,
> free and unbound, only then will you be able to
> see this saying about Great Compassion.

Yamada Roshi himself had serious reservations about the
way this matter of non-attachment had been historically
misconstrued and manipulated in the years and months leading
up to WWII and during it. He once remarked to me on the
Japanese military's slogan of "all under one Great Roof" (Hakkō
ichiu[176] 八紘一宇) as a grave mistake (*o-machigai*). And this
theme has been extensively explored in Brian Daizen Victoria's
highly controversial book, *Zen at War*.[177]

Almost 400 years earlier, Shakespeare had a different answer
on the great matter of non-attachment. In the latter part of the
play *MacBeth* (Act IV, Scene 3), the hero MacDuff discovers that
Macbeth has slaughtered his wife and children. He cries out in
despair and disbelief:

> "What, all my pretty chickens and their dam/At
> one fell swoop?"
> Malcolm, another lord, cautions him: "Dispute it
> like a man," meaning "keep a stiff upper lip."

MacDuff answers him pointedly: "I shall do so, /
But I must also feel it as a man."

It takes great courage to allow ourselves, like MacDuff, to
feel, to have hearts of flesh that otherwise can turn to stone.
When we cut off all of our feelings, our emotions, we lose a part
of our humanity. Finding balance and equanimity in the midst
of our anguish and despair is one of the mythic labors of the
hero's or heroine's journey.[178] Fierce courage to step into the
Void of uncertainty and not-knowing is also one of humanity's
collective challenges in a world that appears to be accelerating
toward chaos.[179]

Finding dynamic balance between non-attachment and
compassion is among our great evolutionary tasks in the 21st
century, and as suggested throughout this book, the energy of
Heart can help us to reconcile the two. In the language of poetry,
Shakespeare's insight points to a path of wisdom, as alive and
pertinent today as it was before the court of Elizabeth I.

Big Heart Intelligence (BHI)—Seeing the Big Picture[180]

BHI offers a vantage point from which to begin formulating
answers to these deep questions about personal wisdom and
responsibility. BHI highlights the centrality of Heart. As the
qigong Master Li Junfeng often observes, "the Heart is the
Governor of the Mind. When we Quiet the Heart,[181] the Mind
also becomes tranquil." In fact, everything instantly recalibrates.

One of Master Li's great teachings is his admonition to "See
the Big Picture." "Seeing" in this context implies not only seeing
with the Mind, through the use of creative imagination, but also
seeing with the Heart. When we see the world thorough Heart,
everything expands. Our petty concerns, fears, and grievances
immediately shrink to more balanced proportions. But there is
another, more subtle dimension to this practice: the Big Picture

is contained in the small. Every atom embodies the whole. The *Book of Serenity* (*Shoyoroku*) offers this commentary (Case 91): "Heaven, earth, and I have the same roots. The myriad things (including mountains and rivers) are one body."

Being able to see the Big Picture, which includes the smallest things, has many practical, positive consequences. First among these may be increased patience, forbearance, and gravitas, or what the English poet Keats referred to as "negative capability"—a term he discerned particularly in Shakespeare, and which he defined as "the capacity to rest in uncertainties, mysteries, doubts, without any irritable reaching after fact and reason." Negative capability is itself closely tied to flow. We simply follow the river without needing to know its destination, to be willing instead to navigate the current of the unknown.

In negotiations, Seeing the Big Picture—when we observe and listen with Heart—enables us to go behind the mask that people wear. As our own mirror-mind illuminates and clarifies the images appearing before us, we are not afraid to see the world with fewer distortions, just as it is.

An interesting exercise is to place BHI at the center of the Explorers Wheel, described in the last chapter, and then observe what happens when we spin the Wheel. I find that each moon is transformed when it is imbued with the intelligence of Heart and Love. Past grievances and hardships soften; future possibilities, including hope, brighten. Creative powers that we did not sense before become available to us. We are moved to reach out and touch the lives of our fellow travelers and all living creatures.

Faten Amal Harby[182]

This is a compelling Egyptian video series portraying the valiant struggle of a divorced woman, Faten Amal Harby, to shield and retain parental guardianship of her children when confronting the brutality of her traditional husband. Faten faces almost insuperable odds to secure her constitutional rights as a woman and mother within the complex religious-secular legal system of modern Egypt, a country undergoing evolutionary change.

At one point in the drama, Faten's husband Seif hears that Faten has been unfaithful to him with a young cleric, Sheik Yahia. Seif confronts the sheik and threatens to assault him. Here is what happens next (somewhat paraphrased):

> Seif: "Hey! You, with the holy books. I know you. You are the one who is playing around with my wife. I will have my honor!"
>
> Yahia: "Why do you say this thing? Your wife, Faten Amal Harby, is a courageous and honorable woman. She is fighting for her rights, which are guaranteed by our Constitution. I am only advising her based on what our holy law teaches. You slander her and demean yourself by saying such things."
>
> Seif: "Nonetheless, you are having sex with her, admit it!"
>
> Yahia: "I am doing no such thing. Why do you make this claim without proof, my brother? Who has told you such things?"
>
> Seif: "It doesn't matter. You are a scoundrel, and I will have your blood." (Seif shakes his fist in Yahia's face.)

> Yahia: "My brother, why would you want to injure an innocent person? How will you feel when you discover that you have made a terrible mistake? Why would you injure yourself in this way?"
> Seif is non-plussed, and Sheik Yahia calmly walks away.

For me, there are several remarkable lessons to be learned from this encounter. The first is Sheik Yahia's utter lack of fear—serenity in the face of imminent violence. The second is that, at some level, he succeeds in breaking through Seif's emotional wall and touching his heart, and Seif yields. Third, in showing compassion for his suffering, Sheik Yahia is giving Seif a priceless gift: Sheik Yahia is demonstrating serenity in the midst of utmost violence, which allows him to respond with compassion. But Seif fails to understand this gift, and that is Seif's tragedy—for as the drama proceeds he descends by his own actions into abject misery.

Conscience[183] and Daimon[184]

When Lincoln faced the prospect of war and struggled with the tragic choice before him, he sought guidance from his conscience. As Jon Meacham writes in his recent biography of Lincoln, *And There Was Light* (2022), "conscience in America has been largely rooted in religious traditions… To Lincoln, God whispered His will through conscience to live in accord with the laws of love." In 1862, Lincoln closed a message to Congress by speaking of "my great responsibility to my God and to my country." Although Lincoln was not a religious man in a conventional church-attending sense, God, country, love, and generosity of spirit all merged as he sought inspiration from both Mind and Heart.

There is a strong parallel between Socrates' dialogue with Callicles and Lincoln's conscience. Like Socrates, Lincoln was reputed to have a logical mind as powerful and unyielding as a bear trap, which he cultivated as a youth by studying Euclid and probably Plato. Like Lincoln, Socrates had a moral compass, which Socrates called his "*daimon*" or his inner channel to the gods. Socrates encouraged his disciples to engage in this internal dialogue with their own *daimon*. The *daimon* was a demi-god, who expressed the larger principle of order and knowledge of the cosmos that Greeks called the *Logos*.[185] In other words, for both Lincoln and Socrates, logic and the inner voice were closely linked. It is interesting that in Greek the term "eu-daimon," or literally good daimon (daimons could also take self-destructive forms) is the root of "eudaimonia," the Greek word for "happiness."

Big Heart Intelligence draws upon and integrates these deep ethical and spiritual antecedents. And it is emergent, pointing to this living moment, illustrated in the simple story of Sheik Yahia, in which each of us can find inner peace, serenity, and love, no matter what is happening in the outer world. It affords a way to witness and to accept the paradoxes of tragic and false choices, and to transcend these contradictions. This intelligence of Heart is not fleeting. Like the sound of a distant temple bell, it reverberates. Along with the practice of *Just Click!* introduced in Chapter 3, the reader may wish to enter this place of refuge now, where all phenomena merge—to pause and enjoy this unique rendition of the Pachelbel Canon in D[186], arranged for cello and piano.

As I continue to explore BHI more deeply, I am discovering that each one of us—indeed humanity as a whole—has the capacity by actively cultivating Heart, along with creative intelligence, to stand up to the shadowy forces that would overwhelm and enslave us. We have free will and can choose, far more that we suppose, to influence, if not control, our destinies.

Now it might seem that such questions have little or nothing to do with the practical affairs of business. Indeed, many in business will assert that the demands of business necessitate its own separate track, even its own separate ethical track. However, those of a different mind, who may share the perspective of the author, will counter that especially today business—no longer government, academia, or the church—is a primary agent of change, and can benefit from the light of Wisdom. The next chapter explores some of the complex choices and tradeoffs when Wisdom is put to the hard test of practical business realities.

Chapter 8: Wisdom in Business

Someone's sitting in the shade today because someone planted a tree a long time ago.

Risk comes from not knowing what you are doing.
—Warren Buffett

As explained in this chronicle, my personal life's journey as an explorer and my professional life as a public interest lawyer and advocate have been from early on closely, perhaps inseparably, entwined. We arrive now at a cause where I am passionately engaged that is testing the mettle of all that I have learned. It is the massive exposure of the general public and the workforce to continuous, high levels non-ionizing radiation (NIR). I will explain in plain terms what is NIR, why it is dangerous and should concern the reader, what can be effectively done about it, and why NIR is my prime exhibit in the case for a shift toward Evolutionary Values.

NIR Basics[187]

Non-ionizing radiation defined—In technical terms, as explained in Wikipedia, "NIR refers to any type of electromagnetic radiation that does not carry enough energy per quantum (photon energy) to ionize atoms or molecules—that is, to completely remove an electron from an atom or molecule. Instead of producing charged ions when passing through matter, non-ionizing electromagnetic radiation has sufficient energy only for excitation, the movement of an electron to a higher energy state." The essential question for the public is whether NIR entails significant biological effects.

The US Department of Labor/Occupational Health and Safety website contains this further explanation:

> NIR is described as a series of energy waves composed of oscillating electric and magnetic fields traveling at the speed of light. NIR includes the spectrum of ultraviolet (UV), visible light, infrared (IR), microwave (MW), radio frequency (RF), and extremely low frequency (ELF). Lasers commonly operate in the UV, visible, and IR frequencies. Non-ionizing radiation is found in a wide range of occupational settings and can pose a considerable health risk to potentially exposed workers if not properly controlled.

NIR is continuously emitted from a broad range of wireless devices, including smart meters, computers, routers, cell phones, small cell and macro cell towers, base and earth stations, electric cars, automated vehicles, medical devices, and a host of other products.

There are over 4000 peer reviewed studies[188] in scientific journals confirming the biological effects of NIR. Hundreds of prominent scientists around the world and hundreds of thousands of concerned citizens around the world are today speaking out on the hazards of NIR. And their voice is increasing. The interested reader can quickly gain an insight into the complex scientific issues by perusing 2012 *Bioinitiative Report* and the recent 2022 Research Review by the newly established International Commission on Biological Effects.[189] There is little or no research on the epigenetic effects of continuous and cumulative NIR exposure of the present generation on future generations. (See Chapter 16 on the new scientific field of epigenetics.)

What is the problem?

Here is a brief summary of the present situation:

There has been until very recently a massive blackout on NIR by the mainstream media, which is one reason the reader may not be fully aware of it.[190] When I was first embarking on this venture in 2019, one of our BBILAN benefactors who was supporting our challenges to the "Space Experiment" (Chapter 15), introduced us to a publicist. The first thing this experienced professional did was to warn us, "I cannot help you if you want to discuss NIR, or 5G in particular. No mainstream media outlet will touch it. None." Despite his caveat, he was able to secure interviews with The Hill, Fortune, Forbes, WSJ, and other leading newspapers and magazines. The interviews focused mainly on our work with satellites and industrial infrastructure. The journalists indicated that they loved our balanced approach and were eager to publish the story. But with one exception, their editors refused to run the interviews.

At the same time the wireless industry aided by its captive[191] federal, state, and local agencies are continuously and effectively promulgating a series of closely woven false narratives, fed to them by the wireless industry with the principal assertions that:

o Continuous NIR exposure of the general public is safe, including exposing the most vulnerable—children, disabled persons, elderly, pregnant women, fetuses, and minorities. (There is ample documentation in the scientific literature of these risks.)

o The environmental effects are negligible.

o The Congress has mandated a broadband wireless infrastructure and states and local communities' "hands are tied", or in legal terms local action is preempted.

o Personal privacy of users of wireless devices and corporate/government surveillance are non-issues that can be dismissed.

o Wireless products are faster, more cybersecure, energy efficient, and climate change friendly. Moreover, wireless infrastructure offers an immediate solution to the Digital Divide, where rural and minority communities are being denied equal access to the internet.

o There exists no viable, immediately available alternative.

In fact, none of these false narratives, when exposed to the light of independent, unbiased, and uncompromised review, holds water.[192]

The nature of NIR itself and the way its harms are presenting themselves also provide good reason to explain why most of the public feels helpless before the Wireless Juggernaut:

o NIR is invisible which distinguishes it from other air pollutants, and other toxic and industrial hazards, including lead, poly vinyl chloride, or asbestos.

o   To my knowledge, no one appears to be continuously monitoring the continuous or cumulative effects of NIR. No one in the federal, state, or local governments, and certainly, no company in the wireless industry is doing so, even though technology for continuous and accurate monitoring exists, is readily available, and reasonably priced.[193]

o   No one really wants to know. From a legal perspective, the telecom corporations certainly don't want to know, because if there is strong evidence that they are aware of the harms and did nothing to prevent them, the harms could be deemed "foreseeable" by a court of law. Foreseeability will in turn help to establish defendant's violation of a duty of care and negligence.[194]

o   Parents of children being exposed to NIR don't want to know because they are intimidated by school administrators, who themselves are fearful of lawsuits by the telecom providers.

o   The harms are expressed in many ways—sleeplessness, behavioral changes, cognitive impairment, cancer, increased oxidative stress[195] (the root cause of many illnesses), anger, depression, suicide, as well as a diagnosed illness, "Electric Hypersensitivity" or "Microwave Sickness", now officially recognized by the Federal Access Board.[196] The medical literature is clear that continuous NIR exposure can seriously complicate existing life-threatening illnesses, including cancer, cardiac illness, diabetes, and various neurodegenerative diseases through the mechanism of oxidative stress.

o   At first and often for months and even years the victims of NIR fail to connect their symptoms to an NIR source; and even when they do, their bosses, or government officials discount or trivialize their complaints, or even worse, expose them to insults and other abuses, and in some instances, outright retaliation.

o Few doctors or other healthcare providers in the country have had any professional training in EHS, and are simply relying on the shibboleth "the government says it's safe"— which is actually an accurate statement as the FCC and FDA are widely disseminating the false claims that chronic NIR exposure, even to young persons[197] is safe, notwithstanding the medical evidence of gliomas and brain cancer risks. In some parts of the U.S. doctors are performing ablations for heart arrythmias on patients living in the vicinity of macro cell towers when a simple move away by the patient, or a dismantling or reasonable adjustment of the cell tower might have abated the arrythmia, which was caused by continuous NIR exposure.

o The federal government has cut back on research on NIR health and environmental effects, while even refusing to accept the scientific findings of its own ten year $25 million National Toxicology Program (NTP) study.[198] As early as 1996, the Congress voted to shut down all funding to the EPA's Office of Radiation and Health which was responsible for enforcement under the Clean Air Act of NIR as an air pollutant.[199] It is one of those quiet acts of legal menace of which the great majority of the public is unaware. Because if NIR is recognized as an air pollutant, the burden of demonstrating its safety, regulation, monitoring, and control will shift away from the public to where it should be, i.e. upon the government and the wireless industry.

o There is no practical way for a helpless public to opt out, or even to have a meaningful voice (the right to be heard is a fundamental right guaranteed by the U.S. Constitution and many state constitutions) in decisions made by remote actors whose agendas are to advance corporate profit not public health and safety.

o   The telecom industry has vast political power and almost unlimited funds to employ high priced attorneys who are more than willing to employ their expertise and experience in the service of advancing the telecom agenda. There is a serious professional ethical issue here that has rarely been discussed.[200]

o   A wireless national communications infrastructure has been a work in progress for over a decade and countless long term contracts with telecom companies have already been signed. Wireless is ubiquitous and *fait accompli.*

o   And, finally, the public is hungry for wireless products. Most consumers do not have the time, interest, legal or political knowledge, expertise, and, ultimately the power to effectuate safer, more private, more energy efficient, and actually faster and more reliable alternatives.

Under these conditions, do reason and balance stand a chance? And if so, where is the path?

The NIR problem is complex, multi-dimensional, and entwined with powerful political currents in societies around the world. At the same time it deeply concerns our most fundamental civil, environmental, and human rights and liberties, which are being systematically stripped away before our sleeping eyes. In my view a path of balance can be found by first distinguishing truly tragic choices from manipulated false choices, as illustrated in the following cases.

Tragic Choices and False Choices

Wisdom is most challenged when life conditions present us with tragic and false choices. "*Tragic Choices*"[201] is the title of a book by the former Yale Law School Dean Guido Calabresi and Philip Bobbitt. It refers to situations where societies confront problems whose apparent solutions cannot avoid inflicting great suffering on many people. Many such "tragic" choices are false choices, masquerading or being promoted as tragic choices, when in fact they are not, and are amenable to creative problem solving. BHI offers a practical way to pierce the veil and to distinguish between tragic and false choices. BHI treats Wisdom not as a static set of values, but rather as an evolutionary process. Building upon a foundation of ethics, conscience, and logic, the living moment reveals compassionate decisions that include, and also transcend complexities and contradictions.

Perhaps the most poignant example of a tragic choice is the American Civil War. Both sides fervently claimed they were upholding higher order, spiritual and religious values and cited scripture as authority, especially with respect to slavery. But as Abraham Lincoln eloquently wrote:

> Both parties deprecated war, but one of them would *make* war rather than let the nation survive; and the other would *accept* war, rather than let the nation perish... And the war came."[202]

Roughly two percent of the population, an estimated 620,000 men, lost their lives in the line of duty.[203]

Below I describe three business cases in which I am professionally engaged as a lawyer where the opposing parties are framing the situation as "tragic" choices, but that, in fact, are amenable to practical, wise, and balanced solutions.

Case # 1—Employee Safety v. Core Corporate Value

What happens when a company sacrifices its core values, arguably its Evolutionary Values, for profits or other corporate interests? I am currently involved in a legal case that raises this question.

The case involves a company that is recognized as a crown jewel of the US semiconductor industry. I was closely involved with this company almost forty years ago when I co-chaired the Japan Industrial Policy Group at the State Department and got to know its visionary founder. The company proudly claims in its employee handbook and other promotional materials that employee safety is among its highest corporate concerns, and advertises the importance of the Christian values of care and compassion for its corporate family in its efforts to recruit able new employees, especially women of Hispanic descent.

My client is a highly skilled program manager, a Latina, who worked at the company for seventeen years, with a four year break, until she was fired in April 2022. During her time with the company she was continuously exposed to high levels of NIR as all the company's campuses added wireless internet in 2003. My client became seriously ill in the fall of 2021 (long-term radiation exposure is cumulative; its hazardous effects may not manifest for many years, until they reach a tipping point), and was told by the company's health care department that she was experiencing menopause and should consult an endocrinologist. It was only after she found a physician trained in the new medical field of clinical electromagnetics that she began to connect her symptoms to a recognized medical diagnosis, Electromagnetic Hypersensitivity (EHS), or Microwave Sickness. She was allowed paid leave for her disability for over a year on the understanding that she was planning to return to work. Free of RF/EMF exposure at home, she was, in fact, making excellent progress; both she and her physician had the realistic expectation that she would be able to resume work at the company early in 2023, especially if she could work in a nontoxic environment. On that condition and with that understanding, she received a "reasonable accommodation" from the company to continue her healing process, as is required under the Americans for Disability Act (ADA).

All went well for several months, but in early spring 2022 my client was summarily terminated from her job, and her benefits were cut off as of September 2022. She was offered no explanation by the ADA manager, except for her arbitrary and unsupported opinion that she would never be healthy again. The manager denied having agreed to the 2023 return-to work date, even though there is clear record of the accord. In our negotiations, the company's legal department asserts that the company is complying fully with federal FCC guidelines for maximum RF/EMF radiation exposure, and "when the federal government changes its policy, our company will consider changing." The federal guidelines, which date from 1996 (over 25 years ago, when cellular networks were only at 2G!), are widely discredited by thousands of independent scientists, and there are thousands of peer-reviewed scientific papers confirming the strong connection between chronic RF/EMF exposure and a wide variety of discrete and recurrent symptoms. Moreover, EHS is a recognized disability under the guidelines established by the Federal Access Board. My client believes that thousands of other company employees are suffering from the same RF/EMF radiation exposure, reporting similar symptoms, and being misled in the same manner.

During this period the company's stock price has plummeted (over 40 percent since 2021). It is likely that senior management sincerely believes it has acted in the best interests of the company—meaning on behalf of its owners, investors, and shareholders—to trim costs by terminating disabled employees (even those whom it has played a strong role in disabling) and, in my client's case, that it has treated her fairly. Moreover, acknowledging the likelihood that harmful levels of NIR are being emitted by wireless devices on its campuses could likely open a Pandora's Box of problems. For the company, the smartest business strategy is to shut the problem down quickly and quietly.

So, what is the path of wisdom in this case, and what will it cost the company not to follow it? From my client's perspective, the path of wisdom is for the company to treat her with dignity, negotiate a fair retirement package, and investigate and address compassionately the real possibility that the toxic work environment on its campuses is causing extensive NIR-related injuries to the company's employees. Suppressing information about the imminent dangers of NIR radiation and retaliating against whistleblowers may offer an expedient short-term solution. But in our view the problem will not go away, because it is likely many other employees are being injured. Some day, perhaps sooner than the company expects, the victims will initiate mass tort litigation.

Is there a way for this company to reconcile its corporate values of safety, compassion and integrity in its dealings with its employees, with the financial interests of its investors and shareholders? In fact, there is such an alternative. The company has a unique opportunity to become the industry's leader in workplace safety by providing its employees with largely radiation-free workplaces, following the principle adopted by the Center for Disease Control and Prevention (CDC) of "As Low As Reasonably Achievable (ALARA)."[204] Of all the companies in the semiconductor industry, this company is perhaps uniquely positioned to innovate and to compete on safety; to establish a powerful competitive advantage with breakthrough patents, which it can license, and its ability to recruit the most talented, health-conscious, and environmentally aware employees. Although the company can easily finance internally this shift in corporate policy, there is also ample federal funding under the Broadband Equity, Access, and Deployment (BEAD) Program[205] and other critical national infrastructure programs to defray the costs.

As with personal life decisions and community decisions, the path of wisdom in business—arguably the only path to corporate survival—depends on Evolutionary Values. Notwithstanding their complexities, these decisions will shape the destiny of corporations and are largely a question of choice.

Case # 2—Fiber First Los Angeles[206]

During the past several years the telecom industry has succeeded in persuading the Los Angeles County Planning Department to issue permits under an accelerated "ministerial" review of the installation of small cell and macro cell towers in residential communities and public rights of way. Ministerial review will remove all administrative discretion and strip away the public's right of due process; in other words, the right to effective prior notification and hearings. There will be no environmental assessment, as required by the California Environmental Quality Act (CEQA), or a risk assessment of the adverse impacts on historic sites protected under the federal Historic Sites Preservation Act. The ministerial review process also permits telecom providers to register their own new independent addresses of the towers they are erecting, notwithstanding that these towers may be located on private property. This practice will enable the telecom providers to circumvent California's well-established conditional use permit system. It will also establish property rights to these towers without any just compensation for private property taken from the original owners. In our legal team's opinion, the Los Angeles Planning Department's program is illegal under both the federal and state constitutions, as well as federal and state laws. On January 10, 2023 the Board of Supervisors voted to approve two ordinances that essentially codify ministerial review, and thereby bypass the discretionary conditional use permit system that has worked well for over 20 years.

The telecom companies' stated goal is to blanket all of Los Angeles County with small cell and macro cell towers which will expose the County's most vulnerable citizens—including children, disabled and elderly residents, and pregnant women—to high levels of potentially dangerous non-ionizing radiation (NIR). The telecom purveyors must justify their actions. They cannot admit that their real goal is to generate huge corporate profits on top of a massive public fraud perpetrated over thirty years that has cost Los Angeles County billions of dollars.[207] Rather, they must scheme and assert a legitimate "higher" public goal that all can readily agree on, which is to close the Digital Divide. The Digital Divide refers to the gap between those with access to high-speed internet and those living in remote or economically disadvantaged areas, especially minority communities, that do not. The telecoms assert, and the Los Angeles Planning Department adopts their argument, that the accelerated installation of small cell and macro cell towers will "solve" the Digital Divide in a far more immediate and effective way than other broadband alternatives, such as optical fiber cables connecting the internet to the home and workplace. To deny and to discriminate against digitally disadvantaged persons will permanently ensure that these communities can never succeed in the Digital Age. It is a compelling "tragic choice" argument.

In fact, the very opposite is true. As investigator Bruce Kushnick documents[208], the practices of the telecom industry over the past 30 years have actually delayed the implementation of the viable, far more effective optical fiber alternative, and have diverted billions of dollars in taxpayer and ratepayer revenues designated for optical fiber (what Al Gore referred to decades ago as the "information superhighway") to wireless infrastructure. The optical fiber infrastructure has already been well funded by these payments. But instead, the wireless industry has used these funds to push a wireless internet solution that is less safe, more energy intensive, more polluting, much less reliable, and that needs to be constantly upgraded to keep up with the blazingly fast speeds that fiber optic and cable internet provide. Moreover, billions of dollars in federal funding are also available to Los Angeles County under the new infrastructure BEAD program mentioned above. Finally, as is well documented, cell towers catch fire. The Board of Supervisors by it's January 10, 2023 action has committed Los Angeles County to an inferior technology that will require upgrading within a few years but will never be as effective or fire-safe as the wired internet infrastructure promised decades ago.

So, how can this clash in values be addressed? How to distinguish what is truly tragic from what is false? In other words, what is the path of wisdom in this situation? Our legal team is urging that the most basic and responsible action by the Board of Supervisors is to pause and become better informed; to listen to the concerns of grassroots community groups like Fiber First Los Angeles;[209] and to assess the immediate benefits to Los Angeles County of receiving billions of dollars in federal support to close the Digital Divide over the next three to five years, while delivering the last mile of optical fiber to millions of Los Angeles County residents who still do not have it to their homes. In short, the Board of Supervisors must reconsider and revoke the two amendments and work with our legal team to fashion a balanced solution.

Unfortunately, the odds are overwhelmingly against County residents.

Case # 3—NIR Exposure of Military Personnel

This case occurred on Kirtland Air Force Base (KAFB) in Albuquerque, New Mexico. According to Wikipedia, KAFB is the "home of the Air Force Materiel Command's[210] Nuclear Weapons Center (NWC)[211]. The NWC's responsibilities include acquisition, modernization and sustainment of nuclear system programs for both the Department of Defense and Department of Energy." The injured parties, my clients, are a licensed nurse and her husband, a retired Air Force security forces professional. The illness reported by the nurse was the direct result of NIR exposure emanating from two smart meters installed on the opposite side of the wall from the head of her bed. The specific and likely cause was the massive pulses of NIR energy that are emitted from the smart meters. These smart meters have clear biological effects, especially on the brains of those who are exposed during sleep.[212] Shortly after moving into KAFB base housing she began experiencing classic and serious symptoms which required hospitalization. A doctor who is a clinical professor at the University of New Mexico School of Medicine diagnosed my client's illness as Microwave Sickness. We made a concerted effort to alert the Commander of the KAFB and the responsible housing authority. When these local actions failed, we wrote to the Secretary of the Air Force and the Surgeon General of the Air Force urging that the unsafe housing conditions not only on KAFB but also many other bases, involving some 53,000 Air Force personnel, must be thoroughly investigated. To the best of our knowledge the situation has never been investigated. At the time it was dismissed as a local landlord tenant dispute.

The tragic versus false choice presented in this case is this: what is the military generally, and the Air Force in particular, willing to do about the health risks to military personnel from continuous and cumulative NIR exposure from multiple devices? The "Havana Syndrome"[213] is one case that has received some press coverage. The documented risks to pilots[214] who become disoriented from NIR exposure is another. The unstated premise—the ostensible value proposition behind the Air Force's cavalier treatment of this issue—is whether "national security"—however the Air Force defines this term—demands that some lives be sacrificed. It is not clear at all that the Air Force's response would have been the same if the KAFB smart meters had been installed next to the Air Force Commander's bedroom, as they are currently being installed in housing for lower ranking, retired Air Force personnel. The more precise, legally technical way of stating the problem is, once again, who should have the burden of proof of showing causation of harm, the installer and others who are responsible, or the public? Of course, some medical and scientific consultants to the wireless industry will assert that the data are insufficient to reach a conclusion that continuous NIR exposure of military personnel is unsafe.

The important point here is to observe what happens when there is a shift that gives priority to Evolutionary Values. If the Air Force will recognize that the safety of military personnel and their families is of high priority, it would take my client's report and other reports concerning NIR related harms seriously and investigate. It will then discover that there is a perfectly sensible and balanced alternative, which is to order the contractor at its cost to remove the smart meters next to active duty, civilian, and retired personnel's bedrooms on KAFB and other bases and to install these smart meters in garages or other locations where they will do far less or no harm. Moreover, of all federal agencies, the Air Force is in a uniquely informed position to develop protective regulations to shield Air Force pilots[215] from the dangers of NIR, which can then be adopted by the FAA for commercial airlines. Again, a clarification of values,

Evolutionary Values, can help us to pierce the veil of false choices masquerading as tragic choices.

Case # 4—Protecting Children's Health

A large number of independent scientists, with no ties to the telecom industry, and a significant body of peer-reviewed scientific papers, confirm the special vulnerability of children to continuous, cumulative, synergistic exposure to non-ionizing radiation (NIR). A child's brain is still developing and the blood-brain barrier is more easily compromised. The associated symptoms and illnesses include cognitive impairment, cancer, neuro-behavioral disorders, fertility impairment, DNA damage, loss of sleep, Electrohypersensitivity (EHS), oxidative stress, and aggravation of chronic illnesses. These special risks to school children from NIR was the subject of a three part series of webinars sponsored by Tech Safe Schools,[216] a project of Americans for Responsible Technology. The long term epigenetic effects of continuous NIR exposure on children and future generations have scarcely been studied. (See Chapter 16 for a brief discussion of epigenetics.)

There has naturally been strong pushback from governments and the cell phone and telecom companies against assertions that NIR emitting devices are unsafe. As I write this chapter, our legal team is currently in negotiations with the Food and Drug Administration (FDA) to remove false and misleading images and text from its website[217] that convey the strong impression to teenagers that it is safe to hold a cell phone against their ear, despite the risk of gliomas and brain cancer. To date the FDA has refused to withdraw or correct the text under these misleading images.[218] As of this book goes to press, the FDA and FCC still refuse to promulgate special guidelines or regulations that focus on the special health risks to children from non-ionizing radiation (NIR).

In Lake Tahoe, a massive macro cell tower has now been erected, hovering over a ski slope in winter and a playground for children during the warmer months. As we see in many similar situations, it is likely to be only a matter of months after the tower is turned on when parents in Tahoe begin noticing symptoms in their children playing under this monster. At first the parents and children will not pay attention to the symptoms; then the symptoms will become more serious, and finally someone will connect the dots and realize that the symptoms are related to NIR radiation exposure from the tower. The Tahoe macro cell tower is not an aberration. We have several other cases where telecom companies are locating massive macro cell towers in school playgrounds, heedless of the dangers to children.

Special Challenges of Schools

The response of school administrators when alerted to the special health risks to school from NIR illustrates the complex issues at stake, including some of the practical challenges of adopting Evolutionary Values. When Tech Safe Schools initiated a pilot study and contacted 300 school administrators on the East Coast and California, we did not anticipate the response. Except for a few lukewarm responses, school administrators were unconcerned or even interested to learn more. And this notwithstanding that we sent a legal advisory[219] I drafted and signed by several prominent attorneys, confirming the legal responsibilities and potential liability of public schools and school administrators in failing to provide safe learning environments for children, teachers, and staff.

I have thought deeply and have tried to understand the perspective of school administrators and have come up with these insights:

o Most school administrators are already beleaguered with COVID. They simply do not have bandwidth to deal with another complex problem for which they have no scientific or medical expertise. **It is better not to know.**

o In many cases the telecom companies are themselves providing grants or are working with state boards of education to provide funding for the adoption of wireless products in public schools. Financially challenged public school administrators are reluctant to cut off this funding source.

o There is massive market demand by young customers for cell phones and other NIR emitting wireless products, such as lap tops, which are widely used in public schools.

o Parents are largely uniformed and in some instances are actually being threatened, bullied, and intimidated by school administrators.

o There is virtually no monitoring of NIR emissions in school environments from multiple devices. So almost no one is aware of the risks.

o Even when parents notice that their children are getting sick, they are not connecting the dots and tracing the illnesses to the sources of continuous and cumulative NIR exposure.

o Public school administrators are relying on false narratives from the federal government, in particular the FCC and FDA that chronic NIR exposure is safe.[220]

So, under these conditions, what constructive role, if any, can Evolutionary Values play? The crucial guiding principle must be informed consent. If school administrators and parents who are the guardians of children are well informed of the risks, and with full knowledge freely accept these risks, a fair argument can be made that the evolutionary position is to respect this decision. But there are three caveats:

o   First, it is highly unlikely that under present conditions of massive disinformation both by industry and our own government such consent can really be said to be fully "informed." Still, even if impartially informed, the final decision is up to the parents.[221]

o   Second, there is the legally complex question of the rights of the child. Do children who are at risk have an independent right to be fully informed and to withhold their consent to NIR exposure, separate from the decisions of their parents? Various European countries recognize the principle that children must be consulted[222] and participate in parental decisions that affect their health and welfare. (This issue has in recent years become important in the context of treatment and precautions relating to COVID protections.)[223]

o   Third, Evolutionary Values as their name suggests "evolve." In this context, this principle suggests that as school administrators, parents, and children become better informed about the risks, they are entitled to change their minds and withdraw their consent. It is likely that a reasonable court would not permit a telecom company, school, or local government to rely on a defense that parents and children have waived all rights by initially consenting. The contingent liability of wireless purveyors (and public schools) for harms knowingly inflicted on children highlights the importance of continuing education both about the risks as well as Evolutionary Values.

If we go behind the mask, and cut through the persiflage, we will quickly observe that corporate power, money, and influence are held to be of greater value than the lives of children. For in the end—and this is the essential Sophist position—*might makes right*. It is the identical claim advanced by Callicles in Plato's dialogue *Gorgias*.[224] Callicles asserts that Socrates's "morality" is so much nonsense, that the powerful have a natural right to dominate the weak and to take from society all that they want to satisfy their personal needs.

In response to the claims of the telecoms, the Broadband International Legal Action Network (BBILAN) team, with contributions from many colleagues, has produced a *Blueprint for Legal Action to Protect Children's Health*[225] from non-ionizing radiation (NIR). It is a living text that will be available and revised, as this book moves out into the world. The Blueprint provides a collaborative framework and a practical process for lawyers, scientists, grassroots organizations, and policy makers to challenge the Wireless Juggernaut where it is endangering children anywhere in the world. It is among the first calls for global action that explicitly confronts the deeper ethical choices facing governments and the telecom industry respecting children.

Coda—Blood on Our Hands

As I am reviewing this matter of tragic choices, two events occur. The first is a colleague recommends Amitav Ghosh's stunning book, *The Nutmeg's Curse: Parables for a Planet in Crisis*[226], which analyzes in compelling detail the historic exploitation of indigenous and impoverished peoples, beginning with the Dutch extermination in the early 1600s of the inhabitants of the island of Banda in the Indonesian archipelago, as part of western civilization's relentless and omnicidal assault[227] on the natural world itself. The second is I learn about the current litigation[228] brought by attorney, Terrence Collingsworth, on behalf of unnamed maimed and killed children, enforced to labor in cobalt mines in the

Congo.[229] It is a compelling indictment of desperate poverty and enforced child labor in the production of cobalt and other essential minerals that are essential components in lithium batteries that are key components for cell phones, computers, and the gigantic emerging market for electric vehicles.

The case also catches my eye because these very same products, electric vehicles and their supporting infrastructure, will be among the highest emitters of NIR. At first glance a tragic Net of Indra[230] appears at work: the tree's root, as *The Nutmeg's Curse* recounts, is based on human and environmental misery and exploitation; its branches—widespread NIR exposure of the general public— are fed by the same soil. And yet, as I think more deeply, I understand that the matter is far more complex. If we accept the premise or fact of climate change, electric vehicles and their supporting infrastructure, appear an intelligent step toward the goal of reducing carbon emissions based on fossil fuels. And there can be no doubt that the introduction and wide use of electric vehicles will save hundreds of thousands of lives that will be compromised by air pollution caused by toxic emissions from millions of vehicles' combustion engines.

At least at present, cobalt seems to be the essential mineral for lithium batteries which are currently the battery of choice for electric vehicles, and a small impoverished part of the Congo today provides 70% of the world's cobalt. So does this mean that over 35,000 poor Africans, including many children, must lead hellish lives and suffer ignominious deaths to service the rest of the world's need for gadgets or climate friendly products?[231] The answer is perhaps "not". Actually, this tragedy has been reported and the industry has known about it for several years, and looked the other way in its obsession to maximize profits.[232]

Once again, there are practical alternatives to what appears a tragic choice. They entail multiplying positive effects, once we decide as a global society to ask different questions and actively seek solutions to these questions by opening our hearts and minds.

o   A first step is to focus world attention[233] on this atrocity, and the value choices that underlie it.

o   The second legal step is to employ existing laws more effectively, such as The Trafficking Victims Protection Reauthorization Act which is the basis for the children's damage action. In addition, U.S. Customs has the legal authority, if it decides to exercise it, to stop illegal imports of products based on enforced child labor in their tracks. For example, Section 307 (§ 307) of the U.S. Tariff Act (19 U.S.C. §1307), states:

> All goods, wares, articles, and merchandise, mined, produced, or manufactured wholly or in part in any foreign country by convict labor or/ and forced labor or/and indentured labor under penal sanctions shall not be entitled to entry at any of the ports of the United States, and the importation thereof is hereby prohibited, and the Secretary of the Treasury is authorized and directed to prescribe such regulations as may be necessary for the enforcement of this provision.

An immediate administrative action would be a Citizen's Petition to U.S. Customs to interdict imports of lithium batteries containing cobalt that are based on coerced child labor.

o   A third step is for national governments actively to support research and accelerated development of batteries that do not depend on cobalt and other toxic materials. Such batteries are already available on the market[234] and other options like supercapacitors will become available for widespread and safe commercial use in the near future.[235]

The world needs to know the human price of delaying such innovations.

o   A fourth (karmic) step is to raise an international fund to support the transition of these impoverished workers, especially children, to safe, soul-rewarding, socially and environmentally beneficial work that will give them hope that their country and the world cares. One immediate source of funding would be a surcharge levied by U.S. Customs and other countries' authorities on all imports of batteries or products containing lithium batteries containing cobalt mined by enforced labor in the Congo.[236] The international community possesses many ways today to finance the immediate removal of children from the equation.

There is no single solution. Many strategies can be effectively combined. The process can begin, and must begin, by articulating basic human values—core Evolutionary Values—and then asking the deep questions they invite. It is critical that commercial enterprises begin to assess carefully the human and environmental risks **before** releasing such harmful products into the market.[237] For example, in the present case the evolutionary path would have been to plan the design or sourcing of batteries for electric vehicles to avoid foreseeable harms, such as endangering the lives of children in the Congo. The solutions exist already well within our imaginative and compassionate powers. They are waiting for us, if we will care enough collectively to look for them.[238] As Albert Einstein wrote:

> The world is not dangerous because of those who do harm, but because of those who look at it without doing anything.

As the reader may have observed, chance and fortune play a role in all the above cases, as they do in all our personal and professional lives. We assume that chance and fortune are disembodied forces separate from ourselves, that influence our lives for good or ill. But is this narrative true? For most of my life I didn't realize that chance and fortune have been given more formal academic names. They are called "Coincidence, Synchronicity, and Serendipity (CSS);" and as I have discovered, it is not at all clear or certain whether CSS events occur "outside" or "inside" us, or are essentially a singular phenomenon.

Chapter 9: Synchronicity

A monk asked Joshu in all earnestness,
"What is the meaning of the patriarch's coming from the West?"
Joshu replied, "The oak tree in the garden."
—*Book of Serenity*, Case 47

"The real voyage of discovery consists, not in seeking
new landscapes, but in having new eyes."
—Marcel Proust, *La Prisonnière, Remembrance of*
Things Past

"Name the greatest of all inventors. Accident."
—Mark Twain

"Things that accord in tone, vibrate together; things that
have affinity in their innermost natures, seek one
another."
—*I Ching*

Does an objective universe exist separate and apart from our personal experience and the meaning we give to it? We are conditioned from birth to believe that we are separate: I/thou, we/they, subject/object. But what if "reality" is more complex, more interesting than we suppose?[239]

Coincidence, Synchronicity, and Serendipity (CSS), which I define below, seem to run like an aquifer just below the surface of my professional life. Here is one example of what appears to be a mystery.

Just as I am writing the above section on Equanimity (May 11, 2022), I glance at the crawl from the Daily Mail on my computer. It is reporting that a passenger has just landed a single-engine Cessna 208 after the pilot had "gone incoherent." "He was really calm," the flight controller, Robert Morgan, reported in an interview following the successful landing. "He said, 'I don't know how to fly. I don't know how to stop this thing if I do get on the runway.'" According to the press report quoted here, Morgan himself had never flown this model Cessna, but he pulled up a picture of the instrument panel's layout and started guiding the passenger step-by-step. "Try to hold the wings level and see if you can start descending for me. Push forward on the controls and descend at a very slow rate," the air traffic controller is heard telling the fledgling pilot in Live ATC audio. Together, they guide the Cessna to touchdown on the runway. The landing rated 10 out of 10 in Morgan's view. "In my eyes, he was the hero," Morgan said. "I was just doing my job."

I am amazed at the synchronicity of my writing this section of the book and a perfect illustrative example appearing at the same moment in the news.

And here is another example of CSS with practical applications in my professional work. As I discussed in Chapter 7, our legal team is engaged in a landmark case to save Lake Tahoe from being blanketed with small cell and macro towers.

Mark Twain described Lake Tahoe:

> As it lay there with the shadows of the mountains brilliantly photographed upon its still surface, I thought it must surely be the fairest picture the whole earth affords.

The principal defendants are the City of South Lake Tahoe, the Tahoe Regional Planning Agency (TRPA), and a major wireless telecom purveyor. A core legal issue is whether the TRPA is legally obligated to prepare a Comprehensive Programmatic Environmental Impact Statement (EIS) under Article VII of the California-Nevada Compact which Congress established in 1968. Our clients have submitted over 4,000 pages of evidence of the environmental consequences of exposing residents, animals, and plants to continuous cumulative NIR radiation. The TRPA is defiantly ignoring our Article VII argument, and the case rumbles along.

One day a member of our extended litigation team, Alex, who is a reclusive but observant genius, decided to take a stroll in the mountains (reminding me of the *koan* in Chapter 3). And what does he discover by absolute chance? Fake plastic needles, numbering in the hundreds, that had fallen from monopines and lay scattered everywhere around a macro cell tower. A monopine is a vertical tubular steel cell tower camouflaged by attached faux fiberglass, reinforced plastic pine tree branches, and needles. These monopines contain tons plastics that fragment and eventually degrade into toxic microplastics including lead, polyvinyl chlorides, and other carcinogens. The wireless telecom companies use them to camouflage their macro cell towers (generally unsuccessfully), to comply with a basic condition of their conditional use permits requiring them to address aesthetic impacts. Monopines are, in our clients' opinion, an aesthetically hideous solution to the ugly, stark macro towers rising far above the natural tree line. But apart from this, monopines (and other similarly disguised plastic cell towers) are known to shed highly toxic needles that break down into microplastics, which have been detected in human and animal blood and lungs.

Alex's descent from the mountain like Moses with *manna,* in the form of a bag of monopine needles he had picked up off the ground, has provided a powerful new set of arguments to present to the federal judge in our case. There are directly applicable federal laws, such as the Clean Water Act, and various California state laws that together impose strict limitations on the discharge of hazardous chemicals into Lake Tahoe which provides drinking water not only to residents of the Tahoe Basin but also downstream through the Truckee River all the way to Reno Nevada. Moreover, we discovered that one of our team members had served on the local Lahontan Water Quality Board and understands its methods and procedures. Thus the playing field for our negotiations has become a bit more level, thanks to CSS. We now have a real shot at averting an environmental catastrophe at Lake Tahoe.

Defining Coincidence, Synchronicity, and Serendipity (CSS)

Besides many online discussion groups there is a growing body of scientific studies on CSS, and even a Serendipity Society[240] based in the Netherlands, whose academic researchers explore what has generally been regarded until recently as a fascinating, although somewhat "weird" and inexplicable, phenomenon. Weird because such occurrences appear to defy our ordinary sense of reality.[241] For me the most astounding example (described in Chapter 1) was my chance meeting on a late summer Santa Barbara afternoon with Brother David Steindl-Rast, who lives in a remote monastery in Austria. Our life paths intersected, for a brief moment, just as I had been reflecting for the past hour with gratitude upon his practice of *Stop, Look, Go!*

There is in fact considerable overlap in the use of the terms Coincidence, Synchronicity, and Serendipity. *Coincidence* is a more general, all-inclusive reference. *Synchronicity* is a term first clinically used by the eminent Swiss psychiatrist, Dr. Carl Gustav Jung, which he defined as "meaningful coincidence" and which describes the specific joining in a moment of time of apparently causally unrelated external or internal events. *Serendipity*, a word coined by the English historian and Whig politician Horace Walpole, refers to a happy chance discovery. With all three, the event in question can be deeply meaningful, even life-changing, but the cause, at least in a conventional sense, is not well explained by western science. The absence of an apparent causal link to CSS phenomena is especially unsettling in a world that has become accustomed to a Cartesian worldview[242] that posits a mechanistic, non-fluid universe in which the behavior of everything, including human beings, can be explained as resulting from the complex interactions of material parts. However, some researchers are beginning to favor a non-mechanistic view. As the pioneering CSS investigator and psychiatrist Dr. Bernard Beitman writes in *Connecting with Coincidence*, "These coincidences suggest we live in a world of unbounded links to one another, especially those we love, especially those with whom intense emotion has forged a bond beyond our current understanding."[243] After several years of hard work Dr. Beitman and his colleague Julia Trail have launched a Coincidence Project, based on the reported phenomena of *Meaningful Coincidences* (the title of his 2022 book) from hundreds of active participants in many countries.[244]

For me, CSS events make the mundane magical. They offer a first taste, immediate and palpable, of our connection to another dimension of life, seemingly beyond time and space. It is a world of miracles where we can actively play and participate.

What is the Mechanism?

It is a natural question as we humans are curious creatures who have become accustomed to viewing our experiences through the lens of science and technology. In response, Dr. Beitman, posits a "psychosphere"—a network of mind that he believes can explain many of these events. A quantum physicist might see an intriguing link with the phenomenon of "quantum entanglement." A neurologist may search for explanations in mirror neurons, or in the brain's connectome, a neural map of its connections. These are all interesting speculations, but in fact, no one really knows.

There is another possibility. What if CSS events point directly to an alternative path, like a Zen *koan*,[245] and we fail to see what is under our very noses? One of my favorite *koan*s conveys this alternate way of seeing, which discards a strictly rational approach and embraces a deeper, more intuitive perspective:

> An old lady raised a goose in a bottle. As it grew, she wanted to release it. Please help the old lady release the goose without breaking the bottle. To "solve" this *koan* the reader is invited for a moment to put aside logic, and simply merge with the goose, or the bottle, or the old lady, and allow the *koan* to speak to you. You and the *koan* simply dissolve into thin air.

What if an important lesson of CSS events is to show us a different, non-mechanistic view of reality—one that encourages us to put aside the part of our mind that insists on clarity and knowing and is intensely uncomfortable with uncertainty? What if we let go of our need to find a cause or a logical explanation? What if CSS events are meant to encourage our

sense of wonder, mystery, and simple gratitude for the
strangeness and beauty of the universe? What if CSS events
point directly to a different mode of being in a world based on
alignment, not-knowing, and flow?

Case 2 in the *Blue Cliff Record* invites us to pursue this line
of exploration. It states:

> If you want to attain intimacy don't seek with
> questions. Why? Because the question is in the
> answer, and the answer is within the question.

Inner/Outer Alignment

My first introduction to the terrain of Inner/Outer
commenced with my serious practice of Zen. I had just
established the Pacific Law Group in Tokyo in 1984 in
partnership with another American lawyer, and two retired
senior Japanese officials, the former president of the Bank of
Tokyo and the former chief of the Tax Bureau in the Ministry of
Finance. In those days, I led a Clark Kent kind of life—
international business deals during the week, retreats to Yamada
Roshi's zendo in Kamakura during the weekends. I was never a
great Zen student, especially during *sesshin* which are extended
periods of concentrated meditation under the stern supervision
of one of the "teachers," who walked up and down with a *bo*
(bamboo stick) and pummeled the adepts to awaken their
consciousness. I was fine during the first few days of this ordeal,
but then the fevers came, as they invariably did, and my resolve
would weaken. Stealthily I would escape to Sabatini, one of
Tokyo's finest Italian restaurants. I was guiltless. I once had a
dream in which we Zen students were given a grade by the roshi.
I got C+. When I reported the grade to Yamada-Sensei, he
laughed and told me that was a pretty good grade for a Zen
student.

The Great Koan Mu (無)

The first *koan* we are given in the Sanbo Kyodan tradition is the great *koan* Mu. Literally, *Mu* (or *Wu* in Chinese) can be translated as "nothing." You are being asked to solve nothing. You may expand the "meaning" of something which is intended to be meaningless as "vast spaciousness," "boundlessness," or "emptiness," but these are, really, all conceptual crutches. You sit on your *zabuton* (pillow) and work on nothing… nothing at all.

In other words, there is a distance between the meditator and the *koan.* However, slowly over the weeks and months, with guidance from the *roshi,* the gap closes. One day we realize, before we can put words around it, that the "outer" Mu and the inner are one and the same. In the Zen tradition this is called *kensho,* early realization. I like to think of it as analogous to the first taste of romantic love (in Japanese *hatsu koi no aji*).

Sometime during that period the thought occurred to me that if the inner and the outer are inextricably connected, or even of the same essential essence, perhaps we might apply this insight to accelerate the discovery of solutions to some of the great challenges facing humanity. I was encouraged when I "discovered" that the Latin root of the word "discover" in English is *discooperire*, meaning to "uncover." In other words, what we are attempting to discover already exists; we simply fail to see it. What if it is just a matter of stripping away the mental blocks that cloud our vision, so that we suddenly come to see clearly, rather than as Mark Twain humorously described it, "through a glass eye darkly." Excited by this core insight, I recruited a few friends and colleagues and we established a Discovery Society in Japan, with a diverse group of engineers, scientists, historians, and entrepreneurs. The Discovery Society disbanded after I left Japan, but my own journey of exploration continued.

One day I came upon Elmer and Alyce Green's classic book, *Beyond Biofeedback*. The Greens were pioneering explorers of human consciousness during the 1960s and 1970s, and *Beyond Biofeedback* describes their encounters with an Indian yogi (Swami Rama), a Native American shaman (Rolling Thunder), and a Dutch yogi (Jack Schwartz). I was fascinated by *Beyond Biofeedback* and immediately called Elmer, who founded and headed the psychophysiology lab at the Menninger Institute in Topeka, Kansas. The operator rang right through to Elmer, who seemed to know who I was even before I described the Discovery Society in Japan. I was delighted when he invited me to come to Topeka to attend a workshop that he and Alyce and their partners, Dr. Pat Norris, Dr. Dale Walters, and Rex Hartzell, were conducting to introduce participants to the technology of "brain wave biofeedback," or "psychophysiological self-regulation." Our synergy was powerful. I never looked back.

Soon after I proposed linking the Menninger team's research to my Discovery Society in Japan, and thus was born a commercial company, Discovery Engineering International (DEI). DEI's mission was to introduce the insights and practical skills that Elmer and Alyce and their colleagues had perfected over decades to enable explorers, especially those transacting business, to apply these skills to creative problem solving.

Research

As DEI was taking off I reviewed many scientific studies on Zen meditators, discovery, problem solving, and in particular, "creative reverie." Prominent among these were books by Andreas Mavromatis (*Hypnagogia*) and Robert Root-Bernstein, (*Discovering*) which contain many fascinating accounts, including the revelation that came to August Kekulé in a dreamlike state of the organic structure of benzene, and Alexander Fleming's discovery of penicillin.

To this day I am fascinated by the phenomenon of "stimulus diffusion," which is well-documented in the anthropological literature.[246] An example: Two indigenous fishing communities, separated by an impenetrable mountain escarpment, face a common problem. Their traditional lore maintains that the most fertile fishing areas are beyond the reefs, but they lack the technology to reach them. Famine is common. It is critical that they devise a means to travel beyond the reefs, but how to do it? Only the gods know such things. One day a genius lady pearl diver in one of the villages on the eastern side of the mountains comes up with an amazing invention. It is called a "canoe". With this extraordinary invention her people (it is a matriarchal society) can travel beyond the reef. Famine is forever averted because the fish are endlessly plentiful. A month later, with no contact whatsoever between the two communities, another brilliant person on the other side of the mountains makes the identical discovery. He has had a dream or has heard from the village shaman that such a thing is indeed possible. Simply the recognition of that possibility triggers his discovery, and it is revealed.

Beyond Biofeedback—Coincidence Control

Elmer Green called the technique he was developing "coincidence control," a term I have never been very comfortable with, especially since the key to all biofeedback training is to "give in" or to "release" control. However, I soon came to understand through my own direct experience with brainwave biofeedback and other biofeedback modalities Elmer's subtle insight that the most advanced form of "control" involves allowing, alignment, and flow. His *Beyond Biofeedback* advances a profound philosophical and scientific proposition that the entire universe is a feedback process, and that biofeedback technologies offer one of many modalities to take us directly through the portals. (The reader may enjoy meeting Elmer in this video,[247] which conveys the essence of this unique human being I was proud to call my friend.)

During our DEI days Elmer and I had two entertaining adventures worth reporting here, because they lend texture and color to this inquiry into the relationship between inner and outer.

An Experiment with Time

I first encountered the idea that time might be nonlinear and serial when Roger Fisher, my friend and colleague at Harvard Law School, casually made a present of his copy of J. W. Dunne's *An Experiment with Time*, first published in 1927. Dunne was a British soldier, aeronautical engineer, and philosopher who had a series of precognitive dreams that he was able organize into a system, based on a theory of time that he called *"Serialism."*[248] Although never accepted by mainstream science, Dunne's book was widely read, and nearly a century later I am still influenced by his ideas.

I myself have experienced CSS time distortions. While writing this chapter, I watched the video *The Beatles in India,* about their sojourn in India and their friendship with Ravi Shankar and Maharishi Mahesh Yogi.[249] While viewing it, a memory of a chance meeting ten years earlier suddenly surfaced. I hadn't given it a second thought since then. In the spring of 2012 I was in the exercise room of the Okura Hotel in Tokyo when Yoko Ono suddenly appeared and mounted the exercise bike beside me. I almost blurted out, "My name is also Julian (referring to her son with John Lennon), how do you do!" But I didn't. Respect for her privacy took precedence over my curiosity to explore this remarkable chance encounter.[250]

The interesting question for me is whether CSS can reach backward in time, prompted by present events. This, of course, depends on our construction of time. If we allow that time has many dimensions, only one being linear, I might interpret this chance meeting with Yoko Ono as somehow related to my viewing the Beatles movie today. Just as the past can reach out to the present, the future and present, as suggested by my DEI experience with a Midwest foundation, described in Chapter 2 and below, may under some conditions reach backwards to the past.[251]

When I posed this question about whether CSS can reach backward in time to Dr. Bernard Beitman, he replied, "Eric Wargo and his 'time loops' answer your question in the affirmative."[252]

Creative Reverie

Soon after we established DEI with the help of Elmer's connections, we received a grant from a foundation in the Midwest that was interested in supporting research into human consciousness. The foundation's president, Dr. Glenn Olds, a former US ambassador to UNESCO, invited our team to the newly designed headquarters to meet with the entrepreneur founder, and then months later to conduct a workshop introducing the DEI system to the foundation's board and staff. Dr. Olds and his staff participated. Our system consisted of equipping each participant with our "discovery brainwave biofeedback unit" (designed by engineer Rex Hartzell) and then analyzing the data through a Fast Fourier Transform (FFT) algorithm to follow the brainwave cycles. FFT provided the metrics, but the prize was the images reported by participants. These suddenly appear as participants journey into "hypnagogic[253] and hypnopompic[254] reverie," a subliminal state of awareness at the border of sleep and wakefulness, where our subconscious and superconscious[255] mind become available to us in the form of images that are projections from the subconscious mind, and in some instances from the "higher consciousness." At the close of each session, the explorer is instructed to record his or her images.

The images reported by some of the board members and staff were eerily similar, and disturbing: a great storm gathering; a shipwreck, a wolf's head, a swamp, a drowning in quicksand, and a decapitation. Although many of the images were unique to one individual, but some overlapped and were shared by several participants.

We prepared a report to the president and offered an interpretation. We suggested that the group's combined imagery pointed to an imminent upheaval, a palace coup, where the president and his team would be removed, where others in the foundation (wolves) were preparing to attack and to devour Dr. Olds' ambitious and visionary plans. There would be a shipwreck, and his expedition would be "lost at sea."

No one paid attention to our Cassandra-like premonitory report. A few months later, the precise events that the images foretold happened. The ax fell. Dr. Olds and his team were out.

I encourage the reader to refer back to Chapter 2, on the Shadow. One of the lessons of the foundation case is that the Shadow can be an ally and friend, offering warning signs of danger ahead, if we will only heed its deeper messages.

Participants in our workshops often reported seeing identical images, without discussing them beforehand. In a program we conducted for the Congressional Office of Technology Assessment some participants in the room laughed as one of their buddies sketched in his Discovery Log another explorer's images, as if he were taking direct dictation from a larger mind field. "We learned this technique from working with the Navajo," the participant, who worked for the Defense Intelligence Agency, remarked casually. This was the era of intense interest in the federal government and Congress led by the late Senator Claiborne Pell of Rhode Island in Russian advances in the field of parapsychological research. Our DEI team speculated that we all share overlapping states of consciousness which at times surface in CSS events—another way of describing Dr. Beitman's proposed "psychosphere."

Graphing CSS Events

As I have reflected on my business negotiations during the 1980s and 1990s in Japan and elsewhere around the world, I have continued to explore these inner/outer connections, which are described in my books *Piloting Through Chaos (1995)*, *The Explorer's Mind (2013)*, *Laughing Heart (2019)*, and *Integral Resilience—Helping Communities Thrive (2020)*. Early on I developed a simple tool to track and then depict on a graph how our inner and outer processes interact. The reader can easily validate that interaction by using this simple graph and tracing CSS events as they appear his or her own life.[256]

(see next page)

CSS Events: Inner/Outer Graphs

External_____
World

Inner_____
World

Integrity/Field_____
Independence

Need_____

Heart
Energy_____
Love (BHI)

Paying_____
Forward

                              Diagram 4

Instructions:

o **External World.** On the top line you simply trace the flow of
   your external life as it is happening during a single day.
   Above the line record "good" or "positive" things; below the
   line note what you perceive as adverse events, at least in this
   moment.

o **Inner World.** Below the line record what is happening in
   your internal world. I have revised the graph based on my
   original rendition in *Piloting Through Chaos* and simplified
   it to focus on a few of the most important variables.[257]

o **Integrity/Field Independence.** This line reflects to what
   extent you are dependent on or thrown off course by what is
   happening in the external world. Above the line note

activities or events that suggest you are less dependent, below the line those where you appear more dependent. Elmer Green refers to this measure in *Beyond Biofeedback* as your degree of "field independence." People who are field dependent are tossed here and there by what happens in the external world. Our goal is to reclaim control over our internal balance or equilibrium (integrity) by becoming independent of the "field" around us.

o **Need.** I define "Need" as the unchallenged and largely delusory belief that we will die as a result of some event in the external world. In fact, we will survive most of the pains of life—disappointments, professional reverses, lack of recognition, business failures, even our own illnesses, or the injury or death of a loved one. No matter what our anxious or terrified mind tells us, these events will not physically kill us, although we may suffer deeply because of them. Most of us are in this sense "field dependent." In other words, when something untoward happens in the external world, our Need increases. The goal is simply to observe the process of how meaning and stories begin to cluster around Need, and by simply witnessing to maintain some degree of mental and emotional detachment. You may note that when Need decreases, positive events start happening above the external line.

o **Heart Energy Field of Love.** The German word for "anxiety" derives from the Latin verb *"ango"* (noun, *angustus, Greek* ἄγχω (*ánkhō,* "to choke") meaning to "constrict." This is actually an accurate description of what happens to the blood vessels, including the heart, when we are in high Need (in psychological terms, in "fight or flight" mode). Our heart literally constricts.

o The most powerful way I know to build field independence is to cultivate the Heart energy of Love, as discussed in

Chapter 3. The graphs allow us to record this simple process of opening the Heart's energy field of Love and then observing what happens internally, first to Need, and then to balance. During the past few years I have discovered something quite remarkable, (described in Chapter 3, Just Click?) When I send out Love to the universe I receive instantly, almost like a boomerang, a reply of Love, and it compounds. I sense that everything—the sky, animals, and plants, even stones—emanate Love. I am reminded of the Biblical passage, "Give and ye shall receive."

o   When we explore how our inner and outer worlds interact, we may not at first perceive anything happening. I have found that sometimes it takes time for the "signal" that marks a CSS event to return as feedback. But if we are patient, our synchronization of Heart and Mind will heighten our perception of CSS events.

o   **Paying Forward**[258]. I experience this exchange of Love with the world as happiness, and for that I am deeply grateful. The most powerful means I know to repay the world for this experience of Love and to "reset" the dial, to turn the rudder toward hope, is the act of Paying Forward. In other words, when we consciously recognize the goodness that is happening in our life right now, at this very moment, and pass it on, without asking anything in return, a beneficial process seems to be set in motion. Watch what starts to happen around the upper line depicting the external world when we act without any expectations or assumptions. Why should the simple deed of Paying Forward have any influence at all on our external life? But it does, and I am pleased to see that what I have discovered empirically is now being studied by the scientific community (e.g., the Science of Paying Forward).[259]

○ **Integrity of Data.** It might be argued that much of the data underlying the graphs is entirely subjective, therefore rendering them unreliable for any practical use. I have given a lot of thought to this challenge, and I have found that as our integrity increases—in other words, our ability to see the world as it is without the distortions of ego and personality—our assessments in the Graphs become more insightful and accurate as a guide for practical action. Again, the reader need not take this finding on faith. Please verify it for yourself.

○ **Working with Misfortune.** There is for me an especially interesting supplement to this process. It appears that analyzing our interactions with the inner and outer worlds by means of the Graphs may also offer one way to interrupt deeply unhealthy patterns before they cripple us. What happened to an old friend who recently resurfaced in my life is one example of this kind of course-correction. His daughter was killed in a car accident when she tried to avoid hitting a deer on the road. Instead of blaming each other, however, and spiraling further downward in mutual recriminations, as often happens in family tragedies, he and his wife decided not to divorce but instead chose to embrace life together. They pooled the outpouring of donations from friends and family given to assuage their grief, and chose to build and finance a school for aspiring young social entrepreneurs in Tanzania, which they visit every year. The school has flourished over the past decade. It has opened new campuses, and has proved a deeply gratifying experience for my friend and his wife to learn about and contribute to this economically impoverished, but spiritually rich country.

Timing (CSS) in Business and Law

Good timing can turn a mediocre product into a breakout success; bad timing can destroy an otherwise successful career. In business, **timing is everything.** However many business people think timing is just like luck. Even some of the best and brightest treat timing as an afterthought.[260] Generally speaking most lawyers pay little heed to CSS events, although an understanding of CSS has important implications for a number of areas of law, where at present it is *terra incognita.*[261]

Meaning Making

It is one thing to "seed" CSS by paying close attention to the images that emerge from our unconscious mind. It is quite another to understand the meaning of the important hidden signal that is often embedded in these images. Carl Jung wrote extensively on this subject, and even posited that meaning is encoded in universal images, resonant across various cultures and across time, which he referred to as humanity's collective "archetypes." DEI participants invariably reported experiencing these archetypal images.

Through DEI we developed a simple and practical way to "decode" the signal. It involved a facilitator, who asks the explorer to imagine that he or she has just arrived from another planet and is unfamiliar with how words are customarily used here on Earth. In other words, the Explorer's Mind becomes a blank slate. Following this protocol, the facilitator helps the explorer parse each element of the image, beginning with the most recent part to appear, as the explorer remembers it. (This is an important subtlety because hypnagogic-hypnapompic images are delicate and fleeting, similar in this respect to dream images.) The facilitator inquires of the first element "What is an "X?", and listens intently. Not what does X mean, but simply what is an X before meaning is assigned to it. So, what is X? Then what is Y? Then Z, until the entire image is recomposed, relived, and reflected back. Finally the facilitator asks a key question: "What might be happening in your present life, or in the past, or possibly in the future, that this image is speaking to?" Far more often than not, the explorer will discover a significant connection.

Here's an illustration. Soon after I met Dr. Beitman I began to notice an increase in CSS events. One of these was especially evocative. Hummingbirds suddenly started to appear everywhere in my life. I practiced *Just Click!* and a hummingbird would whiz by. My wife Angela says over lunch, "You must see this lovely email from my cousin Paula in Australia. It is called "hummingbird pool party."[262] I go to the supermarket, and the first thing I see is a shopping bag with a hummingbird design on it. So, what's the meaning of these CSS events?

To find out, I use the DEI method. I resist impatiently seeking for meaning, and I temper the impulse to settle too quickly on one interpretation. Instead, I ask a different question. I ask myself, "What is the first thing I notice?" It is a whirr of wings. What is whirr? It is pure energy. What are wings? Wings are means of flight. What is flight? A way of conveying a living creature or indeed anything through the medium of the air. I proceed. What's the next thing I notice? Beauty. I am struck by how beautiful the little creature is and how miraculously fast it is, like lightning. What is Beauty? It is for me a transcendent energy that connects us to all that is fine, nourishing, and noble in the world. What is a miracle? That which rises above our ordinary reality, that speaks to a higher intelligence. What is speed? Extraordinary energy in motion. Slowly, methodically, I approach an important question, "What is a hummingbird?" And the answer comes quickly to me, as it does again at this very moment. One voice that I hear says, "why it's a pretty little bird, that's all." But another voice speaks to me at the same time, especially as the lovely little creature appears suddenly and in many forms. "Yes, it's true, it's a lovely little bird. "But," the voice whispers, "what if it is an angel?" An angel is a messenger between different levels of reality.

The important practice is not to discern the "real" or "correct" meaning of the CSS experience. The essential point is to recognize the emotional, even numinous connection, the affirmation that the arrival of hummingbirds has brought to me. It is that the Tao, or the Logos is an immediately available, ever-present beneficial force in my life. I've had a hummingbird baptism. I can no longer think of hummingbirds as I did before, for now they hold a special place in my Heart.

Delusion—A Tale of Bird and Kettle

We must approach this business of meaning making carefully, however. There are traps. The other night as I am lost in meditation I am delighted to hear the call of a bird in the night. It is a sweet and beautiful song. Now, one of life's great mysteries for me is why birds stop singing at night, and don't start until dawn wakens them. I sense that I am on the verge of a major scientific discovery—birds singing at night! But then I listen more attentively. What's this I'm hearing? It's the kettle screeching on the stove! I hasten to turn off the stove before the house burns down.

Murmuration

CSS suggest that even the smallest events (e.g. special providence in the fall of a sparrow[263]) are part of a grander design that we cannot fathom with our limited human perception. The extraordinary natural phenomenon of the murmuration of birds—the collective expression (or emergence) of many individual expressions—is one of those synchronistic events that leaves us awestruck and speechless. Typically seen among starlings, a murmuration is a large flock of birds (hundreds or even thousands) that fly together and become an undulating, morphing collective. The constantly shifting shapes they make are mesmerizing and imply the sense of a kind of higher order; but the shapes are completely emergent and arise as a natural consequence of the changing position of each individual. No bird is leading, but the intention of the flock is internally consistent. Each bird is aware of a few of the birds around it and simply responds to their constantly changing positions. Yet, from the ground, we can observe the constantly changing shape as order within chaos.

Re-enter the Shadow: Manufactured and Contrived Reality

In this *Age of Surveillance Capitalism* (the meme coined by Professor Shoshana Zuboff in her book of that name), can we really distinguish any more what is authentic from what is fake and contrived? Our most intimate behaviors, tastes, and proclivities for good or ill are being influenced, even controlled, to suit some corporate agenda, and by the puppeteers who run these behemoth corporations to feed their appetites for power and profit. We are no more than flies to these twenty-first century gods who manipulate us for their sport.

There is a darker side to CSS that we must be aware of, if we have the curiosity and courage to enter this terrain. It is called apophenia[264] defined as an "abnormal" tendency to perceive meaningful connections between ostensibly unrelated things. Some psychiatrists view apophenia as an early stage of delusional thought based on self-referential over-interpretations or distortions of actual sensory perceptions.[265] A tragic example is Mark David Chapman, the assassin of John Lennon.

Chapman was obsessed with John Lennon, and one day appeared at his residence, The Dakota in New York City and shot him. As he later explained, "because my voices told me to do so." In a world of billions of snooping wireless eyes and ears that make up the "Internet of Things" (more accurately termed the Internet for Things), where personal privacy no longer exists, and where government and industrial surveillance is now commonly used to manipulate our most basic behaviors, how can we ever know that the CSS event we have just experienced is real or contrived? How can we know whether the negative "voices" that urge us to act against our better judgment are not intentionally being implanted in our minds by these same remote interests that profit when society becomes ever more divided, polarized, and violent?

We needn't be slaves to our own meaning making. We needn't believe our own thoughts. In fact, we have far more dominion over the meanings we ascribe to people and events, and how we respond to them; to the stories and narratives we create based on our emotions (for, after all, how can our own feelings lie to us?), and to the behaviors and actions predicated on them. One shortcut is to look to the data, the most basic, easily available, neutral source of information on the world. If we can prune biases in the way we or others interpret data, we have a practical means to see the world as it is before our imaginations begin adding color and creating a narrative. As we cultivate this skill[266] of questioning and exploring our own meaning making, we acquire the ability, individually and collectively, to gain useful glimpses or intimations of the future, to decipher patterns, and to intercept the tide of events, which in turn can influence CSS and other occurrences in our lives. Thus, by cultivating this potential to determine the meaning of our experiences we create a spiraling positive feedback loop that can strongly shape our destinies.

Seeing the World as It Is

The path of wisdom and integrity involves seeing the world just as it is, accepting all its distortions. How can we see the world just as it is? By seeing and feeling not only with our five senses, but also with our Heart and gut[267]. It is easy to put this method to the test. Take any important decision you are about to make. I have noticed that if I decide using only my brain and logic, I will get one answer. If I ask my Heart, I get a different answer, and if I consult my gut, still another. But when I balance and consult all three, I will arrive at what appears to be a wise path which I can then validate through experience. I am also fine with not knowing, with getting no immediate answer. Jizo's instruction[268] is invariably helpful: *"Not knowing is most intimate."* I wait, I observe, I am okay with uncertainty; I get closer to the question, more intimate with it. An answer usually reveals itself in time. The world evolves at its own pace. Our task is to attune. For me the process is more important than any specific answer. This same approach works especially well when interpreting CSS occurrences, which, as I am suggesting, point us to embracing flow rather than seeking a specific causal explanation.

Just Click! Revisited

One of the important findings of Dr. Beitman and other researchers is that CSS events occur far more frequently than is generally supposed, and CSS can be actively encouraged by the exchange and telling of them. The practice of *Just Click!* invites us to consider the possibility that CSS events are ever-present, indeed a natural part of humanity's common heritage. (In Christian terms, "The kingdom of God (the miracle) is at hand.") What can bring us rapidly to this realization is Love. Because when we infuse any encounter—with another person, an object, an event, even an idea—with the powerful energy of Love, a dialogue begins, and together we create a powerful energy field. I experience this exchange as personal happiness, enhanced life force, and gratefulness.

This state of expanded awareness and vitality can also provide a place of refuge when we encounter the Shadow, within ourselves and the outside world. This is because the Shadow tends to lose its grip when we can recognize, accept, and flow with it. I believe this insight can help us to cultivate balance and courage, and to nourish hope in a world that is increasingly spinning out of control.

Chapter 10: Humor and Resilience

Humor is another of the soul's weapons in the fight for self-preservation.
—Victor Frankel

Angels can fly because they can take themselves lightly.
—G.K. Chesterton

Humor along with Love, Beauty, and Vitality is a refuge from the craziness and cruelty of the world. It is available to us at any moment. If we look carefully, we can discover humor in the most improbable settings. It is said there are two kinds of humor: "sacred" humor, which helps us to transcend, and "profane" humor that appears in the exigencies of everyday life.

Man's Search for Meaning by Viktor Frankl is an example of sacred humor. It describes how humor saved his life, and the lives of other prisoners in the Auschwitz extermination camp. Humor was his soul's weapon for self-preservation. He survived by caring for his fellow prisoners and made them smile. It was his personal defiance against the Nazis. He writes:

I trained a friend of mine who worked next to me on the building site to develop a sense of humor. I suggested to him that we would promise each other to invent at least one amusing story daily, about some incident that could happen one day after our liberation. He was a surgeon and had been an assistant on the staff of a large hospital. So I once tried to get him to smile by describing to him how he would be unable to lose the habits of camp life when he returned to his former work. On the building site (especially when the supervisor made his tour of inspection) the foreman encouraged us to work faster by shouting: "Action! Action!" I told my friend, "One day you will be back in the operating room, performing a big abdominal operation. Suddenly an orderly will rush in announcing the arrival of the senior surgeon by shouting, 'Action! Action!'"[269]

Dr. Frankl continues:

The attempt to develop a sense of humor and to see things in a humorous light is some kind of a trick learned while mastering the art of living. Yet it is possible to practice the art of living even in a concentration camp, although suffering is omnipresent."...

Everything can be taken from a man but one thing: the last of the human freedoms — to choose one's attitude in any given set of circumstances, to choose one's own way.

This is the first key. We have a choice.

The King's Fool in Shakespeare

In Shakespeare's King Lear, Act 1, Scene 5 the Fool observes to the King who finally realizes the folly of giving his kingdom away to his evil daughters.

> "Thou shouldst not have been old till thou hadst been wise."

There is a terrible irony here; we don't know whether to laugh or cry, or both at once. The English word "irony" derives from Latin *ironia*, and from Greek *eironeia* "dissimulation, assumed ignorance," and *eiron* "dissembler." Irony tears the fabric of our "reality." Things are out of sync with what we are accustomed to believe.

The Fool is Lear's companion on his journey into madness and eventually death. Just before Lear's death, the Fool is hanged by Lear's enemies, his two daughters and their husbands. The Fool is Lear's conscience. His Fool is wise and constantly commenting on Lear's relentless folly.

There is a Zen *koan* that invites us to dialogue continuously with our inner wise Fool:

> "Every day Zuigan would call out to himself, "Master! Master!" and he answered, "Yes, Sir!" Then inquired, "Thoroughly awake and Present?" to which he answered, "Yes, Sir! Yes Sir." Don't be deceived by others!" he cautioned. "No, Sir! No Sir!" he replied. (Case 12 *Mumonkan Gateless Gate*).

Metamorphosis

I have a special feeling for Charles Dickens, who was among the wittiest of writers. "Lighten it, brighten it," was his editorial advice to young writers.

Here's a brief sampling:

> He appeared to enjoy beyond everything the sound of his own voice. I couldn't wonder at that, for it was mellow and full and gave great importance to every word he uttered. He listened to himself with obvious satisfaction and sometimes gently beat time to his own music with his head or rounded a sentence with his hand.

The last paragraph of *A Christmas Carol* reflects my own philosophy:

> Scrooge was better than his word. He did it all, and infinitely more; and to Tiny Tim, who did NOT die, he was a second father. He became as good a friend, as good a master, and as good a man as the good old city knew, or any other good old city, town, or borough in the good old world. Some people laughed to see the alteration in him; but his own heart laughed, and that was quite enough for him.

A part of Scrooge lives in most of us, but we can transform him with our heart and laughter.

Marriage

If I were to ever write a less serious book, I would write one about my wife, Angela, who, in addition to her other wonderful qualities, is unpredictably hilarious. We spend substantial time each day laughing. Here are two samples:

Talmudic Complexity

> A man is walking by himself in the woods without
> his wife and he has an opinion. Is he still wrong?

In my private survey, I have yet to encounter a husband who didn't think this was funny.

Enlightenment

In my early days of Zen practice, I began to discover an affinity with everything. One afternoon I rushed home with a great discovery.

> "I can become a tree!" I burst out with delight.
> "How wonderful!" Angela observed mildly, "Can
> you become a broom and sweep the deck?"

This happened years ago, early in our marriage. About five years later I compiled a book of her witticisms with a picture of a giant spider hovering above both of us at a pumpkin sale. I like the absurdity of it. One never knows when we will suddenly tangle with the spiders of life. (see below)

I am reminded of Woody Allen's profound treatise on Wisdom, entitled: *Evet Ama, Bir Lokomotif Bunu Yapabilir mi Bakalım*? Do you know it?

> "Arayan cinayet masasından Çavuş Reed'di.
> "Hâlâ Tanrı'yı arıyor musun?"
> "Evet."
> "Yaradan, Var oluş Nedenimiz, Yücelerin Yücesi Rabbimiz mi?"
> "Doğru."

Marriages tend to acquire over time their own Cubist dimensions and rhythms that may be only hilarious to those inside them. I do believe it is a part of love to laugh a lot together.

Developing Personal Resilience

As I describe in *5 Minutes to Resilience*,[270] it is extremely easy to discover hilarious moments in everyday life. They help to strengthen resilience by restoring balance and perspective. These moments are everywhere. I encourage the reader to pause and to watch the excerpt from Sid Caesar's *This is Your Life*, or the broadcast by the BBC newscaster. Such things really do happen to us.

Children Interrupt BBC Newscaster[271]
Sid Caesar - This Is Your Life[272]
Sid Caesar Visits a Health Food Restaurant[273]

There is a powerful *qigong* practice that releases lung energy by shouting Ha, Ha, Ha!! three times a day each week. Just try it! A related practice is *Simply Smiling*.[274] Scientific studies confirm that smiling can alter our brain chemistry in healthy ways. (See: Scientific American, *Laughing Lots, Live Longer*)[275]

Here are a few other tips to cultivate resilience in the face of loneliness, isolation, and despair.

- Quiet and Open the Heart
- See the Big Picture
- Trust in the Connection
- Find your Inner Power
- Increase Flow
- Connect to Nature
- Open your Heart, forget yourself
- Pay Forward

These are all ways to become free like the image of this happy little fish:

21st Century Divine Comedy

I have often wondered why Dante chose to entitle his epic poem, *Divine Comedy,* when the first book is about Hell and all those who enter are warned at the threshold to "Surrender All Hope." Dante was greatly influenced by the classic Greek conception. He called his epic poem a "comedy," because unlike tragedies that begin on a high note and end tragically, comedies begin badly but end well.

Can we say the same for the divine comedy in which our present world is engaged? The following chapters offer one path, hopefully among many, of how Big Heart Intelligence and Evolutionary Values can help us navigate through the gathering storm.

BIG HEART CONNECTOME

Chapter 11: Roots of Crisis

Where there is no vision, the people perish.
—Proverbs 29:18, King James Version

The artist, however faithful to his personal vision of reality, becomes the last champion of the individual mind and sensibility against an intrusive society and an officious state.
—President John F. Kennedy (Amherst College Address)

Over the next few years, the entire Earth, the Heavens, and the Oceans will be invaded by billions of wireless devices. A few powerful actors within remote mega-corporations, captive government agencies, and the global military establishment will lead the onslaught. The Wireless Juggernaut will enable governments and corporations to surveil and intrude on our private lives and will dramatically increase the chances of global conflict, especially between the West, Russia, and China. It is happening before our very eyes, and the threat will only increase unless we are willing to act collectively, and soon. However, a large part of the population on Earth is uninformed about these dangers, and even those who see and understand them, feel overwhelmed, defeated, and helpless. It is an unfolding catastrophe.

In ancient China, when the ruler acted against the natural order of things (Tao),[276] the signs of disharmony would appear everywhere: dikes would collapse and floods would destroy crops; drought, famine, and pestilence would ravage the land; "barbarian" hordes of non-Han peoples would breach the Great Wall. If the ruler failed to heed the signs, the kingdom would inevitably perish and a new dynasty would replace it.

There is a striking parallel in today's breakdown of cities, the breach of borders, widespread depression and mental illness, a global crisis of meaning, pandemics, violence against children, government arrogance, cynical disregard of law, widespread disinformation and manipulation of facts, concentration of economic power in the hands of a very few. It is also evident in the destruction of habitat, climate turbulence, regional wars, accelerating US/China conflict, especially around the tinderbox of Taiwan, a sudden uptick in threats of preemptive nuclear strikes and retaliation. All these trends attest from the perspective of Chinese philosophy that the Mandate of Heaven[277]—requiring that government power be used benevolently and in accord with the natural order (Tao)—has already been lost.

The Rainmaker

In these conditions, what would the ancients advise? There is an old Chinese story that can serve as a prelude to the discussion of the Big Heart Connectome (BHC), which is the subject of this section of the book. It is entitled "The Rainmaker."

A farming village had been suffering drought for many months and was now facing the danger of famine, as the crops were beginning to fail. The village elders decided to call in a

Rainmaker. When the Rainmaker, who was also a Taoist shaman, arrived, the village council asked him what he required. "Just provide a small hut outside town and leave some drinking water and simple daily rations outside the door," the Rainmaker replied. And that is what they did.

A few days passed without rain. The council members began to doubt their decision, and even to quarrel. When the Rainmaker received this report from a messenger, he simply advised, "Tell them to be patient," which is what the messenger reported back to the village. And so, the village was patient, trusting in the skill of the Rainmaker.

Suddenly, at the end of the week, the clouds darkened, and it began to rain buckets. The villagers surrounded the hut, and clapping their hands in gratitude, called on the Rainmaker to reveal how he had caused the miracle. "It was nothing special," the Rainmaker observed mildly. "When I came to the village, I noted much discord and conflict. I saw that I had to remove myself to a place some distance away, which allowed me to work on behalf of the village and to allow the village to begin to return to balance and harmony with the Tao."

Is it still possible for us, as eight billion plus global citizens to devise a wise and peaceful relationship with each other, the living environment, and the Tao? What if our present catastrophic course contains the seeds of a more loving, creative, and prosperous stage in human evolution? How can we break this murderous downward spiral? We must go to the roots of the problem.

Distortion of the "Free Market"

One important cause of the problem may be a distortion of the original concept of the free market system.

In the *Wealth of Nations*, the Western Bible of free market ideology, the economist-philosopher Adam Smith[278] clearly emphasized the priority of the consumer over producers:

> Consumption is the sole end and purpose of all production; and the interest of the producer ought to be attended to only so far as it may be necessary for promoting that of the consumer.

Over the years Adam Smith's original idea of the priority of the consumer has been replaced by the self-serving assertion that there is no conflict, and when there is, corporate interests must prevail over the interests of consumers (and the environment). "What is good for General Motors is still good for America." attributed to Charles Wilson and later Lee Iacocca.[279] The same kind of thinking has been attributed to conservative economists such as Nobel Laureate Milton Friedman who wrote in *Capitalism and Freedom*:

> There is one and only one social responsibility of business" "[and that is] to use its resources and engage in activities designed to increase its profits so long as it stays within the rules of the game, which is to say, engages in open and free competition without deception or fraud."[280]

My close friend Clinical Professor James E. Schrager, a leading expert on corporate strategy at the Booth School of Business at the University of Chicago, points out that this famous quote, which is still widely cited, has often been taken out of context; and in fact it does not accurately portray Milton Friedman's true thinking, which was far more sophisticated and visionary. Schrager urges that Milton Friedman had an excellent appreciation of what Harvard historians, Richard E. Neustadt and Ernst R. May describe in their 1986 book, *Thinking in Time*,[281] that wise business managers will inform themselves about the history, issues, individuals, and institutions involved in past decisions in order to make better present and future decisions. In short, by looking farther and seeing the Big Picture, wise corporate strategists will take close account of the consequences to their companies if their products and activities violate the law or injure people and the environment.

The modern, narrower, more near term view asserts that decisions concerning corporate social responsibility rest largely on the shoulders of the shareholders; that a corporation is not obligated to engage in any philanthropic or other socially responsible action unless the shareholders decide to do so. Some legal academics[282] go even further, arguing that it is a breach of fiduciary duty for the board of directors of a corporation to invest any of the corporation's assets in any "social enterprise," however "worthy," if these actions are deemed financially irresponsible to shareholders. In doing so directors would be subject to liability in shareholder lawsuits. An untested question is if shareholders of major telecom corporations were fully informed and the matter was put to a vote, would a majority of shareholders consent and approve what may turn out to be the terrible harms inflicted by the NIR emitting products the companies are profiting by? It is unlikely that such a shareholder vote will ever be permitted. Shareholder power is very much curtailed in mega corporations. In fact, our present economic system is rigged to favor management of powerful corporations and against shareholders and the public.

The Rainmaker story and the passing of the Mandate of Heaven provide a philosophical interpretation of our present maladies. The theory of "externalities" and "public goods" from the field of Welfare Economics[283] provides a more specific diagnosis and a remedy.

Negative Externalities

Many of our present challenges—for example, pollution of all kinds (including non-ionizing radiation overexposure from wireless devices)—can be viewed as a dysfunctional aspect of the efficient operation of markets, because the risks and costs of dangerous activities are imposed on the public without its consent. I call this the *Public Pays Principle*, in contrast with the *Polluter Pays Principle*[284], first articulated by the Organisation for Economic Co-operation and Development (OECD) in 1972. The remedy advanced by the OECD was, wherever practicable, to require by law, regulation, and judicial decision, firms to "internalize" these otherwise "external" uncompensated costs (to the victims), which would thereby generate powerful incentives for these firms to innovate safer products and compete on safety. Whereas the OECD's policy has been adopted effectively in many product areas, for example, for seat belts, cigarettes, lead, asbestos, and pesticides, it is openly being defied today by the regulatory agencies, which are captives of the telecom industry. The outcome is a massive regulatory subsidy that is allowing these firms to avoid the costs of their harmful activities and to impose these costs without compensation on the public.

Today a wide range of hazardous wireless products including smart meters, small cell and macro cell towers, cell phones and other mobile devices, computers, routers, and other emitters of non-ionizing radiation are benefitting from regulatory subsidies. The law is contrived to place the burden of proof of harms squarely on the most vulnerable among us—children, parents, pregnant women, disabled persons, economically disadvantaged citizens, and minority groups—who have the least knowledge or access to reliable unbiased information, and lack the legal and financial means to object. In the Kingdom of Wireless, the *Public Pays Principle* today reigns supreme.

Failure to "Price" Public Goods

Public goods are the converse of negative externalities. They are benefits society enjoys that are generally not accurately reflected in the price paid for them. Classic examples are national defense, lighthouses, streetlights, public roads, and clean air. In economics, public goods[285] are referred to as "non-excludable" and "non-rivalrous."

Less well recognized, but important to the ideas we are developing here, are certain values that resemble public goods and, like them, confer unaccounted benefits, but are treated essentially as noneconomic in nature. These values include Wisdom, Beauty, Kindness, Generosity, Creativity, Inventiveness, Happiness, and Love. In recent years there has been some attempt to quantify these values, the most prominent example being Bhutan's Gross National Happiness Index.[286] Beauty is sometimes well rewarded, as demonstrated by the sale of Leonardo da Vinci's Salvator Mundi[287] a few years ago for over $400 million—although the price perhaps more reflected the name value of the artist than the intrinsic beauty of the painting itself. The key point, however, is that although such virtues are often praised (see the Old Testament reference to wisdom as more precious than rubies[288]), the current economic system largely does not recognize them and so assigns to them a value of zero. I will explore the subject of Evolutionary Values more deeply in Chapter 12, as in many ways it is a key to finding our collective way through the wilderness of problems the world now faces.

Below are some other examples of market dysfunction, where those who are providing services that truly benefit society, or technologies that will protect the environment are being ignored or marginalized, and where in some instances the beneficial uses of technology are actually being suppressed to maximize profits, in ways that reinforce the primary goals of our present economic system.[289]

Cultural Creatives

In their best-selling book by that title, published in 2000, Paul Ray and Sherry Anderson estimated that there were over 50 million "culture creatives"[290] in the US collectively helping to transform civil society. The number has likely grown since then. A great many of these cultural creatives are younger people, who are not being paid the true value of their contributions to society over and above the market price of their work. In economic terms, a value of zero is being ascribed to the very real, but largely unrecognized benefits they are providing to society at large.

Public Interest Service Providers

Grassroots consumer, environmental, and civil rights organizations, and the physicians, attorneys, architects, city planners, and other professionals working with them offer the last bastion of protection and hope for society's most vulnerable—the economically disadvantaged, minorities, children, disabled persons, the elderly—and for the voiceless, fragile, rapidly disappearing natural world. These organizations are chronically underfunded and therefore marginalized, whereas their corporate adversaries, attorneys, lobbyists, and consultants receive exorbitant fees from mega-corporations to advance their profit-maximizing agendas. There is nothing inherently wrong with working to generate profits. Many great charitable foundations today have been endowed by fortunes accumulated through capitalist enterprises by men like Andrew

Carnegie, John D. Rockefeller, and Bill Gates. The problem is that the present capitalist system today is wildly out of balance.

Technology's Undervalued Public Potential

Technologies are invariably developed and commercialized to meet highest market demand, not to provide the highest value to society.[291] One example is cell phones. In a recent wrongful death case, *Walker et. al.. v. Motorola et. al.*[292] plaintiffs are alleging that manufacturers currently hold patents to inventions covering safe uses, but are intentionally suppressing these applications, or colluding with competitors to frustrate and to reduce competition that might enhance public safety.[293] The development of artificial intelligence is another example. Some of the smartest people I know are investing their creative genius in companies that are targeting the "big" markets for AI—the financial sector and the military —and leaving the exploration of AI's wider societal potential to the starry-eyed do-gooders, and visionaries.[294]

The Compounding Negative Multiplier

There are also deepening structural flaws in our society, and in particular our economic system that together reinforce one another and multiply their negative effects.

Concentration of Wealth

Today glitz, celebrity, and status are elevated and actively worshiped at the Altar of Greed by millions who yearn to share vicariously the lives of the rich and famous, as they can never do so in their ordinary lives. Meanwhile, wealth as never before has migrated into the hands of the über-rich, who invent rules and pull strings like puppeteers to manipulate the rest of us, but ignore these same rules when it comes to their own behavior.

Hyperpolarization

Hyperpolarization in the U.S. today is one sign of how long-simmering grievances are rapidly reaching a boiling point. One particularly unfortunate trend is the attacks on the classics and excellence in general, which are asserted by some parties to be elitist, even racist. Hyperpolarization is playing into the hands of the Shadow puppeteers, who are playing a far higher stakes game, seeking to profit from societal discord and division that they themselves are actively fomenting. As with China's Cultural Revolution under Mao, dogmatism and intolerance intensify polarization, foreclose opportunities to learn from the past, and prevent open and probing public discourse on the deeper grievances and values various factions are seeking to express. A continuing exploration of Evolutionary Values, especially the energetic power of Love, offers one way to temper and to balance hyperpolarization.

Desacralization of Nature

Another trend—which Rachel Carson alerted us to sixty years ago in her book *Silent Spring*—is the desacralization of nature.[295] As Ben Ehrenreich observes, "Only once we imagined the world as dead could we dedicate ourselves to making it so.[296] Despite the fact that the environmental movement in the US grew from Teddy Roosevelt's creation of the national park system (see Ken Burns' documentary, *The National Parks— America's Best Idea*[297]), it is significant that not one major environmental organization, and not one California senator or governor, past or present, has stood up to stop the desecration of Lake Tahoe. Not one. No public official has spoken against the wireless telecom companies blanketing the entire Tahoe region with macro-cell towers and toxic microplastic waste from the faux monopines that they are using to camouflage these towers. The voices of Mark Twain and John Muir are long silenced. Even the Sierra Club has forgotten Lake Tahoe.

Cynical Manipulation of Law

As our Tahoe and satellite legal cases (described in Chapters 8 and 15) well illustrate, there is today a widespread and cynical disregard by government agencies, in particular the political appointees who run them, of the rule of law. At BBILAN we are finding in all our public interest cases that the law in general is not the main problem. In fact, many of the laws we cite in our cases embody wisdom and balance—exactly as they are written. One notable exception is the 1996 Telecommunications Act. This outdated law is being mischaracterized and asserted by the wireless providers as a *carte blanche* to disempower local communities that widely and incorrectly believe "our hands are tied" and to authorize wireless purveyors to install as many cell towers as they wish, without any safeguards for public health or the environment. The problem is how the power brokers who run these federal agencies, state governments, boards of county supervisors, and city councils are manipulating the law, both civil and criminal, to advance the interests of their corporate patrons.

A stunning case in point is our experience with the Federal Communications Commission (FCC), a highly politicized federal agency that is organizationally subordinate to the traditional Departments of State, Defense, Commerce, Transportation, Labor, and Treasury. The FCC is currently engaged in a power grab that is remarkable in its arrogance and overreach, if the public only knew the facts. The issue is the agency's blanket licensing of over tens of thousands of low-orbit, non-geostationary satellites, which our legal team has challenged on many legal grounds (see March 11, 2021 Citizen's Petition for Rulemaking[298]). One concern is the FCC's current position on US liability[299] for catastrophic damages resulting from satellite collisions in Outer Space. (A SpaceX satellite narrowly missed the Chinese space station in 2021. See Chapter 15[300]) The FCC explains in its official documentation that the United States will not be liable for these accidents under the Outer Space Liability Convention, a signed and ratified multilateral treaty, because, implausibly, the FCC itself lacks statutory authority to approve the launch of these satellites in the first place! (The FCC's official position is so Orwellian, the reader may want to read this last sentence again.)

Quietly, without Congress or the public noticing, we have entered an age of supra-constitutional agency power and authority. In our experience the FCC and other agencies like the FDA, treat their responsibilities under the law not as required mandates but simply as discretionary guidelines.

Mainstream Media Blackout

A vast majority of the public is unaware of the Wireless Juggernaut that is driving the rollout of 5G infrastructure, and someday soon 6G, which will include wireless transmission of power. Why? Because, as noted previously, there is currently a blackout by most of the mainstream media outlets regarding any expression of concerns over 5G, and more generally the risks to public health and the environment of NIR emissions from wireless products. As one of the very few lawyers working in this field, I know first-hand that the nation's mainstream media outlets have an active policy not to investigate the takeover of our critical national infrastructure by the wireless telecommunications industry.

The biggest "bait and switch" in US history (scrupulously documented by my colleague Bruce Kusnick, founder of the Irregulators[301]) has been ignored by the media and continues largely unnoticed. Billions and billions of dollars collected from tax and rate payers, originally intended to fund fiber optic communication infrastructure to homes and workplaces across the US, have instead been diverted, and continue being diverted even as I write these words, by the wireless telecom companies for wireless applications, including 5G and future generations. It is a bipartisan failure in political leadership to ignore this situation. If the public were properly informed, the great majority of voters would, I believe, never consent to having their hard-earned tax dollars misappropriated and diverted to uses for which they were never intended. As noted earlier, the greatest source of this evil is the Telecommunications Act of 1996, signed by President Clinton,[302] which disempowers state and local communities and gives the telecommunications industry vast leeway.

Loss of Privacy, Disinformation, and Government Surveillance

This topic is insightfully discussed by Harvard Business School Professor Shoshana Zuboff in her magisterial book *The Age of Surveillance Capitalism*. Her main point is that our most personal data is now being captured, converted, packaged, and sold without our knowledge, or at least without our explicit consent. Data has become as valuable as gold; we ourselves have become the "product." As Mark Zuckerberg is famously reported to have quipped in the early days of Facebook, "Can you believe these dumb f**** are giving us all their personal information!"[303] The underlying goal of data surveillance is to manipulate our behavior in ways that maximize the profit of remote corporate actors. When we succumb to others' profitaggrandizing agendas in this way, we begin to lose control over our lives.

Addiction and Behavior Modification

There is mounting scientific evidence that continuous use and dependence on cell phones and social media overstimulates the user's sympathetic and parasympathetic nervous systems (which regulate the fight-or-flight response) and interferes with the functions of the *vagus* nerve which controls and maintains balance for a wide array of biological and biochemical functions. Clearly there is an unhealthy synergy at work: the business model is designed to profit from a dearth of accurate information and the absence of informed consent by consumers. The very mechanism of delivery is addictive; consumers become ever more dependent on the product, even as they grow physically weaker and less mentally discerning. In systems theory, cell phones and social media create a destructive "self-reinforcing feedback loop."[304]

Political Polarization

While the general population is becoming ever more dependent and disempowered, the political system is becoming more geriatric, decrepit, dysfunctional, and polarized. As the people are robbed of their power and their voice, a dysfunctional political system becomes ever more the tool of the wealthy and powerful few.

Disdain for the Classics and the Humanities

The classics and the humanities generally have been in decline for over a decade in the curricula of many schools, colleges, and universities.[305] The trend is accelerating downward into the lower grades, prompting proposals to revise and to curate a multitude of cultural treasures—for example, to rewrite Shakespeare, pruning pronouns and what are judged to be culturally incorrect metaphors to meet standards that today's censors deem acceptable. As many of those who participated in China's Cultural Revolution later realized to their regret, when we revile the wisdom and beauty of the past, we deny ourselves the opportunity to deepen and enrich our lives, and to learn from our common cultural heritage.

Social and Environmental Injustice

The growing concentrations of wealth and power in the U.S. today are taking a pernicious, largely unnoticed form through the wireless telecom industry's efforts to bypass due process and thereby blanket every community, especially economically disadvantaged and minority communities, with ubiquitous NIR emitting devices. These include small cell and macro cell towers and smart meters that will support an 'Internet of Things." It is not generally appreciated that this same multitude of devices can be deployed as an effective tool for personal surveillance and crowd control of these same communities.[306] In Chapter 9 I described our current litigation against the Los Angeles Board of Supervisors (BOS) on behalf of Latino communities and grassroots environmental organizations to defend these communities' constitutional right to be heard.

Under US law and that of many other legal systems, the burden of proof falls most heavily on the most vulnerable. There is currently no administrative system for compensation to assist the victims of NIR. The benefits of this industry strategy largely go to the shareholders (in reality, the major wealthy owners and senior management) and the costs are borne by an uninformed and non-consenting public.[307]

So, what's to be done? We possess the power to break free from these life-suppressing doctrinal shackles. What if there are practical ways for most of us to realize more abundant lives by discovering our "soul's work" and being paid fairly for it? The Latin root of the word *vocation* means "voice." How might we design practical incentives to encourage the expression of these inner voices even within present unbalanced economic institutions?

Chapter 12: Evolutionary Values

Sir, I cannot with my little learning and my common way tell the gentleman what will be the better of this—though some working men of this town could above my powers— but I can tell him what I know will never do it. The strong hand will never do it. Victory and triumph will never do it. Agreeing to make one side unnaturally always and forever right, and the other side unnaturally and always forever wrong, will never, never, do it. Nor yet letting alone will never do it. Let thousands upon thousands alone, all leading the like lives and all falling into the like muddle, and they will be as one and you will be as another, with a black unpassable world between you, just as long or short time as such-like misery can last. Not drawing near to folks with kindness and patience and cheery ways, that so draws near to one another in their many troubles, and so cherishes one another in their distresses with what they need themselves—like, I humbly believe, as no people the gentleman has seen to all his travels can beat—will never do it until the Sun turns to ice. Most of all, rating them has so much Power and regulating them as if they were figures in a soom (seam) or machines: without loves and likes, without memories and inclinations, without souls to weary and souls to hope—and when all goes unquiet, dragging on with them as if they were nothing of the kind, and when all goes unquiet, reproaching them for their wants of such humanly feelings in their dealings with you-- this will never do it, sir, till God's work is unmade.

Author's Translation of the Statement of Stephen Blackpool, a worker in Coketown, excerpted from Charles Dickens *Hard Times* 1854[308]

Dickens was a passionate voice of reform for the grinding working conditions of early 19th century England. Coketown is a metaphor of extractive capitalism at its worst demanding change. And over the 19th and 20th centuries change came in a shift in values that protected the dignity and human rights of the poor and defenseless. In "modern" industrial countries Coketowns have largely vanished, although in places like the Congo children still labor in cobalt mines under hellish conditions, as described in Chapter 8. Throughout human history a shift has occurred when societies evolve upward to meet new challenges of complexity. Such I believe is our moment today when climate change, the exploitation of Space, the proliferation of electronic devices releasing dangerous levels of NIR pollution, and a host of other problems engulf us. In this context it may be useful to journey back to a time when all of Europe slept, and then awakened to an evolutionary shift that broke forth brilliantly in the Italian Renaissance, and soon after in other parts of Europe.

In his magisterial biography of *Leonardo da Vinci*, Walter Isaacson provides a vivid picture not only of the transcendent genius Leonardo, but also of the fertile seedbed of fifteenth- and early sixteenth-century Florence that nourished him. During those years Florence experienced a flowering of beauty, creativity, scientific inquiry, and technological virtuosity. The vaulting spirit of the Renaissance arose from a shift in societal values called Humanism, expressed by the youthful Giovanni Pico della Mirandola in his *Oration on the Dignity of Man*:

> We have made you a creature neither of heaven nor of earth, neither mortal nor immortal, in order that you may, as the free and proud shaper of your own being, fashion yourself in the form you may prefer. It will be in your power to descend to the lower, brutish forms of life; you will be able, through your own decision, to rise again to the superior orders whose life is divine.

Humanism took its inspiration from the great works of art, philosophy, and science of the classic past, especially Greece in the fifth-century BCE. Those who were inspired by the Renaissance were not limited by intellectual silos. Many, like Leonardo, were uniquely gifted artists, but they were also highly skilled craftspeople, architects, goldsmiths, engineers, inventors, and scientists. They created their masterpieces at the intertidal frontiers of knowledge. Although some, like Michelangelo, preferred to work in seclusion, many collaborated, living and working in a studio known as a *bottega*. Here apprentices like Leonardo contributed to the works of an experienced proprietor—in Leonardo's case, Verrocchio, a grandmaster in his own right. We know the geniuses—Leonardo, Michelangelo, Raphael, Botticelli, Brunelleschi, and many others. But just below the surface, the entire city swarmed with creativity. Most likely there were thousands of geniuses who participated in collaborative guilds but remain unknown today. Leonardo's disciple and heir, Francesco Melzi, is a good example. His portrait of Leonardo[309] is a masterpiece. But who today, outside of art historians, has ever heard of Melzi?

It was also an age of trade that produced fundamental inventions like Gutenberg's printing press and double-entry bookkeeping that are foundations of our modern commercial world. And overseeing this seedbed of invention and creative expression was the generous patronage of the great families like the Medici, not aristocrats by birth, but bankers, men and women of commerce, who controlled Florence and elevated themselves to become dukes and popes. It was also the age of terrestrial exploration and conquest. Leonardo had just resettled in Florence after several years in Milan when Columbus returned from his first successful voyage to the New World.

The European Renaissance looked back to the glory of Greece and the grandeur of Rome. To meet today's urgent problems, a 21st Century Renaissance must look backward and forward at the same time, focusing the Promethean power of science and technology on their most beneficial uses for the planet as a whole. Guided by the wisdom of Heart and new Evolutionary Values, the vitality and creativity of cities and local communities will be its wellspring.

Big Heart Connectome

In neuroscience the "connectome"[310] is a comprehensive map of neural connections in the brain that can be thought of as its "wiring diagram."[311] An organism's nervous system is made up of neurons, which communicate through synapses. A connectome is constructed by tracing these neuronal connections. Big Heart Connectome (BHC) adopts the metaphor of the connectome, viewing it as a living, dynamic, ever-changing and evolving system. The term BHC also suggests the centrality of Heart, along with Mind and Hand, to connect communities in ways that support their noblest aspirations and highest creative potential.

Foundational Principle

A basic and focused goal of the Big Heart Connectome is to create and to accelerate the provision of well-paying, personally rewarding, and meaningful jobs. The Big Heart Connectome addresses what occupies most people, most of the time—their work. It creates a parallel market and exchange where the participants' highest values, talents, aspirations, and activities are recognized and rewarded, thereby offering an alternative to the dominant economic model where they are undercompensated or not rewarded at all. In the quote in the chapter headnote, Charles Dickens eloquently expressed, over 150 years ago through the voice of a coal worker in *Hard Times*, industrial society's dilemma. George Bernard Shaw observed "*Hard Times* to be a novel of "passionate revolt against the whole industrial order of the modern world". In modern times, an increasing number of visionary companies and organizations are now recognizing that the values of the Big Heart Connectome hold the key to achieving a resilient advantage in the competitive marketplace. (See Michael Porter and Mark Kramer, *Creating Shared Value*[312]; and Julian Gresser, *Beyond Shared Value: Character as Corporate Destiny*.[313])

Values

A Big Heart Connectome (BHC) shares with the Humanist perspective of the Renaissance a recognition that societies can rapidly change for the better when there is a shift in values. The concept of the BHC is, I believe, one the first attempts to articulate a set of critical life-affirming values and align them with technological and scientific virtuosity in an economic model that addresses urgent local as well as planetary needs and concerns.

We are paying a terrible price today for divorcing compassion from the workplace. This is the somber legacy of the East India Company,[314] the first corporation, founded in 1600 by a cartel of English entrepreneurs who received a Royal Patent to exploit and to profit from the resources and cultural treasures of India and China. There is no intrinsic reason that trade and commerce must be predicated on human suffering and the despoliation of Nature, or that they are incompatible with Heart.[315]

Big Heart Intelligence (BHI)

Love is the cardinal value of BHI. BHI presents an alternative to the aggressive, centralized, dominating culture that currently prevails in both the East and the West. BHI also celebrates and incorporates other values, such as wisdom, balance, beauty, kindness, generosity, gratitude, integrity, humor, resilience, courage, and abundance.[316] Moreover, BHI offers a plausible means to assess and to measure these values. Although these BHI metrics are admittedly subjective, there is a positive twist: the more we cultivate the values that constitute BHI, the less we are caught up in self-delusion. BHI transforms our experience of "reality," and we lose our fear to see and to accept the world just as it is. Also, as our propensity for self and collective delusion declines, BHI metrics become increasingly useful as a tool for describing and predicting individual and community behavior.

Paying Forward

As noted in earlier chapters, our decision to embrace the practice of Paying Forward immediately resets and recalibrates our behavior toward others. Until very recently I viewed Paying Forward, as described by Emerson and by Indian sages like Vivekananda in his classic *Karma Yoga*, as an act expressing gratitude by passing along the goodness that comes our way without asking anything in return. However, recently it seems to me that we can go a step further: What if we celebrate, take joy in, and pay forward the good fortune that comes to others?[317] To me this approach adds a new element to the equation that powerfully enhances the momentum of the positive spiral.[318]

In Case 74 of the *Blue Cliff Record*, there is a verse by the monk Xuedou that expresses this idea:

> From among the white clouds, laughter rings out:
> Joyfully he dances;
> He brings the rice in both hands to give to the monks,
> Eat this rice you little bodhisattvas!', he cries in joy.
> A golden-haired lion, they follow him,
> As if they had been the lion's cubs.

This same idea of bounty and abundance is everywhere in Nature. The tree overflows with fruits and flowers. It doesn't bargain with the bees.

Love generates an energy field that connects us to the greater spiraling forces of Abundance. One expression of this phenomenon is Coincidence, Synchronicity, and Serendipity. An increase in the number of positive CSS events we experience is one powerful indication that the Universe in its deep heart's core is designed to be friendly. The practice of Just Click! allows us freely, and at any moment, to verify this principle.

Chapter 13: Organizing a Big Heart Connectome

But you were always a good man of business, Jacob,'
faltered Scrooge, who now began to apply this to himself.
'Business!' cried the Ghost, wringing its hands again.
'Mankind was my business. The common welfare was my
business; charity, mercy, forbearance, and benevolence,
were, all, my business. The dealings of my trade were but
a drop of water in the comprehensive ocean of my
business!
—Charles Dickens, *A Christmas Carol*

Defining a Big Heart Connectome Community

The process of creating a Big Heart Connectome (BHC) begins by defining a discrete "community."[319] A community can be a small city like Santa Barbara, a for-profit corporation, a large public interest organization, or a nonprofit foundation and its associated networks. BHCs can be organized around urgent public concerns, such as climate change, urban violence, homelessness, drug abuse, and pandemics; or they can be designed to create markets for environmentally protective and energy efficient technologies, such as intelligent solar microgrids, or fiber optic infrastructure that connect homes and workplaces to the internet. BHCs succeed when they deliver effective solutions to urgent community needs.

The Players

Every BHC requires a champion who detects an important unsolved problem or unmet societal need. That challenge establishes a potential market. As in the parallel free market, there are traditional producers of products and services, and purchasers or consumers. Following the Renaissance model[320] there are also patrons, who can be wealthy investors, benefactors, foundations, venture philanthropists, and also socially concerned corporations. BHCs create value for existing products and services by combining utility with beauty and wisdom.

BHCs actively seek to foster collaboration among cultural creatives, public interest advocates and entrepreneurs, and others who struggle and compete constantly for financial support. BHCs also extend special consideration and care to society's most vulnerable citizens, namely the poor, minorities, children, the disabled and the elderly—not so much as victims of the system, but as reservoirs of untapped experience, talent, and wisdom, who are marginalized and rarely given an opportunity to realize this potential.

Visionary leaders in corporate enterprises, whether traditional C-corporations or benefit B-corporations, can become change agents. We have ample case studies proving this. Harvard Business School professor Michael Porter has well documented how corporations that "create shared value" gain competitive advantage; this competitive edge will be further enhanced by BHI values and protocols within a BHC. BHCs complement the current free market economy in important ways, generating both ROI and SROI (Social Return on Investment) based on the dedicated cultivation of a community's creative potential.

Cultural Creatives[321]

As noted, there are millions of artists, musicians, writers and poets, architects, filmmakers, actors, designers, and others who are actively engaged around the world in addressing urgent societal and planetary problems. Art can empower action.

Beethoven's *Eroica* Symphony was inspired by the ideals of the French Revolution and dedicated to its hero, Napoleon, who at that time appeared to be a great liberator.

It has often been suggested that a number of Shakespeare's plays, attributed by many scholars to Edward de Vere, the 17th Earl of Oxford, were written to advance the political agenda of his patron, Queen Elizabeth I.

Picasso's Guernica[322] is the artist's *cri de coeur* against war.

The *Battle for Los Angeles County—People's Tsunami* is an image by the author[323] intended to help millions of people in Los Angeles County stand up to the barrage of wireless small cell and macro towers threatening their communities.

A Big Heart Connectome will not only support individual creative expression, it will also cultivate the creative potential of the entire BHC network of producers, consumers, and patrons. An MIT colleague, Peter Gloor, describes this phenomenon as *Swarm Creativity*.[324] As Walter Isaacson points out in his biography of Leonardo da Vinci, you don't have to be a towering genius Leonardo to learn to think like him. BHCs can introduce and promote Leonardo's precepts in collaborative learning communities.

- o   Be relentlessly curious.
- o   Seek knowledge for its own sake.

o   Retain a childlike sense of wonder.

o   Observe and pay attention to details.

o   See things that at first glance are unseen.

o   Go down rabbit holes of discovery.

o   Allow yourself to be distracted.

o   Think visually.

o   Connect conceptual silos through intertidal thinking.

o   Combine fantasy, art, and science.

o   Collaborate.

o   Create for yourself as well as for patrons.

o   Be open to the mystery.

Metrics of Success

It is often said that if you can measure something, you can change it. A BHC lends itself to metrics, but at the same time it is highly qualitative, dynamic, and expanding. This combination of quantitative and qualitative invites new horizons of thinking.

As BHCs are mission-driven, the first way to gauge and measure a BHC's success is by the terms of the mission itself. For example, if the mission is to increase affordable housing within a community, one metric of success, which can be defined at the outset, is to set a baseline of present units versus the number of new units built, or the number of low-income people who benefit from new housing over a specified time. The mission is to accelerate optical fiber installations to the home and office and to attract millions of dollars in federal and state funding. The metrics of success could therefore include the number of successful installations, along with the avoided harms (costs) to human health, the environment, or privacy; or the benefits of faster internet speed, lower latency[325], and greater energy efficiency.[326]

There is a substantial body of writing by professional economists on the social returns from investing in human capital,[327] which can also be useful in measuring the performance and assessing the success of BHCs. The most immediate and well-established of these are the methodologies being used to determine the Gross National Happiness[328] index created by Bhutan. In economic terms, a BHC is at its core a social invention that will enhance a community's human capital, and while there are analytic tools to measure a community's human capital,[329] the Big Heart Intelligence Quotient (BHIQ) offers another method.[330] Although entirely subjective at first, the BHIQ can become a powerful predictive instrument, for the reason that the data become less distorted as the analyst becomes more willing to see the world with a clearer mind and heart.

However, there are dimensions of a BHC that will render it especially resistant to meaningful measurement. A BHC by its very nature is designed to be open, dynamic, and nonlinear. Paying Forward can generate surprising clusters of generosity. At first glance we could not have anticipated them. In reality, the seeds will have been germinating just below the surface for some time. And when the conditions are ripe, the community's creative energies will likely align and breakthroughs may start to happen, at any moment and under the least likely circumstances.

Chapter 14: Empowering Local Communities
—A Case Example

The best education I received was working with people in the community on a grassroots basis. Because what it taught me was that ordinary people, when they are working together, can do extraordinary things.
—Barack Obama

There is a remarkable confluence between the capacity of BHCs to empower local communities and a recent shift in federal policy on critical national infrastructure, toward prioritizing broadband optical fiber to homes and workplaces. Optical Fiber First (OFF) offers an immediately viable, safe, cybersecure, fast, resilient, sustainable, energy-efficient, climate change-friendly, and more equitable alternative to the Wireless Juggernaut that is currently being imposed on local communities around the world. Contrary to the claims of the wireless industry, a predominantly wireless internet will not solve the Digital Divide, where economically disadvantaged, predominantly rural and minority communities are being denied high speed and reliable access to the internet. In fact, overreliance on wireless technologies and devices, many of which will become obsolete in the next few years, will only increase the Digital Divide, which some commentators suggest was caused by the wireless industry in the first place.

As visionary engineer Tim Schoechle writes in *Re-Inventing Wires: The Future of Landlines and Networks*,[331] "Communities have a basic right to build their own public infrastructure and to have local control over issues related to public health, safety, and environment." In fact, optical fiber networks afford an opportunity for local communities to own, operate, control, manage, and generate revenues from their own utility and communications infrastructure. They are independent of centralized control by remote corporations that show little or no concern for the needs of local communities.

On May 13, 2022, the National Telecommunications and Information Agency (NTIA), a part of the Commerce Department that advises the President, issued an extraordinary announcement declaring that "Priority Broadband Projects" are an essential part of national broadband infrastructure. The term "Priority Broadband Project" is defined as a project that will provide service via end-to-end fiber-optic facilities to each end-user premises.[332] NTIA's announcement surprised and delighted all of us who are striving for some reasonable balance in the accelerating deployment of wireless devices. NTIA will begin investing billions of dollars to support state and local initiatives to prioritize the "last mile" of optical fiber to homes and workplaces. This sudden shift in federal policy giving priority to optical fiber broadband coincides perfectly with the actions our legal team is taking to challenge an imminent decision by the Los Angeles County Board of Supervisors (BOS).[333] The timing of these two events, even for a dedicated student of Synchronicity, is stunning.

Santa Barbara Pilot

The City of Santa Barbara, where I live, is an ideal location to undertake an experimental pilot program to demonstrate how a BHC can operate in practice. Santa Barbara has a tradition of concern for community and a political awareness dating from the days of its Center for the Study of Democratic Institutions (1959-87). The city has more registered nonprofit public interest organizations than any other small metropolis in the US. It supports a vibrant arts and theater community, has an excellent hospital established as a nonprofit corporation, and numerous charitable organizations that care for the poor, elderly, and disabled. It has an active food bank, a dedicated community foundation, a strong pool of philanthropic capital, and an active Social Venture Partners network that collaborates closely with the foundation. Santa Barbara is also the headquarters of a few socially concerned billion-dollar companies like Deckers Outdoor Corporation.[334] The city's proximity to Los Angeles (~90 miles) will make it easier for its BHC innovations to scale rapidly throughout California.

BHC Exchange Essentials

Leadership—Every successful strategic alliance begins with a champion. The same is true for a BHC, which is essentially a network of alliances. However, a BHC is far more polycentric, dynamically evolving, and emergent than a simple business alliance. A BHC's fluid structure encourages new and creative leaders to step forth as the BHC proves its value and expands.

Mission—The primary mission of the BHC Exchange that I am proposing is to generate hundreds of deeply meaningful, creative, well-paying new jobs ("soul's work") within the first year and thousands within five years. Specifically, the Exchange will actively support members in identifying and realizing their creative talents and capabilities, while connecting these talents to the important social, economic, and environmental challenges facing the Santa Barbara community. Many of these challenges are described on the Santa Barbara Foundation's website and in its annual report.[335] The annual report provides a useful starting point and focus for transactions on the Exchange.

Values—The BHC is based on twenty-first century Humanist and Evolutionary Values as described in Chapter 12 and other parts of this book.

Product/Service Providers—The providers (sellers) will ideally be those with products and services, skills, and capabilities that match the community Exchange's mission and values. These include cultural creatives and public interest organizations of all kinds, but also participants with special skills who have assumed there are simply no buyers for them. The Exchange supports transactions in products and services that reflect its values, and will also be a crucible for inventions and innovations that address the community's challenges.

Example: What is Your Soul's Work?

This afternoon I had the following conversation with my hairstylist Brook after describing the BHC. As she expressed an interest, I invited her to explore how she might become involved.

> J: "What if there is practical way for you to realize your soul's work and get paid well for it?"
> B: "Wow! What a question. I'll have to think about it. I love what I already do, cutting hair."

J: "Might there be some new use for what you already do so well that might help others in the community?"
B: "Mmm... I'll have to think about it."
She paused.
Then suddenly...
B: "I'd help poor people, street people, who don't have a chance for a nice haircut. I have had that idea for a long time, but I assumed it would not be possible."
J: "Great! Here's how the BHC would work. You would post your aspiration on the BHC Dashboard. It is quite likely that someone in BHC—another person who is paying forward, or a company, or some nonprofit organization— would see a fit. And you'd receive the following communication: 'We would like to sponsor five haircuts a week for twelve weeks.' And, Brook, you are off to the races."
B: "Sounds great to me!"

What if Brook's good "luck" is multiplied by thousands? The beneficent soul of the community will emerge, like a butterfly from its chrysalis.

And here is a living illustration. I am conversing with my physical therapist, Laura, who is helping me with my ankle and the conversation turns to her husband, who she is telling me is good at his current sales job, but finds it unrewarding. His real talent and passion lies in making and editing films. So, I ask Laura the same question I asked Brook and described the Santa Barbara Connectome. Right away she volunteers, "Your haircutter should contact the Organic Soup Kitchen,[336] they might welcome this idea." "Yes," I say, "and your husband might find sponsors for him to film the event, and start his career as a public interest photographer." Her eyes light up. When I tell Brook about the Organic Soup Kitchen, she says, "I never thought of that. I will contact them directly." "And now you will have a local organization to partner with," I observe. The Positive Multiplier of a BHC can begin even when it is only still a concept.

Second Example—A Caregiver

Doug is an experienced caregiver with innovative ideas on helping families in hospices navigate the transition of death. He was deeply moved by the video *Alive Inside* (Chapter 6) and has some ideas about how to introduce Dan Cohen's work to Santa Barbara. He completes the BHC onboarding questionnaire (Appendix 1) and posts it on the Dashboard, introducing his vision of his "soul's work," the contribution he wishes to make to the community, and his estimated budget to carry out this project. He connects through the Visual Matching Engine (VME), described below, with other members who may have been thinking along similar lines, as well as potential funders. The chances of his finding collaborators and benefactors are high.

BHC Consumers—These are BHC customers, who will find value in, and in some cases even be willing to pay a premium for the products and services on the Exchange. Other consumers will be potential employers of those who produce the products and services.

Market Makers—These are interested organizations, like the Santa Barbara Foundation or other public foundations in the city, or public-spirited individuals, that see potential value for Santa Barbara in funding the Exchange.

Price Discovery—Pricing for the products and services offered on the Exchange is determined via established lines of Bid and Ask,[337] through negotiations facilitated by the Exchange on behalf of its members.

Collaborative Innovation Clusters

The Exchange will actively encourage members to form collaborative innovation clusters. An excellent candidate to stimulate an innovation cluster would be to design the BHC Exchange on an optical fiber infrastructure, including an Intelligent Solar Microgrid (ISM).[338] An ISM offers a fast, safe, cybersecure, cost-effective, energy-efficient, sustainable (solar) technology that will support Santa Barbara in power outages during the next wildfire or earthquake. Combined with an Optical Fiber First platform, ISMs can themselves become magnets for collaborative creativity and innovation.[339]

As noted in earlier chapters, I pay attention to CSS signals. Just as I am writing this section I receive an unsolicited email from the Clean Coalition,[340] a Santa Barbara organization dedicated to advising and installing intelligent solar microgrids. I call its founder, Craig Lewis. He is an experienced, no-nonsense engineer and we have an immediate rapport. It turns out he lives across the street, and has been my neighbor for the past five years.

Good News—A large segment of the public is weary of the constant stream of bad news broadcast by the mainstream media. BHC-based communities will offer their members positive news in the form of inspirational stories of how their participants came to discover work that is deeply meaningful to them and to their community.

Arts, Lectures, Theater—Santa Barbara already has a vibrant Arts & Lectures Program[341] at the University of California; and the community regularly draws on art and theater to celebrate festivals such as Cinco de Mayo, or the Madonnari that recognizes mainly local artists in front of the Old Mission; or to come together around a community tragedy, such as after the great fire and mudslides of 2017-2018. There are thousands of residents who might welcome the Exchange as an outlet for their creative work.

Santa Barbara's Wisdom Exchange Platform and Dashboard

Onboarding—Visual Matching Engine—The first step to participate in the Exchange is to create a market. This can be facilitated by an established technology, a Visual Matching Engine (VME), invented by a Santa Barbara entrepreneur, Mark Sylvester, and his company introNetworks.[342] The VME can help to onboard participants—BHC producers, consumers, market makers, cultural creators, public interest advocates, and others—and then connect them with each other by degrees of affinity. Given the core values of the BHC, the process of connecting through a VME will immediately begin to generate momentum, especially when participants are motivated by the powerful incentive to secure meaningful and remunerative work.

Price Discovery—Bids and Asks for work are posted on the BHC Exchange's Trading Board where interested parties introduce themselves. Participants negotiate transactions directly online or offline.

Transactions on Blockchain—BHCs can be designed to run on advanced blockchain technology that is already proven to support the tracking, accountability, and integrity of complex community-wide transactions. A blockchain guarantees the fidelity and security of a data record and generates trust without the need for a third party.

Intelligent Collaborative Learning Platform—As the Santa Barbara pilot program delivers value to the community, many technical options are already available to enhance the participant's experience. The BHC platform, employing artificial intelligence, can itself become an active contributor—conducting research, generating its own ideas, and making new connections on behalf of the community. A BHC will afford wonderful opportunities for coupling AI with BHI principles in addressing urgent community challenges.

Paying Forward—The BHC platform can amplify the power of Paying Forward by linking the process to existing apps such as Givelify.com which already has over one million users.[343]

Power, For All[344]—In their 2021 book by this name, Professors Julie Battilana and Tiziana Casciaro challenge some prevailing assumptions and misconceptions about power. Although absolute power may corrupt absolutely, the authors document how power is an essential asset that is available to all of us, especially when used wisely and compassionately. The book provides a useful technique for mapping power structures as a way to locate actionable points of leverage. Every BHC is well advised to develop maps of its community's power networks.

This book amplifies Battilana's and Casciaro's findings in several ways. First, it focuses on energy—indeed special forms of energy, Love and Qi. Power derives from energy and is defined in physics as the amount of energy divided by the time it takes to use this energy. Power is not only static. It also flows. Second, the process of exploring Evolutionary Values is itself energy generating and transforming, and among its most important drivers is Paying Forward. Third, as noted, acts of Love and Paying Forward have the peculiar ability to compound their energy (and power) by giving it away. As already noted, this possibility turns scarcity economics on its head. BHCs will provide marvelous laboratories to test these propositions.

BHC Ownership and Management

Utility Ownership—The City of Santa Barbara will own, operate, and control its communications infrastructure instead of Southern California Edison. As the owner and operator, the City of Santa Barbra can generate its own revenues through the sale of services, issue social impact bonds, and, as discussed in a moment, even make available its own alternative currency secured by future revenues.

Nonprofit Organization—BHCs can be established under US law as 501(c)(3) tax- exempt organizations. Donors' gifts and grants will be fully tax deductible.

Charter—Santa Barbara's BHC like every successful alliance network should have a "Strategic Alliance Charter," a visionary statement that expresses its high purpose, values, and important protocols governing communication.

Management and Operations—A BHC's management will include individuals with passion for the mission and practical experience in managing business enterprises and collaborative public interest innovation networks.

Collaborative IP in the Creative Commons—As enterprises actively encouraging collaborative innovation, BHCs must necessarily address core issues involving the ownership of intellectual property. Based on many years of experience as a practicing lawyer, I believe the most congenial arrangement is a "mixed" system with a "Creative Commons License" as the foundation, offering participants the opportunity to generate freely their own proprietary intellectual property based on the terms of their collaboration. The leading precedent for this arrangement is the Linux operating system, which basically places the core IP in the public domain, inviting programmers around the world to improve on it. Linux then produced for-profit spin-off ventures like Red Hat that became multi-billion-dollar ventures. Under this arrangement BHC participants would be free to develop their own collaborative IP portfolios, including "mega-patents,"[345] a concept that the author has helped to develop.

Privacy—In a world of surveillance capitalism, BHCs built on a foundation of optical fiber will have a significant leg up, because Optical Fiber First platforms are far more private and secure than those based on wireless technologies, which are easily compromised. In addition to the basic architecture, BHCs will afford a clear, easily understood means for participants to opt out and to maintain control over their private information, as required by California's Consumer Privacy Act of 2018. BHCs will not transact, bundle, sell, or resell their members' data, even when it is anonymous.

Shadow—However inspired the intention and mission of a BHC, the Shadow is an essential part of the human psyche. There will be some members who will seek to game the system, while others will not even know they are doing so. BHC communities will be better able to address such destructive behavior because the managers will be well trained in the principles of Resilient Negotiation,[346] which themselves are based on the principles of Big Heart Intelligence. The most successful BHCs will make the principles and skills of Resilient Negotiation freely available to their members, which in turn will produce beneficial cascading effects.

Business Model

The chances of a Santa Barbara BHC model securing seed funding and achieving early financial sustainability are excellent.

Seed Capital—The traditional way in which a new and innovative public interest venture is launched is by philanthropic seed capital. A practical baby step is to raise modest funding to produce a feasibility study and White Paper that will engage a core group of thought leaders. The White Paper then becomes a "single negotiation text" that is a living Charter for the BHC. It reflects the creative contributions and concerns of the promoters, and is continuously deepened and refined. This process will in turn attract and engage early stakeholders, some of whom will become champions and funders.

Government Funding for Infrastructure—Santa Barbara can begin immediately working with the state and federal government to secure its fair share of Optical Fiber First infrastructure funding.

Tax Deductible Grants—As a 501(c)(3) tax-exempt organization, the Santa Barbara BHC can accept grants from local foundations and philanthropic individuals. In the future, the BHC can itself make grants to support important community causes.

Sale of Products and Services—The Santa Barbara BHC will be self-financing to the extent that it is actively supporting transactions that create jobs for its members. An important early decision will be whether the BHC should charge a modest commission for each transaction on the Exchange, or instead rely on Paying Forward by the beneficiaries.

Philanthropic Capital—As described, the Santa Barbara BHC will likely develop its own IP portfolio and own shares in spin-off for-profit social ventures. This close connection between the BHC and the venture philanthropy community will in turn generate virtuous circles of funding for the BHC itself.

Public Banking—Santa Barbara is well-suited to establish its own public bank, as it is also home to the Public Banking Institute.[347] As noted on its website, a public bank is an organization that is operated in the public interest, through institutions owned by the people through their representative governments. Public banks can exist at all levels, from city to state to national. Any governmental body that can meet local banking requirements may, theoretically, create such a financial institution. As of this writing, the US Congress is deliberating a National Infrastructure Bank Act of 2021[348] that would establish public banking as an important national resource and priority.

Complementary Currency (Solar Dollars)—As Thomas Greco, the leading theorist in the field, explains in *Solar Dollars: A Complementary Currency that Incentivizes Renewable Energy,*[349] a Solar Dollar is a private community currency issued in the form of vouchers by electric utility companies based on their willingness and ability to provide their customers with energy derived from renewable sources. By monetizing the value of renewable energy in the form of a community currency, Solar Dollars help to solve several critical problems at once. They incentivize a more rapid shift to renewable energy, help communities become more resilient and self-determined, and enable the decentralization of economic and political power. A Santa Barbara Public Bank working in close collaboration with a locally owned Santa Barbara Optical Fiber Utility is ideally positioned to underwrite the Solar Dollar as a complementary currency that can be used to augment and to reinforce transactions on the BHC Exchange.

A Santa Barbara BHC offers a practical example of how one community can begin imaginatively to reclaim control over its communications infrastructure, while at the same time produce new jobs that enable people to work for what they love most and be paid well for doing so. Some utopian visions like a Santa Barbara BHC can take form rapidly if their champions stay sharply focused on the mission. A BHC is a living not a fixed entity. It is a dynamic, experimental, emergent process that manifests the dreams and aspirations of its community. Because BHCs augment our present reality, they will take time to grow and flourish. But I have found few things of real value happen in this world without our paying dearly for them.

Gaiapolis

Just as this book nears publication, chance arrives again. I reconnect with a colleague, Sheridan Tatsuno, who participated in my Harvard Law School class fifty years ago, and is now a visionary city planner and prolific author. Sheridan has written a book, *The Gaiapolis Strategy*, that outlines a practical roadmap to create a global network of 10,000 sustainable cities by 2030.

Gaiapolis will:

o   Draw upon the proven 20 year track record of Technopolis, a unique project based at the University of Texas' IC^2 Institute in Austin in which Gaiapolis' founders were directly engaged. Technopolis has already shown the power of "strategic" technologies and industries in economic and urban development.

o   Implement an AI-based intelligent collaborative learning platform to support change agents of all ages at the grassroots level.

o   Offer practical training in a wide range of skills, including
    evolutionary values, ethical AI, community organizing,
    global collaboration, leadership, negotiation, mediation and
    other core competencies.

o   Aim to increase grassroots ownership, control, and
    financing of local infrastructure in place of top down control
    by remote centralized corporations.

o   Foster collaborative innovation, including a U.S.-Japan
    technology partnership emphasizing optical fiber to homes
    and workplaces, intelligent solar microgrids; and
    highlighting European cities as drivers of financial
    innovation.

o   Learn from and collaborate with the Integral City,
    Compassionate Cities, Mayors for Peace, and other
    initiatives.[350]

o   Support potential early adopters such as Santa Barbara,
    Santa Fe, and Seville, Spain.

o   Follow best entrepreneurial practices: experiment, harvest
    errors, adapt, and evolve.

Gaiapolis can be the mother ship for thousands of allied
BHCs in the coming years.

HEALTHY HEAVENS TRUST

Chapter 15: Let Us Not Go Mad

O, let me not be mad, not mad, sweet heaven.
—Shakespeare, *King Lear*, Act 1 Scene 5

Reverence for Life.
—Albert Schweitzer

Meanwhile, a few powerful commercial companies and the military are conducting a Space Experiment on the rest of us without the normal precautions of due diligence and premarket testing. The prospect for profits is simply so vast that very few in authority are willing to assess the planetary risks. The challenges in effecting some legal constraint, notwithstanding many applicable national laws and treaties, are formidable.

Have a look and see for yourself the Starlink Satellite Mesh that will soon obscure the evening skies forever.[351] The debris from these satellites is traveling at extraordinary speeds, and the risks of collisions increase exponentially with the proliferation of satellites. I would like to believe that partially in response to our March 11, 2021 FCC Petition for Rulemaking filed by the Healthy Heavens Trust Initiative (HHTI)[352] and other organizations, the FCC is reported in *Scientific American* to be updating its agency review of satellite debris.[353] In addition, the FCC has canceled Starlink's $886 million grant, citing ex-FCC Chairman Ajit Pai's mismanagement of the public auction, which the March 11, 2021 Petition also challenged.[354] And finally, the Congress' Government Accountability Office (GAO) has just issued a report: *Large Constellations of Satellites: Mitigating Environmental and Other Effects*[355] possibly also influenced by the HHTI Declaration and Petition.[356]

Despite these positive steps, the FCC persists in granting blanket licenses for millions of base stations[357] that will be continuously communicating with constellations of satellites, and with each other. Sensors are also being installed by the military for a wireless Oceans Internet of Things that will detect every object and every sea creature that passes by. This network of networks encompassing earth, sea, and sky is so vulnerable that an average hacker can create havoc in just 30 seconds, or even weaponize a satellite.[358] The Chinese Ministry of National Defense has publicly stated on its website that it can and will target and destroy the nerve plexus of the Satellite Mesh.[359] A recent report quotes several US generals who predict that a war in Space between the US and China is almost inevitable.[360]

And for every positive advance, there seems to be a setback. As of this writing, SpaceX is lobbying the FCC to reinstate its $886 million grant for Starlink. At the same time, SpaceX is seeking approval from the FCC to expand its current Starlink fleet, which comprises 3,200 satellites and is permitted to increase to 12,000. The new authorization for SpaceX's Gen2 request will bring the company's total fleet to roughly 42,000. The Gen2 satellite is considerably larger[361] than any of the more than 2,500 Starlink satellites now orbiting 340 miles above the Earth's surface. Gen2 satellites are 22 feet long and weigh 2,755 pounds. By contrast, the first-generation satellites weigh just 573 pounds, or about one-fifth as much as Gen2.

Diagram #5 depicts eight domains that present immense risks arising from the Space Experiment.

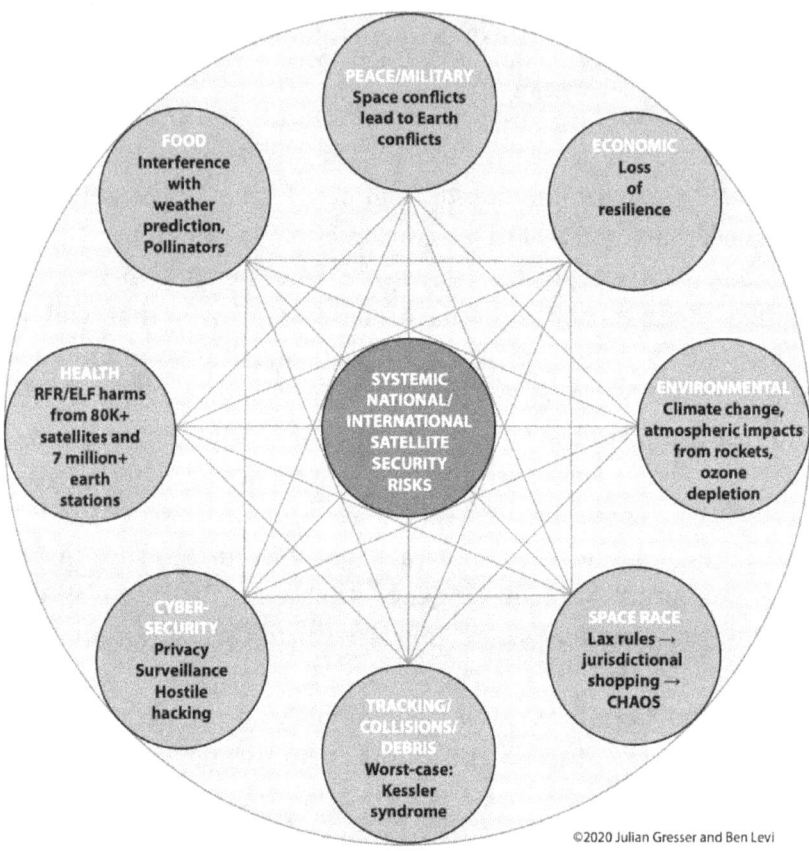

Diagram 5

As of this writing, we are unable to identify anyone in federal government or even the private sector who is currently conducting a comprehensive and systematic assessment of the synergistic and compounding risks of failure of any part of these tightly coupled systems. We have the analytic tools[362] to conduct such a comprehensive programmatic risk assessment. It is a complex task, but even more formidable is the problem of how to secure these tightly coupled system in the midst of the cascading effects of a major systems breakdown, or an intentional disruption or attack. Meanwhile, as we ignore and leave the risks unattended, the probability of even a small event precipitating a massive systems collapse is extremely high.[363]

Recent Events

○ Every one of the national security risks portrayed in HHTI's original March 11, 2021 FCC filing is increasing, including cybersecurity[364] and conflicts in Space.[365]

National and International Satellite Risks

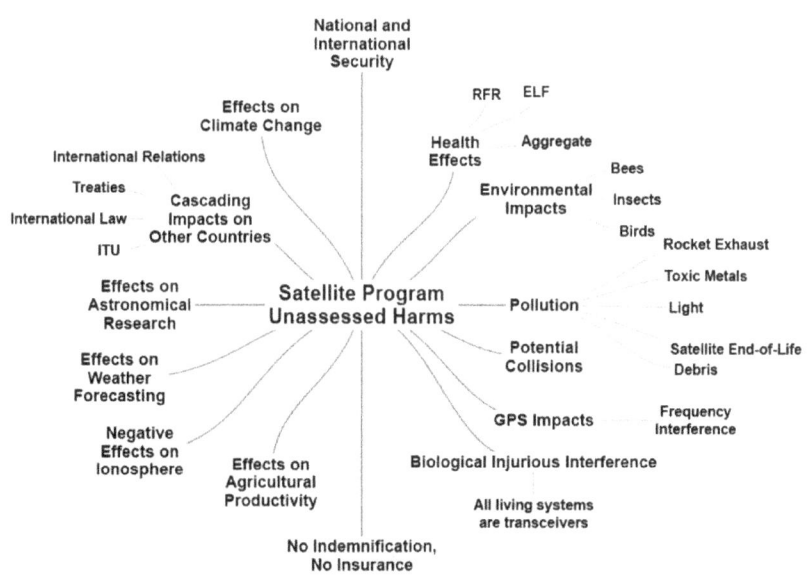

Diagram 6

- On January 9, 2023 the FCC issued Order 23-1[366] establishing a Space Bureau and Office of International Affairs, and eliminating its International Bureau, which has previously overseen all satellite licensing.[367]

- Over the past two years, the FCC has received applications for 64,000 new satellites and witnessed an eight-fold increase in the number of applications for fixed-satellite service gateway Earth stations.[368]

- Increasing private and public ventures, and public/private partnerships are precipitating a Space Race, and SpaceX is indisputably among the leaders driving this space renaissance. The company has launched over 3,000 Starlink satellites since 2019 and built impressive vehicles to lower space transportation costs. In 2023 Amazon is set to launch its 'Project Kuiper' low Earth orbit (LEO) satellite broadband service. Amazon is planning to launch 1,500 satellites over the next five years to support Kuiper as it goes head-to-head against SpaceX's Starlink. Boeing, Inmarsat, Astra, Intelsat, Hughes Network, OneWeb, SpinLaunch, and Telesat are some of the other companies that have asked the FCC for access to V-band spectrum for their services. In total, the FCC has been asked to approve over 38,000 satellites. The formation of a dedicated Space Bureau is seen as vital to handling the growing demand.

- The close integration of military and commercial deployments in the Space Experiment is also increasing. On January 15, 2023 it was reported SpaceX's Falcon Heavy rocket launched a classified mission for the US Space Force.

- The USSF-67 mission carried a military communications satellite and five smaller payloads to orbit. "The mission of CBAS-2 (Continuous Broadcast Augmenting SATCOM) is to augment existing military satellite communication capabilities and continuously broadcast military data through space-based satellite relay links."[369]

o Dark-Sky Association Appeal. On December 29, 2022 a non-profit group, the Dark-Sky Association, filed a Notice of Appeal with the DC Circuit challenging the FCC Order granting in part and subject to certain conditions the application of Space Exploration Holdings, LLC ("SpaceX") "to construct, deploy, and operate a constellation of 29,9881 non-geostationary orbit (NGSO) satellites."[370] This is an important legal challenge that builds on the earlier Healthy Heavens Trust Initiative (HHTI) Declaration and FCC Petition filed by BBILAN on behalf of the HHTI.[371]

Untested Assumptions

In Chapters 7 and 8 we pointed out that an essential element of Wisdom is to challenge and explore critical assumptions. What are some critical assumptions underlying this massive Space Experiment? Here are a few:

o Protective technological innovations will keep pace with the increasing density of satellites launched into the Earth's orbit, and the associated debris they cause. The Kessler Syndrome[372] can and will be avoided, even though there appears to be no plan in place in case it cannot be avoided.[373]

o With eight million earth-based terminals and dozens of base stations licensed and operating, there will be no adverse impact on human or environmental health by the NIR emissions from this equipment.

o Light pollution from the 12,000 currently licensed satellites, (including second-generation Starlink which are 5 times bigger than the first generation[374] will not interfere with astronomic research sufficient to warrant any conditions imposed on new satellite licensing.

o The FCC Fact Sheet[375] claims that satellites will result in total satellite disintegration upon reentry, and there is zero human casualty risk; thus there is no need for accident liability insurance. FCC Rule 22-91[376] (released 2022-12-1) states that its second generation satellites will also "totally demise" upon reentry.

o Starlink and other low Earth orbit (LEO) satellites will not affect weather forecasting.[377]

o Increasing rocket launches of satellites will have no negative impacts on the environment and climate change[378] (This is disputed here by a military professor at the Stockton Center for International Law at the U.S. Naval War College).

o Military use of mega-satellite constellations will not result in increased threats of war in Space.[379]

o The threat of cybersecurity attacks on mega-satellite constellations will not be significant enough to affect increasing deployments.[380]

And here are some further basic assumptions:

o There is no need for wisdom, balance, forbearance, and caution in the Space Experiment because the unquantified benefits greatly outweigh the risks that are also unquantified.

o It is unnecessary to conduct any comprehensive and systemic environmental risk assessment as required by the National Environmental Policy Act of 1969. The FCC is asserting its licensing program is categorically exempted as a matter of law.[381]

o The risks noted in the above charts must be underestimated and ignored because national security requires it.

○ It is better not to understand the risks, even if we have the tools and capacity to identify and analyze them, because then we will have to do something about them.

○ Commercial and military interests, which are increasingly entwined, must take priority over all other interests.

○ The living Planet Earth and its surrounding Heavens are dead "things" to be exploited for commercial and military gain.

○ Because the Earth is not considered to be alive, it cannot possibly be recognized to have juridically recognized legal rights, even though other things like corporations and ships have legal rights and standing to sue.[382]

○ It may be regrettable, but millions of human, animal, and plants lives must be sacrificed to carry out the exploitation of Outer Space.

○ The Space Experiment is too important to be made transparent, so most of the real agenda must be concealed from the public whose consent doesn't matter anyway.

○ The U.S. does not have the luxury of time to pause and to reflect upon the Space Experiment, because other Space players will seize upon this weakness and gain competitive advantage in the Space Race.

Few people today in this or any past administration, in Congress, the media, or even grassroots organizations are probing these fundamental assumptions. And few also are asking questions such as:

○ Why is the FCC (which, remember is only a "Commission" established by Congress in 1972 under the Federal Advisory Committee Act) allowed to usurp the traditional powers of the established cabinet level agencies without any effective Congressional oversight?

o   Which other agencies, beginning with the White House, the National Security Office, DOD, NASA, State Department, Department of Commerce, NOAA, Department of Transportation, Department of Agriculture, EPA, CEQ, and other agencies, should play a critical role in these decisions, which the FCC is today making unilaterally?

o   Why is Space not considered part of national critical infrastructure when satellite deployment is increasingly being integrated with national infrastructure, and the multiple hazards of the Space Experiment are placing U.S. national infrastructure itself at increasing risk?[383]

o   What constructive role can the public play in this vital national enterprise?

o   What is the most effective process to support wise decision making in the exploration and exploitation of Outer Space?

o   What are the unstated values and assumptions that the present Space Race embodies?

o   What alternative Evolutionary Values will increase the chances of our planet's survival?

o   Drawing upon the deep insights of many of the world's wisdom traditions, what if Planet Earth, the Heavens, and the Oceans are not separate from ourselves? By wreaking havoc above and below we are hastening our own demise.

We must summon the courage to challenge these controlling assumptions and to ask such inconvenient urgent questions. Our lives and those of our children and future generations may depend upon it.

The Broadband International Legal Action Network (BBILAN) is one of the few groups in the world today that is seeking to restore sanity and balance as the Satellite Experiment unfolds. BBILAN's website offers our legal templates freely to all, including a Declaration by the Healthy Heavens Trust Initiative, signed by concerned citizens in 60 countries, and a Citizens Petition for Rulemaking concerning the FCC's blanket licensing of over 100,000 satellites (March 11, 2021).

There may still be time, even before midnight. The Doomsday Clock indicates 90 seconds remain.[384] The perpetrators of this silent crisis are a few mega corporations, the military, and captive government agencies. They have virtually unlimited resources and are well organized. But they are not monolithic. We are discovering, as in the case of *Viasat, Inc. v. FCC*—a collaborative action between a major satellite company and a citizens' group challenging the FCC's approval of the largest orbit elevation change in history—there are responsible actors in industry and government who can tolerate complexity, oppose greed, and believe in wise precautions. These are our potential allies. And we, the people, have the law on our side.

Right now we have a unique, historic chance to pause and to reflect. Let us not be afraid to ask difficult questions and to take courageous actions. Let us listen carefully and respectfully to the cry of the heart of our fragile planet.

EVOLUTION

Chapter 16: Our Noble Chance

When every morning brought a noble chance.
—Alfred, Lord Tennyson, *Morte d-Arthur*

Great ideas, it has been said, come into the world as gently as doves. Perhaps then, if we listen attentively, we shall hear, amid the uproar of empires and nations, a faint flutter of wings, the gentle stirring of life and hope. Some will say that this hope lies in a nation; others, in an individual (sic). I believe rather that it is awakened, revived, nourished by millions of solitary individuals whose deeds and works every day negate frontiers and the crudest implications of history. As a result, there shines forth fleetingly the ever-threatened truth that each and every person (sic), on the foundation of his own suffering and joys, builds for all.
—Albert Camus

One of the startling scientific observations in recent years is MIT researcher Michael Triantafyllou's explanation of how fish can swim upstream and even vault waterfalls, apparently defying the laws of gravity. In explaining his counter-intuitive discovery he notes that trout, like salmon, are very good at conserving their own energy and even extracting energy from the waters surrounding them. But he had no idea that they would be able to draw enough energy from the surrounding water to swim upstream without expending any energy of their own.

As it turns out, objects that block the natural flow of water, like a rock or a boat, create a series of complex vortices[385] in the current as the water navigates the obstacle. Fish are quite flexible along the entire length of their spines, which allows their head and tail to move independently of each other. In certain situations, the array of vortices that form behind an obstacle cause the fish's body and tail to flap in resonance. This tilts the body in such a way that the vortices, which cause a drop in pressure, apply a surge of suction that propels the fish forward and upward.[386]

As Triantafyllou explains:

> You have a flow behind the obstacle, which creates
> a continuous stream of eddies. Each eddy contains
> energy and also causes the pressure in the fluid to
> drop... the eddy causes the body to flap back and
> forth, and the fish manages to extract energy.[387]

The saga of the trout and salmon carries a message of hope for us all, especially if we understand chaordic systems. As its name suggests, a chaordic system combines chaos and complexity, obscuring an underlying order—which means that that little changes in part of the system can lead to larger changes throughout the system. Chaordic systems follow a common life cycle: they are born or initiated; they develop and grow into maturity; they reach a limit to growth, and thereafter die or transform, or they can leap to the next level of complexity and begin a new cycle of development. An important characteristic of chaordic systems is they tend toward a tipping or inflection point. When this point is reached, even a small perturbation can catalyze a massive change in the overall system, for good or ill.

One of the most thoughtful contemporary thinkers about chaordic systems, Dee Hock,[388] was the founder and CEO emeritus of Visa International. He wrote:

> We are living on the knife's edge of one of those rare and momentous turning points in human history. Liveable lives for our grandchildren, their children, and their children's children hang in the balance. The Industrial Age, hierarchical, command-and-control institutions that, over the past four hundred years, have grown to dominate our commercial, political, and social lives are increasingly irrelevant in the face of the exploding diversity and complexity of society worldwide. They are failing, not only in the sense of collapse, but in the more common and pernicious form— organizations increasingly unable to achieve the purpose for which they were created, yet continuing to expand as they devour resources, decimate the earth, and demean humanity. The very nature of these organizations alienates and disheartens the people caught up in them. Behind their endless promises of a peaceful, constructive societal order, which they never deliver, they are increasingly unable to manage even their own affairs, while society, commerce, and the biosphere slide increasingly into disarray. We are experiencing a global epidemic of institutional failure that knows no bounds.

Evolutionary Values and Epigenetics

Will the processes of conceiving and embodying Evolutionary Values have epigenetic effects, individually and collectively, that may be critical for the survival of our species? Epigenetics[389] is a relatively new science that studies changes in organisms caused by modification of gene expression rather than alteration of the genetic code itself. In their important study, *A Review of Epigenetics in Human Consciousness*,[390] researchers Mitchell B. Liester and Erin E. Sullivan, report:

> Epigenetic processes modulate interactions between individuals and the environment. A wide range of environmental factors can trigger epigenetic modifications,[391] including: toxins, alcohol, addictive drugs, diet, physical exercise, in utero exposure to maternal nutritional factors, and stress/trauma. These factors produce lasting epigenetic changes that influence neuronal development, neuroplasticity, cognition, and behavior. Furthermore, through their influence on the genome, epigenetic changes create a bi-directional crosstalk between the genome and the environment, with the environment influencing genetic transcription and changes in genetic regulation influencing the behavior of the individual toward the environment. Epigenetic marks can persist for decades. Epigenetic changes may be transmitted across generations, a process termed transgenerational epigenetic inheritance, in which non-genetic information is transmitted from parent to offspring via germ cells. Such information has been demonstrated to persist for at least fourteen generations.[392]

If environmental stresses can affect consciousness and behavior via epigenetic changes, and these epigenetic harms can be transmitted across many generations, what scientific evidence is there for the converse proposition? An important 2020 study, *Molecules of Silence: Effects of Meditation on Gene Expression and Epigenetics*,[393] reaches this conclusion:

> Growing evidence suggests that epigenetic changes are a key mechanism by which a stressful environment acts on the genome, causing stable changes in gene expression and in behavior that can mediate maladaptive responses. On the other end, the voluntary practice of meditation can be considered a form of environmental enrichment, equivalent to positive external stimulation. Hence, it appears fundamental to understand whether meditation can elicit epigenetic events able to prevent disease and promote health. Relevant examples of stress-related targets of epigenetic deregulation are genes involved in glucocorticoid signaling, serotonergic signaling, and neurotrophins. Surprisingly, meditation practices seem to act on the same gene targets, such as FKBP5, SLC6A4, and BDNF, and promote endocrinal, neuronal, and behavioral functions. This suggests that the achievement of a state of inner silence through the practice of meditation can prevent or reverse the detrimental effects of a stressful environment.[394]

Molecules of Silence explores data covering a wide variety of mindful practices stemming from Eastern traditions that have been introduced in Western societies following the impelling demand to increase self-awareness, improve health, and ameliorate the quality of daily life. These practices include a spectrum of meditations, both sitting (i.e., mindfulness meditation, Vipassana, breathing attention) and moving (Yoga, Tai Chi, Qigong), all of which share the common goal of achieving a state of silence of mind, with positive repercussions on emotional regulation and health.

The strong hypothesis suggested by this book is that the processes of conceiving and embodying Evolutionary Values could indeed have epigenetic effects, individually and collectively, and across generations, and epigenetics will play a powerful, if not primary, role in how our species adapts and evolves to cope with the extraordinary planetary challenges that we now face. This is a testable proposition in an exciting new frontier of science that I would like to explore with interested readers. (See Appendix 1: *Evolutionary Conversations*).

As a planetary community we may be fast approaching a tipping point,[395] wherein a minor event, even a remote, seemingly insignificant perturbation, can suddenly generate instability throughout networks of tightly coupled systems. That extra grain of sand can cause the entire sandpile to collapse.

How to anticipate the tipping point? The signs are everywhere, especially in CSS events, if we will have the interest and courage to look. Some of the tools described in this book may help us catch the warning signal before a tipping point is reached. Like an earthquake, we cannot prevent the tipping point. But we can cultivate the resilience of our response.

Many will feel overwhelmed. Some may decide to retreat and face a wall for nine years, as it is said the fifth-century Patriarch Bodhidharma[396] did in a cave near the Shaolin Monastery. Others will choose to contend with the urgent problems of today. As the story of the Rainmaker suggests, both detachment and active engagement are necessary and complimentary. Although the Western mindset has come to believe that every problem can be fixed by the raw power and genius of science and technology, I believe, as Dee Hock suggests, that the challenges we face are fundamental. Science and technology can no longer be divorced from values, 21st century Humanistic and Evolutionary Values that are also ancient, universal, emergent, and transcendent. The change that is needed and coming will not be brought about by our tools alone, however sophisticated.

Like trout seemingly defying the laws of gravity, we have arrived at a unique historical moment, where we are being called upon, individually and collectively, to swim upward. Although the mainstream media actively encourages a narrative of hopelessness and helplessness, there are many examples of the positive shift in consciousness that is well underway. The work of Ashoka, founded by my Harvard '65 classmate Bill Drayton[397], is one such example. Ashoka's core principle is that everyone can be a change maker, and the organization has supported social entrepreneurs and change agents around the world for over forty years.

This book has introduced a cluster of Evolutionary Values, principles, and practical tools that will enable us to work with and to transcend gravity, and to catch the upward currents of a global awakening as it expands and evolves. Technology can be our ally. Just as massive advances in computer processing, AI, the internet, and social media have encouraged addictive, environmentally destructive, and socially maladaptive behaviors among millions of people around the world, and are doing so today at an ever-accelerating pace, so these same technologies can support evolutionary changes in values, behaviors, and actions. And as this book records, deep epiphanies are at hand. Time is compressed into a moment—this moment. There is a reasonable and practical basis for hope.

o We have the capacity, each in our own way, to achieve a happy, loving, abundant life.

o Collectively, we possess a reservoir of wisdom that we can draw on from our ancestors, and today from within our communities.

o We can use our powers of reason, while drawing upon the deep intelligence in our hearts.

o We can identify the pressure points that will activate a cascade of beneficial results that in turn will multiply our resilience.

o We can learn to recognize and work with Coincidence, Synchronicity, and Serendipity, and ally with these forces. We can rejoice that they are beyond our personal understanding and control.

o We can learn not to fear the Shadow, but rather to recognize these unconscious forces in our deep psyches, and accept their power, beauty, and intelligence.

o We can experiment with paying forward in lightening the burden or increasing joy in someone's life in a modest way.

o By loving one another and all living things, we can discover a world of abundance, not scarcity; and

o Observe how when these forces combine, they will bring us, faster than we can imagine, to an evolutionary tipping point.

Then we will be amazed to see that the leopard can indeed change its spots.[398]

Afterword

The Big Heart Connectome I have described is one example of how twenty-first century Humanist and Evolutionary Values can be practically embedded within the present economic system in a manner that benefits communities. I understand that a BHC is complex, and that there are many moving parts. It will take time and a lot of experimentation for BHCs to reach their fullest creative expression. The first spark can occur simply, as Camus suggests, through a single act, and subsequent acts, like a fluttering of dove's wings.

I am always struck by how much discord can ensue from a single mad act of cruelty—for example, as I noted in Chapter 1, how the assassination of Gandhi changed the course of India forever. But what of the converse? Might a single act of kindness or generosity alter the course of a human life?[87] In *Les Miserables,* Victor Hugo relates how the singular act of enlightened kindness—the Bishop of Digne makes a gift to the hero, Jean Valjean, of the candlesticks he had stolen and dismisses the gendarme. This single enlightened action transforms Jean Valjean's life forever, as well as the lives of every other character in this great novel.

As Jean Valjean is dying, Hugo writes, "He lay back with his head toward the sky, and the light from the two candlesticks fell upon his face."

The practice of Just Click! is a practice that can cause a beneficial shift by manifesting the essential world in an instant. The essential world is here already, right before us. Just Click! invites us to go deeper and to allow our hearts to touch what lies just beyond this simple practice.

I will close this account of my life with three stories from far distant cultures, separated also in time, that for me express the core discovery of this book:

A younger contemporary of Bodhidharma, the Mahassatva Fu, expounded Buddhism to the Emperor Wu of the Kingdom of Liang thus:

> Empty-handed, holding a hoe
> Walking, riding a water buffalo
> Man is crossing a bridge,
> The bridge, not the river, flows.

The flux of the river does not change, because it is always just as it is. That which appears solid and concrete, the bridge, is alive, and so it will change and transform by our experience of it.

Shakespeare expresses in the closing lines of *The Tempest* (Act IV, Scene 1) a similar view of the transitory nature of our personal "reality":

> Our revels now are ended. These our actors,
> As I foretold you, were all spirits and
> Are melted into air, into thin air:
> And, like the baseless fabric of this vision,
> The cloud-capp'd towers, the gorgeous palaces,
> The solemn temples, the great globe itself,
> Yea all which it inherit, shall dissolve
> And, like this insubstantial pageant faded,
> Leave not a rack behind. We are such stuff
> As dreams are made on, and our little life
> Is rounded with a sleep.

But to this somber note, there is again a life-affirming response. It can be found in Case 39 of the *Blue Cliff Record*:

> A monk asked grandmaster Yumen,
> "What is the Pure Body of Reality?"

Yumen replied, "A flowering hedge."
The monk continued,
"What is it like if one goes on in such a way?"
Yumen replied, "A golden haired lion."

As I advance in years I take comfort in accepting that everything changes, everything emerges, nothing is constant...save Love, the Golden Haired Lion, and that is sufficient.

Water Dragons at Play
In the Japanese language the *kanji* for "waterfall" is written with the "water" radical combined with "dragon," which is very apt, as dragons are thought to live near water. They are also creatures of the sky. This calligraphy depicts three dragons at play around a golden *enso,* which suggests their ethereal nature.

Appendix 1: Evolutionary Conversations

Discovery is seeing what everybody else has seen, and thinking what nobody else has thought.
Albert Szent-Gyorgyi, Nobel Laureate in Physiology and Medicine

The questions one asks oneself begin, at last, to illustrate the world.
James Baldwin

Our goal is to begin a global conversation on Evolutionary Values focused on urgent community and planetary challenges. The following summary distills each chapter and asks a central Discovery Question. We invite our readers to email their own questions and insights. It is not about the conclusions we reach, but the process of opening our minds and hearts, and listening deeply to one another. In a hyperpolarized and noisy world, deep listening may itself be an evolutionary value.

BEGINNINGS

Prologue—We cannot solve our problems with the same thinking we used when we created them. Not only new thinking but also new values—Evolutionary Values—are critical for our collective survival.

> DQ: How can communication technologies—social media, internet, cell phones—be practically redeployed and business owners incentivized to accelerate beneficial, life-affirming change and innovations—not over decades but in the next few years?

Chapter 1 My Journey—Traces the author's personal and professional life journey, in particular the pivot point when he realized his time on this Earth was not unlimited. Explores some intriguing questions on the nature of reality, presented by remarkable occurrences of Coincidence, Synchronicity, and Serendipity.

DQ: What if we have a chance, each in our own way, to bring together the diverse strands of our professional, intellectual, and personal lives to contribute to a new and more compassionate world? How can we practically realize this chance?

Chapter 2 Shadow—Explores the domain of the Shadow---not only our subconscious "negative" drives, conceits, fears, rages, and obsessions, but also a vast, yet unexplored source of kindness, compassion, beauty, abundance, charity, warmth, and love.

DQ: What if we can learn to work effectively and compassionately with the Shadow and apply its dark creative energy in addressing the critical challenges before us?

ESSENTIALS

Chapter 3 Just Click!—Introduces a simple practice that can change our experience of life in an instant.

DQ: What do you discover when you practice Just Click!—for one day, a week, a month? What if Just Click! becomes a place of refuge, your constant companion, and friend?

Chapter 4 Love—Views Love as an extraordinary source of freely available energy that multiplies and compounds even as it shared.

DQ: What are some immediate and practical (entrepreneurial) applications of this economic paradox?

Chapter 5 Beauty—Recognizes that Beauty is everywhere when we look out with fresh eyes.

> DQ: What if the "market share" of Beauty in our lives doubles by the month? What if it can continue to do so? How might that phenomenon become a source of comfort and joy?

Chapter 6 Vitality—Points to largely untapped inner and outer reservoirs of essentially free energy of Qi and Love.
DQ: How might becoming alive inside build resilience, transform aging, and create more abundant lives for ourselves and others?

Chapter 7 Wisdom (Daily Life)—Explores wisdom, equanimity, and Big Heart Intelligence in the context of tragic and false choices.
DQ: What if wisdom is a learnable skill that can be applied in every moment?
DQ: How can we balance non-attachment with compassion?

Chapter 8 Wisdom (Business)—Explores how Evolutionary Values can help business managers make wiser decisions and reconcile tragic choices.
DQ: How can the active cultivation of Evolutionary Values expand the core competency of wisdom in business?
DQ: How can Evolutionary Values enhance our creative powers and help to inspire breakthrough innovations for humanity?

Chapter 9 Synchronicity—Observes that occurrences of Coincidence, Synchronicity, and Serendipity (CSS) are far more common than generally supposed, and questions why it is so important to explain the mechanism.

> DQ: What if CSS events increase simply by exchanging stories of their occurrence? Are we all participants in a singular Big Heart Connectome, where CSS is one important manifestation of our deeper connectedness?

Chapter 10 Humor—An Interlude—Offers the reader an interlude to lighten and brighten the journey.

> DQ: How does humor help us restore balance and see the Big Picture?

BIG HEART CONNECTOME

Chapter 11 Roots of Crisis—Focuses on the problem of unpriced "externalities" and "public goods" in the development of the present economic system, in order to set the stage for a discussion of Evolutionary Values.

> DQ: What are some of the most effective ways to motivate entrepreneurs to build enterprises that release technology's highest potential for the good of local communities and our planet?

Chapter 12 Values—Reflects on Humanism and the Italian Renaissance as a useful model for exploring a 21st Century Renaissance.

> DQ: How might Big Heart Intelligence, Paying Forward, and Evolutionary Values provide the basis for an evolutionary shift for meeting the urgent challenges of this century?

Chapter 13 Organizing a Big Heart Connectome (BHC)—Explains how a BHC might be practically organized, financed, and managed.

DQ: What kinds of communities are ideal candidates for experiments in the evolution of kindness, compassion, and Love?

Chapter 14 Empowering Local Communities—A Case Example—Imagines how a BHC might actually be launched and flourish in a pilot community.

DQ: How to measure the social, environmental, and wisdom 'returns' (short term, intermediate, and long term) to a community from its investment in a BHC?

HEALTHY HEAVENS TRUST

Chapter 15 Let Us Not Go Mad—Warns that the world is hurtling toward a precipice by the unchecked, voracious exploitation of Outer Space; urges us to pause and suggests eight fundamental risks that, if effectively addressed, will bring us to a more balanced path forward.

DQ: How can social entrepreneurs take best advantage of new satellite communications technologies that can help humanity address our most urgent challenges?

EVOLUTION

Chapter 16 Our Noble Chance—Explains how our world appears rapidly to be coming apart and coming together at the same time, and the implications and opportunities created thereby.

DQ: Why will the exploration of Evolutionary Values help us to come together and care for one another?

Appendix 2: Big Heart Connectome (BHC) Questionnaire

BHC Champions/General

o What are the Evolutionary Values our BHC embraces?

o What is the core Mission of our BHC?

o What is the "Wisdom Genome" of our community? How can we encode it and make it available as a community-wide resource?

o What are other vital, as yet underrecognized talents, capabilities, and resources of our community that might be directed to addressing our community's most pressing challenges? How best to do this?

o What groups in our community are most vulnerable? Where are we least secure? What environmental treasures are most in jeopardy? How might we live more peacefully and in harmony with Nature?

o How to encourage the discovery of Beauty, however, wherever, whenever.

o How best to organize a Good News Network?

o How to inspire and enlist new visionary leaders, young and old?

o How to create bridges of understanding and effective communication across disciplines, ages, ethnic, and political groups in a hyperpolarized world?

o How to enlist the beneficial *Power of Synchronicity*™ in meeting community challenges? How best to promote a creative exchange between CSS explorers and entrepreneurs?

o What are our success stories, and what are their secrets?

o How to weave these success stories into our community's narrative of our heroic/heroinic journey?

o How to foster the spirit of a 21st Century Renaissance in our community?

o What will be our metrics of success?

o What constitutes true community prosperity?

o What are other important questions this Questionnaire has missed?

Sponsors/Benefactors

o How might a BHC help to address some Big Ideas that we have nourished but haven't had the time to test?

o What are some important community challenges where Collaboration Innovation Networks (COINs) based on intertidal thinking might accelerate breakthroughs?

o What are some good candidates for pilot projects to test this proposition, and how best to organize, launch, and finance these pilots?

o What are the areas of venture philanthropy that our foundation/organization/company has not explored that are well suited to a BHC?

o How to measure the community's Social/Environmental Return on Investment (SEROI)?

o How to encourage Paying Forward?

o What causes matter most to our community? How much progress has the community made to date in meeting these challenges?

o What are other important questions this Questionnaire has missed?

Producers

o   What are some Big Ideas we have had for some time but have not yet had the chance to be realized?

o   What do I envision as my "soul's work"?

o   How can I contribute in my own way to Beauty, Wisdom, Kindness, and Generosity in my community?

o   What if there is a way to be paid fairly for taking virtuous action? How can I contribute to the community by engaging in this way?

o   What fair monetary value do I place upon my proposed "Ask" in order to allow me to continue sustainably?

o   What do I want to leave behind to my children and future generations? (See Sean Rowe[399])

o   How open am I to exploring a new way of seeing connections and solving difficult problems through Intertidal Thinking?

o   As an artist and cultural creative, how can I most usefully employ my talents and energy to raising community awareness of critical community challenges and solutions?

o   What are the most important community challenges where my skills as a lawyer/public interest advocate, physician, architect, city planner, and other professional can be most helpful?

o   What are the leadership challenges I believe are not being met effectively in my community, and how might my vision of new leadership practically contribute?

o   What are some critical community challenges where my leadership could beneficially contribute?

o   What strategic alliances will be most helpful?

o How can I practically go about building new value alliances and networks?

o What are other important questions this Questionnaire has missed?

Consumers/ Other Participants

o What products or services am I looking for that are not readily available in our community?

o What exciting product ideas do I have that will embody Evolutionary Values?

o How might frontier technologies be better deployed in addressing community challenges? What specific technologies do I have in mind?

o How can I use my purchasing power to advance important community concerns?

o What are areas where our community's (consumer) voice must be heard and our consent required?

o How to promote effective engagement between entrepreneurs, artists, and other cultural creatives?

o How to enlist the creative energy of the entertainment industry in promoting Evolutionary Values?

o What are other important questions this Questionnaire has missed?

Appendix 3: Resources

Chapter 1

Julian Gresser
- *Piloting Through Chaos—The Explorers Mind (2013)*
- *Laughing Heart—A Field Guide to Exuberant Vitality for All Ages—10 Essential Moves*
  www. https://alliancesfordiscovery.org/
- *Integral Resilience—Helping Communities Thrive*
  https://resiliencemultiplier.com/
- *5 Minutes to Resilience*
  https://resiliencemultiplier.com/5m2r-details/
- *Big Heart Intelligence*
  web site: www.bighearttechnologies.com
- *Inventing for Humanity—A Collaborative Strategy for Global Survival* https://www.explorerswheel.com/blog/inventing-humanitya-collaborative-strategy-global-survival

Elmer and Alyce Green *Beyond Biofeedback (1978)*

Yamada Koun (teisho) *The Gateless Gate* (translation San Un Zendo) 1979

Brother David Steindl-Rast *Stop, Look, Go!*

Chapter 2

Charles Perrow *Normal Accidents: Living with High-Risk Technologies (1984)*

Julian Gresser
- *Going Behind the Mask (pdf link)*
  https://resiliencemultiplier.com/the-resilient-negotiator/
- *Broadband International Legal Action Network (BBILAN)*
  www.bbilan.org

Chapter 3

Zen Classics—Yamada Koun Commentaries (teisho) 山田耕雲

Yamada Kōun (1907-1989)
https://terebess.hu/zen/mesterek/KounYamada.html
- *Gateless Gate (Mumonkan)* (Translation: Sanun Zendo) 1979

- o *Blue Cliff Record (Hekiganroku)* (Translator Thomas Cleary) 1977
- o *Book of Equanimity (Serenity) (Shoyoroku)* (Translator Thomas Cleary) 1990

John Tarrant *Bring Me the Rhinoceros (2008)*

Li Junfeng
- o *Awakening the Soul Demonstration*
  https://www.youtube.com/watch?v=UHTHko9IygE
- o *Awakening The Soul with Master Li Junfeng - Part 1*
  https://www.youtube.com/watch?v=h-VvfeknzCY
- o *Awakening the Soul with Master Li Junfeng - Part 2*
  https://www.youtube.com/watch?v=oUE5QZtc2X8
- o *Awakening the Soul with Master Li Junfeng - Part 3*
  https://www.youtube.com/watch?v=RZPCNx8ISII
- o Li Jing – *Calming the Heart*
  https://www.youtube.com/watch?v=vO2ytqdoVaM

Beryl Markham
- o *West with the Night,* (1942)

Chapter 4

Barbara Friedrich *Love 2.0 (2013)*

Chapter 5

CSS in Art, Music, and Beauty
- o Search on *"Synchronicity and Art"* images
  https://www.google.com
- o *Synchronicity and Art*—Lauren Kindle
  http://www.laurenkindle.com/blog/2017/3/21/entropy-and-art
- o *Music and Synchronicity* | Psychology Today
  https://www.psychologytoday.com/us/blog/connecting-coincidence/201707/music-and-sychronicity
- o *The Beauty of Synchronicity. Synchronicities are often played out as...* | by Sara Eaton | New Earth Consciousness | Medium
  https://medium.com/new-earth-consciousness/the-beauty-of-synchronicity-24bccf83d32a

- o *Move # 3: Discovering Beauty* – Alliances for Discovery https://alliancesfordiscovery.org/guide/laughing-heart/move-3-discovering-beauty/
- o Kathleen Ferrier sings *Erbarme dich, mein Gott* J.S. Bach (*Saint Matthew Passion*) https://www.youtube.com/watch?v=Sm8CY8kqkXg&list=RDMM&index=2
- o John Dowland, *Now o Now I Needs Must Part* https://www.youtube.com/watch?v=5l6jF8v_Wus
- o Umberto Eco—*History of Beauty (2004)*
- o Zenrin-kushū - Wikipedia https://en.wikipedia.org/wiki/Zenrin-kush%C5%AB
- o Paul Reps, *Zen Flesh, Zen Bones (1998)*
- o Ralph Waldo Emerson—*Essay on Compensation* (1841) https://archive.vcu.edu/english/engweb/transcendentalism/authors/emerson/essays/compensation.html
- o Seamus Heaney Collected Works https://seamusheaneyhome.com/seamus-heaneys-literature/
- o Yeats, *The Lake Isle at Inissfree* https://www.poetryfoundation.org/poems/43281/the-lake-isle-of-innisfree
- o *Laughing Heart*—Alliances for Discovery http://www.alliancesfordiscovery.org/

Music and Beauty in Living and Dying
- o *For me there is a terrible poignancy between Beauty and Dying.* Three of the most beautiful Handel arias I know are sung below by Lorraine Hunt Lieberson https://en.wikipedia.org/wiki/Lorraine_Hunt_Lieberson) Arlene Auger https://en.wikipedia.org/wiki/Arleen_Auger and Kathleen Ferrier https://en.wikipedia.org/wiki/Kathleen_Ferrier, all of whom died very young from breast or brain cancer.
- o *Lord To Thee (Theodora)* https://www.youtube.com/watch?v=6eGPRMrKpD4
- o *Softy Sweet in Lydian Measures (Alexander's Feast)*

https://alliancesfordiscovery.org/guide/laughing-heart/move-3-discovering-beauty/

- o *Art Thou Troubled (Rodelinda)* https://www.youtube.com/watch?v=-tINkGp2axI
- o *What is Life* (Gluck) https://www.youtube.com/watch?v=-tINkGp2axI
- o *He Was Despised (Messiah)* https://www.google.com/search?q=Marion+Handel+he+was+despised&oq=Marion+Anderson+Handel+he+was+despised
- o *I Know That My Redeemer Liveth (Messiah)* https://www.google.com/search?q=I+know+that+my+redeemer+liveth+you+tube
- o John Dowland Songs *Come Again* https://www.youtube.com/watch?v=8iACNRyQm1M
- o *Now o Now* https://www.google.com/search?q=john+dowland+you+tube+now+o+now
- o Handel *Ombra Mai Fu* (*Xerxes*) https://www.youtube.com/watch?v=OdeOyrLHdSg
- o Marion Anderson "*He Shall Feed His Flock Like a Shepherd*" (Handel *Messiah*) https://www.youtube.com/watch?v=6-25tz_reRA
- o Marion Anderson "Erbarme dich, mein Gott" from *Matthäus-Passion* J.S. Bach (BWV 244) https://www.youtube.com/watch?v=_E7zjNiz2ZI
- o Puccini *E Lucevan le Stelle* (*Tosca*) (Enrico Caruso 1904)
- o Mozart *Marriage of Figaro* (Kiri Te Kanawa, final aria: 2:57:25)

Native American Beauty Tradition
- o *Walking in Beauty: Closing Prayer from the Navajo Way Blessing Ceremony* https://talking-feather.com/home/walk-in-beauty-prayer-from-navajo-blessing/

Japanese Tradition
- ○ *Shinrin-yoku (Forest Bathing)*
  https://www.karmatube.org/videos.php?id=8936
- ○ *Shinrin Yoku: The Japanese Art of Forest Bathing* Yoshifumi Miyazaki, June 12, 2018

Chapter 6

Qigong
- ○ Kenneth S. Cohen, *The Way of Qigong* (1999)

Neuroplasticity
- ○ *How to Boost Your Brain Through Neuroplasticity Healing*
  https://drruscio.com/neuroplasticity-healing/
- ○ *Neuroplasticity: How to Use Your Brain's Malleability to Improve Your Well-being*
  https://accelerate.uofuhealth.utah.edu/resilience/neuroplasticity-how-to-use-your-brain-s-malleability-to-improve-your-well-being
- ○ *Neuroplasticity and the Brain-Heart Connection*
  https://www.youtube.com/watch?v=sCsbn6RpIFY
- ○ *The Neuroendocrinology of Love* - PMC
  https://www.ncbi.nlm.nih.gov/pmc/articles/PMC4911849/
- ○ Richard Davidson—*A Neuroscientist on Love and Learning | The On Being Project*
  https://onbeing.org/programs/richard-davidson-a-neuroscientist-on-love-and-learning-feb2019/
- ○ NASA twin study re: resilience and aging
  https://www.engadget.com/2019-04-11-nasa-compared-twin-astronauts-to-see-if-space-ages-the-human-bod.html
- ○ Norman Doidge, *The Brain That Changes Itself* 2007
  https://www.amazon.com/Brain-That-Changes-Itself-Frontiers/dp/0143113100

Chapter 7

Nature
- ○ *Connecting to Nature*
  https://alliancesfordiscovery.org/guide/laughing-heart/move-4-connecting-to-nature/

o   Stephen Harrod Buhner
    https://www.stephenharrodbuhner.com/about/
o   Stephen Harrod Buhner *Secret Teachings of Plants*
    https://www.abebooks.com/Secret-Teachings-Plants-
    Intelligence-Heart-Direct/
o   Stephen Harrod Buhner *Plant Intelligence and the Imaginal
    World*
    https://forthewild.world/listen/stephen-harrod-buhner-on-
    plant-intelligence-and-the-imaginal-realm
o   *The Whole World is Medicine*
    https://tarrantworks.com/2009/10/22/1-the-whole-world-is-
    medicine/

Warlike Zen

o   *Zen at War* is a book written by Brian Daizen Victoria, first
    published in 1997. The second edition appeared in 2006. The
    book explores the contradictions as Zen was interpreted and
    applied by the military clique that seized control of Japanese
    society preceding and during WWII.

Chapter 8 Wisdom in Business

o   Nobel Laureate Daniel Kahneman, *Thinking Fast and Slow*
    2013.

Chapter 9 Synchronicity

Social Media Links

o   Coincidence-Synchronicity-Serendipity Learning
    Collaborative
    https://www.facebook.com/groups/search/groups/?q=synchr
    onicity
o   Linkedin.com Synchronicity search
    https://www.linkedin.com/search/results/groups/?keywords=
    synchronicity
o   Youtube.com Synchronicity search
    https://www.youtube.com/results?search_query=synchronici
    ty&sp=CAM%253D
o   *Neuroplasticity, Neural Networks, and Synchronicity*

https://onlinelibrary.wiley.com/doi/full/10.1111/dmcn.14341
4
o *Randonauts* Reddit https://www.reddit.com/r/randonauts

Timing (CSS) in Business
o *BK Blog | Synchronicity in Business* by Joseph Jaworski
   https://www.bkconnection.com/bkblog/joseph-
   jaworski/synchronicity-in-business
o *Timing Is Everything* | Forbes | 2014
   https://www.forbes.com/sites/groupthink/2014/12/05/when-
   launching-a-business-timing-is-
   everything/?sh=5a4c3cc55820
o *In Business, Timing Is Everything.* | Advisorpedia
   https://www.advisorpedia.com/viewpoints/in-business-
   timing-is-everything/
o *Why Timing Is the Most Important Factor in Ensuring Your
   Startup's Success (and What to Do About It)* | Inc.com
   https://www.inc.com/patrick-henry/want-to-launch-an-
   explosively-growing-startup-heres-why-timing-is-huge.html
o *The Role of Timing in the Business Model Evolution of
   Spinoffs*
   https://www.tandfonline.com/doi/full/10.1080/08956308.201
   9.1613116

Creating Your Own Luck
o *Creating Your Own Luck* | Alliances for Discovery
   https://alliancesfordiscovery.org/#move_nine
o Lyne McTaggart, *The Intention Experiment*
   https://lynnemctaggart.com/intention-experiments/the-
   intention-experiment/

Books
o Bernard Beitman, *Connecting with Coincidence (2016)*
o Bernard Beitman, *Meaningful Coincidences: How and Why
   Synchronicity and Serendipity Happen (2022)*
o Victor Mansfield, *Synchronicity, Science, and Soul Making
   (1995)*
o Andreas Mavromatis' *Hypnagogia (1987)*
o Robert Root Bernstein *Discovering (1989)*

o Julian Gresser, *Piloting Through Chaos—Wise Leadership/Effective Negotiation for the 21st Century* (1995)
o *I-Ching or Book of Changes* (Preface by Helmut Wilhelm, Introduction Carl Jung)
o Isak Dinesen, *Barua a Soldani—Letter from a King*
o Trevor Leggett, *Zen and the Ways, (1978)*
o Trevor Leggett, *The Tiger's Cave* (1988)
o Carl J. Jung, *Synchronicity* (1952)
o J.W. Dunne, *An Experiment with Time (1927)*
o Shoshanah Zuboff, *Age of Surveillance Capitalism (2018)*
o John Vervaeke—Youtube Video Series—*Awakening from the Meaning Crisis*
   https://www.youtube.com/playlist?list=PLND1JCRq8Vuh3fo
   P5qjrSdb5eC1ZfZwWJ

Chapter 10

o *Laugh Lots, Live Longer* – Scientific American
   https://www.scientificamerican.com/article/laugh-lots-live-longer/
o *Children Interrupt BBC newscaster*
   https://www.youtube.com/watch?v=Mh4f9AYRCZY
o Sid Caesar—*This Is Your Life*
   https://www.youtube.com/watch?v=BQBlEnsylIo
o *Syd Caesar Visits a Health Food Restaurant*
   https://www.youtube.com/watch?v=Kpn4_QeS7w8
o *5 Minutes to Resilience—A Simple Smile*
o Charles Dickens, *A Christmas Carol (1843)*

Chapter 11

o Adam Smith, *Wealth of Nations* (1776)
o Milton Friedman, *Capitalism and Freedom (2002)*
o Amitav Ghosh *The Nutmeg's Curse (2021)*

Chapter 12

o Walter Isaacson, *Leonardo Da Vinci* (2017)
o Charles Dickens, *Hard Times (1854)*
o Giovanni Pico della Mirandola, *Oration on the Dignity of Man*

- o Swami Vivekananda
  vivekananda.net/PDFBooks/KarmaYoga.pdf
- o Swami Vivekananda, *Bhakti Yoga (1978)*
  https://www.amazon.com/Bhakti-Yoga-Yoga-Devotion-Swami-Vivekananda/dp/818530197
- o Howard Bloom *Global Brain (2000)*
  https://www.amazon.com/Global-Brain-Evolution-Mass-Century/dp/0471419192
- o Amitav Ghosh, *The Nutmeg's Curse* (2021);

Chapter 13

- o Peter Gloor, *Swarm Creativity* (2005) There are fascinating relationships between Peter Gloor's concept of Swarm Creativity and the science of murmuration in birds, referred to earlier.
- o *Emergence* https://obviousstate.com/blogs/journal/there-s-a-special-providence-in-the-fall-of-a-sparrow
- o *Murmuration in Nature*
  https://www.youtube.com/watch?v=uV540aoSyMc

Chapter 14

- o Tim Schoechle—*Re-Inventing Wires—The Future of Landlines and Networks*
  https://gettingsmarteraboutthesmartgrid.org/wires.html
- o Thomas Greco—*Solar Dollars: A Complementary Currency that Incentivizes Renewable Energy*

Charles Eisenstein

- o *Sacred Economics (2011)*
- o You Tube video: *Sacred Economics* with Charles Eisenstein (2019 Remix)
  https://www.youtube.com/watch?v=-G0FzU3cRE4

Chapter 15 Healthy Heavens Trust

- o BBILAN web site for references to the Satellite Experiment
  http://www.bbilan.org/

Chapter 16

Emergence in fish swimming upstream
o   Trout swimming through vortex
    https://www.youtube.com/watch?v=AWcoi51hE04
o   *How Does a Dead Fish Swim Upstream?*
    http://physicsbuzz.physicscentral.com/2018/07/watch-how-
    does-dead-fish-swim-upstream.html

Chaordic Systems
o   *Chaotic Pattern Recognition: The Spectrum of Properties of
    the Adachi Neural Network* | SpringerLink
    https://link.springer.com/chapter/10.1007/978-3-540-89689-
    0_58
o   https://en.wikipedia.org/wiki/Chaordic_organization

Books
o   Mark Anderson, *Shakespeare by Another Name* (2005)
o   Geoffrey West - *Scale: The Universal Laws of Growth,
    Innovation, Sustainability, and the Pace of Life in Organisms,
    Cities, Economies, and Companies*
    https://www.amazon.com/Scale-Universal-Innovation-
    Sustainability-Organisms/dp/1594205582
o   Geoffrey West – *The Universal Laws of Growth, Innovation,
    and Sustainability* | YouTube
    https://www.youtube.com/watch?v=ncDE_V5RAQc
o   *Scale* by Geoffrey West: A brief summary | by Thomas A
    Dorfer | The Startup | Medium
    https://medium.com/swlh/scale-a-book-summary-
    3d39d16321ef
o   Bruce Lipton, The *Biology of Belief* (2005)

Movies
o   *A Christmas Carol* (original Alistair Sim)
o   *Chariots of Fire*
o   *Velvet*
o   *Brother Son, Sister Moon*
o   *Remember the Titans*
o   *Gandhi*
o   *Seven Samurai*

Glossary of Key Concepts

Act with Integrity   To embody integrity by action. Goethe writes: "It says: 'In the beginning was the word; already I am stopped. It seems absurd. The word does not deserve the highest prize. The spirit helps me. Now it is exact. I write: 'In the beginning was the Act.'" Without using words or thoughts, see if you can express your integrity to someone else, right now!

Agape   In Greek philosophy and later adopted by early Christianity *agape* is the highest form of love, charity, the love of God for man and of man for God.

Ashoka   An international network of change makers established by William Drayton.

Ask Your Integrity   To seek guidance from your innermost core. Timing is important and so is auspices: we pay respect to the source. In Japanese the word for "god," *kami*, is written with the Chinese character "to speak" beside "platform" or "dais." To ask your integrity is to initiate a dialogue with your True Self, face-to-face.

Baihui   A Qi energy point located at the top of the head.

Base Stations/ Earth Stations   A satellite internet, i.e. Starlink, Kuiper, etc., there are two types of "earth stations. The millions of antennas mounted on rooftops are known by Starlink as "CP Terminals," and by definition these are not connected to the terrestrial internet, rather, connect via satellites. The other kind of earth station is also referred to as a "base station," and consists of a small number of facilities, each with many antennas connected to the terrestrial fiber optic network that communicate directly with the satellite constellation.

Big Heart Connectome (BHC)	A community applying principles of BHI.
Big Heart Intelligence	The next frontier after mindfulness which combines the wisdom of "heart", the vision of "mind", and the practical applications of "hand."
Chaordic Systems	The term 'chaord' is formed from the words 'chaos' and 'order'. Chaordic organizations display simultaneous cooperation and competition of the members of a network. The mix of chaos and order is often described as a harmonious coexistence with neither chaotic nor ordered behavior dominating. The chaordic principles have also been used as guidelines for creating human organizations—business, nonprofit, government, and hybrids—that would be neither centralized nor anarchical networks.
Coincidence/ Synchronicity/ Serendipity (CSS)	*Coincidence* is a more general, all-inclusive reference to a chance event.
	Synchronicity is a term first used clinically by the eminent Swiss psychiatrist, Dr. Carl Gustav Jung, which he defined as "meaningful coincidence" and which describes the specific joining in a moment of time of two or more apparently causally unrelated external or internal events.

Serendipity, the English historian and Whig politician Horace Walpole, refers to a happy chance discovery. With all three, the event in question can be deeply meaningful, even life-changing, but the cause, at least in a conventional sense, at present has not been confirmed in western science.

Compromise Integrity	To surrender integrity for something of lesser value.
Connectome	A neural map of the brain's connections
Conscience	The sense or consciousness of the moral goodness or blameworthiness of one's own conduct, intentions, or character together with a feeling of obligation to do right or be good.
Coopetition	A state of simultaneous collaboration and competition.
Cosmos	In Greek philosophy the universe seen as a well-ordered whole.
Creative Reverie	Highly creative liminal state where conscious and unconscious worlds and processes meet.
Cultivate Integrity	Refers to the process by which we gradually build the vessel of character that allows us to navigate productively in the world.
Daimon	Greek for inner guide or spirit.
Dantian	Chinese Taoist term close to the Japanese concept of *hara*, but more focused on the energy field itself.
Digital Divide	The gulf between those who have ready access to computers and the internet, and those who do not.
Dojo (Japanese)	Martial arts practice hall.

Dokusan	Private encounter with a Zen master or teacher.
Dragon	"Dragon" comes from the Greek word "dukein" meaning "to see". There is a famous Buddhist saying, "When the universe roars, only the heavenly dragon watches calmly and with pure delight." The world can be topsy-turvy, but your dragon energy observes, seeing all, understanding all, content in its power. The dragon is the child of the four elements: air, water, earth, fire. The dragon lives in pools, in the bowels of the earth, in the shadows of caves, in the mists. It is your reticulated power. When you connect to your integrity, the power uncoils and then the dragon, in all its glory, steps forth.
Energy Field	A field of energy, often referring to subtle energy beyond the conventional sources of energy recognized in Western physics.
Enhanced Placebo	Enhanced placebo powerfully reinforces the psychological effects of engaging the mind in a healing process by enlisting the energetic power of Heart.
Epigenetics	A new science that studies changes in organisms caused by modification of gene expression, rather than alteration of the genetic code itself.
Evolutionary Values	Values that will help us individually, and collectively adapt, survive, surmount, and rise to a more joyful, peaceful, and creative level in the midst of compounding global crises.
Explorers Mind	The title of a book by the author that introduces a systematic process of

exploration and discovery.

Explorers Wheel	A tool and technique invented by the author to connect large domains of inquiry through the processes of CSS.
Expressionist *Zenga*	The author's term for a new genre of Zen art inspired by and incorporating various elements of nature.
Eudaimonia	Greek word for happiness, literally a good spirit within.
Fall Out of Integrity	To lose your line (connection) to the universe.
Field Effect	In this book, field effect is a change in our individual awareness as the result of changes in another's consciousness, or in the physical environment.
Field Independence	To become self-reliant and in various degrees free from and independent of the superflux of life and the dictates of the Shadow.
Follow Your Integrity	The specific act of being guided by integrity as well as the pursuit of its life-path.
Free Good	In economic theory a "free good" is not subject to scarcity, and therefore is available without limit. A free good has zero opportunity cost to society from its use.
Gather Integrity	To collect one's scattered consciousness by becoming aware and present.
Gravitas	The condition of wakefulness, steadiness, and equanimity derived from the disciplined practice of attending to the present moment.
Gut	Commonly referred to in the West as the area around the physical stomach, but more developed in East Asia as *hara* and *dantian*.

Hara	Japanese term for physical, emotional, spiritual energy field located below and behind the naval, recognized as a source of extraordinary power. In Japanese there is a wide range of characters (kanji) and phrases combining *hara*, including *hara wo yomu* (to read the stomach and thereby discern intention); *haragei*, the art of understanding another's true mind or *hara*; and *hara-kiri*, the less formal term for suicide (literally, cut the *hara*.)
Healthy Heavens Trust Initiative (HHTI)	An international grassroots initiative appealing for respect for the international public trust in Outer Space and the Heavens.
Heart	The faculty of consciousness and intelligence found as an energy field around the physical heart that interplays with the Mind and the gut. In Sheng Zhen *qigong*, the Heart is recognized as the governor of Mind.
Hold Integrity	To maintain integrity, defined as connectedness, coherence, wholeness, and vitality under stress or in the face of pain.
Hypnagogia	Technical term for liminal state between wakefulness and sleep, literally entering sleep.
Hypnopompia	Technical term for liminal state between wakefulness and sleep, literally emerging from sleep.
Integral Resilience	Resilience amplified by integration and expanded connectedness of diverse physical, emotional, psychological, and spiritual functions.
Integrity	Sense of connectedness, coherence,

	wholeness, and vitality.
Internet of Oceans (IoO)	Extension of IoT to oceans and seabed for monitoring and surveillance.
Internet of Things	Describes physical objects (or groups of such objects) with sensors, (IoT) processing ability, software and other technologies that connect and exchange data with other devices and systems over the Internet or other communications networks.
Intertidal Thinking	Creative exploration at the intersection of established fields of knowledge, often leading to important innovations.
Joriki	Japanese term for powerful life force, cultivated through the practice of *zazen*.
Just Click!	A practice created by the author to initiate a dialogue between the energy field of Heart, which is Qi and Love, and the living external and internal worlds.
Kensho	The first taste of Zen realization.
Know Your Integrity	To feel whole and alive, connected and coherent, and willing to let your spirit go fort into the world and be of use.
Kokoro	Japanese term for the energy field of Heart and Mind combined
Laogong	A QI energy point located in the palms of the hand.
Listen to Integrity	We listen to our integrity not only with our ears, but also with our Heart, eyes, stomach, our whole body and mind. It is different from ordinary listening—quieter, more profound. And what we listen for is also different. Our integrity may express itself not only in words or thoughts, but also in images, dreams, or events in the external

world. When we listen to our integrity in this way we open ourselves to the signal wherever it appears.

Lōgōs

In Greek, *lōgōs* meant both the spoken word and the pervading principle of reason. The Stoics saw *lōgōs* as the ordering principle of the universe. Like the Chinese *Tao*, the wise person, they believed, would aim to live in harmony with *lōgōs*. In the prologue of the Gospel according to John, the *lōgōs* is the Divine Word, a self-communicating divine presence that exists with God and is uniquely manifest in Jesus Christ.

Love

The most powerful form of subtle vital energy located significantly as a field surrounding the physical heart.

Maimuki ni (Japanese) *kento shimasu*

To adopt a forward looking attitude.

Makyo (Japanese)

In Zen tradition a still delusory state of mind characterized by revelatory images thought to be important signs of "progress" on the path of spiritual revelation.

Metanoia (Greek)

A change of mind or metamorphosis.

Mind

The faculty of consciousness and thought attributed generally as an attribute of the physical brain.

Mokusatsu (Japanese)

To kill by silence.

Mu (Japanese)

Absolute, spacious, nothingness—our essential nature.

Muses

In Greek mythology the Muses were daughters of Mnemosyne (Memory) and Zeus—the fruits, it is said, of nine nights of love-making. They presided over thought in all its forms: eloquence, persuasion, knowledge, history, mathematics, and astronomy. Hesiod claimed that they accompanied kings and inspired them with the persuasive words necessary to settle quarrels and re-establish peace, and gave to kings the gentleness that made them dear to their subjects.

Mushin (Japanese)   Martial arts term, literally vast, spacious, open, empty mind.

Negative Resilience Multiplier   This principle refers to a falling out of integrity in one place that impairs integrity in another place, and with compound interest. In the history of kings such as Achilles, King Lear, Macbeth, and Othello, the single flaw of hubris—overweening pride—could so eat away at character that the whole person was destroyed. It is the same with organizations, communities, even nations. When integrity is torn, troubles come not singly but in battalions.

Okiya   Japanese term for geisha house.

Optical Fiber Networks   Optical transport networks are based on the use of glass strands of optical fiber, each no thicker than a human hair, that can transmit light pulses, and thus information, with practically no limits on distance, or capacity.

Paying Forward   To celebrate a win and then pass its joy and other benefits onward to another person without seeking monetary compensation or other recompense.

Player Integrity Profile (PIPs)   A key tool in assessing the "source code" of character from the perspective of integrity.

Polluter Pays Principle	An axiom of Welfare Economics first articulated by the OECD in 1972 that polluters ought to bear the full external costs of environmentally destructive actions, thereby generating powerful incentives for innovation and competitive advantage.
Positive Resilience Multiplier	As the number of beneficial deeds increases and their rate accelerates, much like bombarded neutrons in a nuclear chain reaction, a critical mass is reached. Then an explosion can occur of such human warmth, kindness, generosity and cheer that the world might never recover from it.
Psychosphere	The *Psychosphere* is a theory proposed by psychiatrist, Bernard Beitman, which posits mental networks through which information-energy is exchanged. This idea is described in the last chapter of his book *Connecting with Coincidence.* He writes: "Our brains receive information through our senses which includes first sight (or 6th sense). Vision, hearing, smell, taste and touch operate through transducing energy-information in various vibratory forms (like light waves) into nerve impulses to the brain. Most likely we transduce psi information-energy through as yet unknown receptors."
Public Good	Public goods are the opposite of negative externalities. They are benefits society enjoys that are generally not accurately reflected in the price paid for them. Classic examples are national defense, lighthouses, streetlights, public roads, and clean air. In economics, public goods are referred to as "non-excludable" and "non-rivalrous."

Public Pays Principle	The assignment of financial and other costs of harmful corporate activities to the public.
Qi (Chinese)/ *Ki* (Japanese)	Vital subtle nourishing energy.
Qigong (Chinese)	Systematic training and practice to cultivate the subtle vital energy of Qi.
Resilience	The capacity for adaptive vitality, or the ability to turn adversity to advantage.
Roshi	Zen teacher
Samisen	Japanese stringed instrument.
Serialism	A theory developed by J.W. Dunne in his important book, *An Experiment With Time*. Dunne's starting point is the observation that the moment of "now" is not described by science. Contemporary science described physical time as a fourth dimension and Dunne's argument led to an endless sequence of higher dimensions of time to measure our passage through the dimension below. Accompanying each level was a higher level of consciousness. At the end of the chain was a supreme ultimate observer. According to Dunne, our wakeful attention prevents us from seeing beyond the present moment, whilst when dreaming that attention fades and we gain the ability to recall more of our timeline. This allows fragments of our future to appear in pre-cognitive dreams, mixed in with fragments or memories of our past. Other consequences include the phenomenon known as *deja vu* and the existence of life after death. (Wikipedia)
Sesshin	Intensive Zen meditation training.
Shadow	Term from Jungian psychology referring to

the unconscious part of the psyche, which is the repository of fears, anger, trauma, drives, but also a source of great creativity and power.

Tao In Chinese philosophy the great organizing principle of the natural universe.

Teisho Commentary provided by a Zen teacher or master on the Zen classics; also reflections from a Zen perspective on daily life.

Tightly Coupled Systems that are closely linked and interdependent, and especially systems vulnerable to cascading breakdown when tipping points are reached under cumulative stress.

Tragic and False Choices A tragic choice in economics is a situation where any decision will result in tragic and false choices serious harm to someone, often a vulnerable and weaker party. A false choice is a situation masquerading as a tragic choice, where, in fact, such harm can be effectively avoided by adopting a wise course of action.

Vitality Life force

Welfare Economics A branch of economics that uses microeconomic techniques to evaluate well-being (welfare) at the aggregate (economy-wide) level.

Wu (Chinese) Chinese term for Mu, virtually identical in its reference with Mu.

Yongquan Bubbling well energy point located at the center part of the foot.

Yukata Light Japanese wearing apparel

Zen A spiritual practice originating in India and China, then transferred to Japan, Korea,

	and other countries that explores the nature of reality and deep questions of life and death.
Zenga	Japanese term for Zen art.
Zhongtian Movement	A *qigong* practice developed by Grandmaster Li Junfeng that opens the connection of Heart and *dantian* with Heaven and Earth.

Endnotes

To have convenient clickable access to all of the end note links below, please visit JustClick.Earth

[1] Handel Overture (2:25-3:35)
https://youtu.be/hMM_1KsKrSo?t=145

[2] In economic theory a "free good" is a good that is not scarce, and therefore is available without limit. A free good is available in as great a quantity as desired with zero opportunity cost to society.

[3] Julian Gresser, Koichiro Fujikura, Akio Morishima, *Environmental Law in Japan* MIT Press (1981).

[4] Christiana Figueres and Tom Rivett-Carmac, *The Future We Choose: The Stubborn Optimist's Guide to the Climate Crisis* (2021).

[5] https://news.artnet.com/art-world/here-is-every-artwork-attacked-by-climate-activists-this-year-from-the-mona-lisa-to-girl-with-a-pearl-earring-2200804.

[6] See video series, "*While the Rest of Us Die*".
https://www.vicetv.com/en_us/show/while-the-rest-of-us-die

[7] For an overview of tightly coupled systems in the context of infrastructure, see Gresser, "*Inventing for Humanity—A Collaborative Strategy for Global Survival*" also discussed in Chapter 1.
https://www.explorerswheel.com/blog/inventing-humanitya-collaborative-strategy-global-survival

[8] Studies by the World Bank (https://blogs.worldbank.org/africacan/poor-but-happy) and other international development organizations point out that it is a cruel portrayal to suggest that poverty-stricken villages in Africa are somehow "happy" despite their poverty.

As Abraham Lincoln describes his own childhood and early youth, citing Gray's Elergy: 'The short and simple annals of the poor. That's my life and that's all you or anyone else can make of it." And yet here are several examples which suggest that situations of survival can inspire acts of compassion and altruism.

One book is Rebecca Solnit's *Paradise Built in Hell: The Extraordinary Communities That Arise in Disaster* (2010) (https://www.amazon.com/Paradise-Built-Hell-Extraordinary-Communities/dp/0143118072) which describes extraordinary acts of heroism during the 1906 San Francisco Fire. A second is Jacques Lusseyran's *And There Was Light* (2014) (https://www.amazon.com/There-Was-Light-Extraordinary-Resistance/dp/1608682692) which describes how the author was able to survive the horrors of Auschwitz, completely blind—by the cultivation of love—when thousands of his fellow French countrymen and women perished. The third is a video, *Weapons of the Spirit*, (https://www.chambon.org/weapons_en.htm) which describes the altruism of a Huguenot community in Nazi occupied France that sheltered Jewish families under the brow of the Nazi Headquarters. Not a single sheltered Jewish family in Le Chambron-sur-Lignon was arrested, even though the video reports these families went about their natural lives, celebrating births and marriages, and burying their dead—a kind of collective "consensus trance" activated by compassion and love.

See also: Viktor Frankl *Man's Search for Meaning* (1946) in which the author writes "the will to meaning" is the fundamental survival principle, based on his own survival from the Nazi concentration camps. A last and poignant scene is from the movie *Gandhi* where a Hindu man confronts Gandhi during the riots. "They have killed my child" he screams, referring to the Muslim rioters. "I will be revenged." "I know a way out of hell," observes Gandhi who is very weakened from fasting. "Find a little boy, a Muslim child, whose parents have been killed by Hindus. Bring this child into your home. But you must raise him as a Muslim."

[9] NIR is a general term which includes information-carrying radio waves and extremely low frequency magnetic fields that can produce adverse bioactive effects. An important relatively unexplored issue appears to be polarization of man-made electromagnetic fields, in regard to Biological Activity. See Polarization: A Key Difference between Man-made and Natural Electromagnetic Fields, in regard to Biological Activity - 2015.
https://www.nature.com/articles/srep14914

[10] In the case of satellite internet, i.e. Starlink, Kuiper, etc., there are two types of "earth stations". The millions of antennas mounted on rooftops are known by Starlink as "CP Terminals," and by definition these are not connected to the terrestrial internet, rather, connect via satellites. The other kind of earth station is also referred to as a "base station," and consists of a small number of facilities, each with many antennas connected to the terrestrial fiber optic network that communicate directly with the satellite constellation.

[11] This is based on personal experience. Our legal team was interviewed by journalists in many leading media outlets, but the editors of these magazines, for example, The Hill, all denied to publish the interviews because they were critical and precautionary about 5G. Our clients have had the same experience.

[12] Peter Elkind *How the FCC Shields Cellphone Companies from Safety Concerns,* 2022 https://www.propublica.org/article/fcc-5g-wireless-safety-cellphones-risk

[13] See Charles Eisenstein, *Sacred Economics,* 2011.

[14] For an important new book which documents the importance of bringing innovations to reviving local communities, see Michele

Anderson, *The Fight to Save the Town: Reimaging Discarded America* 2022.

[15] BBILAN http://www.bbilan.org/

[16] Queen Ann's Lace
https://en.wikipedia.org/wiki/Queen_Anne%27s_lace

[17] Yamada Koun Roshi
https://terebess.hu/zen/mesterek/KounYamada.html

[18] I was inspired by the term used for the Lewis and Clark Expedition, commissioned by President Thomas Jefferson, "the Corps of Discovery."
https://en.wikipedia.org/wiki/Corps_of_Discovery

[19] Stop Look Go https://gratefulness.org/resource/stop-look-go/

[20] stone striking bamboo
https://www.pacificzen.org/library/koan/stone-hitting-bamboo/

[21] Some might challenge my interpretation by pointing out the "meaning" of 'No Lifeguard on Duty' was just that–a clear warning, not the metaphorical meaning that I saw in it. But as discussed in Chapter 9, this is the point. We can pass the same tree one hundred times and only see a tree. Yet, at the one hundred and first time we pass the same tree, and it becomes a metaphor for the branching possibilities of our life. What has changed? The same tree, but its meaning to us has altered, because we have changed. Possibly, our entire life has changed, simply by this "small" modest internal shift of our mind (and heart).

[22] *Well Tempered Clavier*
https://www.youtube.com/watch?v=nPHIZw7HZq4

[23] pre-stressed and reinforced concrete
https://en.wikipedia.org/wiki/Kahn_system

[24] At thirteen my parents invited me to accompany them on a visit to Japan to meet my brother, Ion, who was the head of the US Army's Camp Zama Laboratory on Rickettsial Diseases. My brother later became a leading researcher on interferon. He died in 2019. I admired him greatly.
See https://www.ncbi.nlm.nih.gov/pmc/articles/PMC7388057/

[25] *Trilogy Life of Miyamoto Musahi*
https://en.wikipedia.org/wiki/Samurai_Trilogy

[26] citizens movement
https://www.bmartin.cc/pubs/88psa/88psa_Satofuka.html

[27] Yokkaichi air pollution
https://en.wikipedia.org/wiki/Yokkaichi_asthma

[28] Japan Center for Human Environmental Problems (JCHEP)
https://www.jstor.org/stable/24111318

[29] Japanese Diet https://en.wikipedia.org/wiki/National_Diet

[30] *Environmental Law in Japan* (MIT Press, 1981), pages 355-368

[31] Hiroyuki Ishi https://www.nippon.com/en/authordata/ishi-hiroyuki/

[32] Hiroyuki Ishi became Ambassador to Zambia and a leading expert in Japan on Africa and FAO.

[33] Richard Holbrooke
https://en.wikipedia.org/wiki/Richard_Holbrooke

[34] neo-mercantilist http://n.wikipedia.org/wiki/Neomercantilism

[35] "Single Negotiation Text"
https://www.beyondintractability.org/essay/single-text-negotiation

[36] *High Technology and Japanese Industrial Policy*
https://books.google.com/books?id=ZQl_tQ-MhLkC&printsec=frontcover&source=gbs_ge_summary_r&cad=0#v=onepage&q&f=false

[37] Sematech https://en.wikipedia.org/wiki/SEMATECH

[38] snapshot
https://www.legacy.com/us/obituaries/washingtonpost/name/william-osterman-obituary?id=6077283

[39] Richard Holbrooke
https://en.wikipedia.org/wiki/Richard_Holbrooke

[40] The polarized characteristics of the waveforms required to carry information that encompass those exposures are bioactive. This is not in dispute. The present FCC SAR guidelines, which are widely promulgated and cited, are based on heating of tissue, which is a measurable form of bioactivity. Panagopoulos et al - 2015 Polarization-A Key Difference between Man-made and Natural EMF.pdf

https://drive.google.com/file/d/1V7wob014_ugdalmHTVbXcXzEI9c9p__5/view?usp=share_link

[41] *Seventh Seal* https://en.wikipedia.org/wiki/The_Seventh_Seal

[42] Toranomon https://en.wikipedia.org/wiki/Toranomon

[43] Yamada Koun
https://terebess.hu/zen/mesterek/KounYamada.html

[44] A *koan* (meaning "public case" in Japanese) presents a challenge or "gate" for the Zen adept to penetrate the world of conceptualization and meaning making to an implicate world beyond form and physical senses.

[45] *Beyond Biofeedback*
https://www.youtube.com/watch?v=mVTAQoykcMU

[46] *Beyond Biofeedback* https://www.amazon.com/Beyond-Biofeedback-Elmer-Green/dp/0940267144

[47] Jim Schrager
https://scholar.google.com/citations?user=JGX7eMwAAAAJ

[48] Jim Camp, 2002
https://drive.google.com/file/d/1zmgTxjCKekNZ13_s-zpGo-mF-RliW65i/view?usp=sharing

[49] Jim Camp, 2007
https://drive.google.com/file/d/1bB_MUtQkXgN1k4QfB3tGd36VX EKVB3dc/view?usp=sharing

[50] judo term https://en.wikipedia.org/wiki/Randori#In_Judo

[51] *Piloting Through Chaos—Wise Leadership/Effective Negotiation for the 21ˢᵗ Century*
https://drive.google.com/file/d/1MNmdEVTjje7pJYTuPsmdBsj1y_5i ko5q/view?usp=sharing

[52] *Inventing for Humanity—A Collaborative Strategy for Global Survival* http://www.explorerswheel.com/blog/inventing-humanitya-collaborative-strategy-global-survival

[53] wicked problems https://en.wikipedia.org/wiki/Wicked_problem

[54] My close colleague, Ben Levi, offers this comment: "Solutions to our most wicked problems require new ways of thinking, something that engaging with one another can enhance (especially with out of the box thinkers). For one real-life example, see: *The Honey Pot—A Lesson in Creativity and Diversity*".
https://docs.google.com/document/d/1BKGmGL2SnMVkhll7pf-qcvHqYeO8K6490u4EQ7XrczU/edit?usp=sharing

[55] *The Explorers Mind* https://www.amazon.com/Piloting-Through-Chaos-Explorers-Mind-ebook/dp/B00DW7RDC6

[56] intertidal thinking http://explorerswheel.com/conversation-among-friends and https://www.sciencedirect.com/science/article/abs/pii/S014829632100 4781

[57] See interview with author:
https://www.youtube.com/watch?v=920VMi4na50

[58] Fukushima Daiichi nuclear accident https://en.wikipedia.org/wiki/Fukushima_nuclear_disaster

[59] Radio Interview with Tim Spangler.

https://www.explorerswheel.com/blog/radio-interview-tim-spangler-fukushima-china-and-piloting-through-chaos-explorer%E2%80%99s-mind-july-6

[60] Open Letter https://www.scmp.com/comment/insight-opinion/article/1464566/abe-must-act-now-seal-fukushima-reactors-its-too-late

[61] Li Junfeng https://en.wikipedia.org/wiki/Li_Junfeng

[62] Sheng Zhen https://www.youtube.com/watch?v=RZPCNx8ISII

[63] *Laughing Heart—A Field Guide to Exuberant Vitality for All Ages – 10 Essential Moves* https://alliancesfordiscovery.org/guide/laughing-heart/

[64] Big Heart Intelligence http://www.bighearttechnologies.com/

[65] Integral Resilience http://www.resiliencemultiplier.com/

[66] 5 Minutes to Resilience https://resiliencemultiplier.com/5m2r-details/

[67] The present risk
(https://www.cnn.com/2022/06/28/opinions/nuclear-war-likelihood-
probability-russia-us-scoblic-mandel/index.html) of nuclear war
with Russia must be viewed in historic context. See: 1983 Soviet
nuclear false alarm incident.
wikipedia.org/wiki/1983_Soviet_nuclear_false_alarm_incident

For an especially grim Doomsday prediction for 2023,
https://www.dailymail.co.uk/news/article-11576737/Doomsday-
warnings-2023-Risk-nuclear-war-highest-ever.html However,
counterbalance these predictions with Steven Pinker's thesis that
violence in the world has been on the decline: *Enlightenment Now*
(2018)

[68] I am indebted to our BBILAN board member Kate Kheel for
bringing to my attention the writings of prominent scholars in *War
with Russia?: From Putin & Ukraine to Trump & Russiagate*, and
journalists who point to the complex issues and interests in the
Ukraine war. See, also, Diana Johnstone *Washington's Iron Curtain
in Ukraine* for one controversial perspective which provides insight
into why Putin and his allies may feel encircled and threatened. The
Ukraine war illustrates several important dimensions and questions
relating to the Shadow at work:

a. How one person's shadow, indeed here a country's shadow, can
become entangled with and constellate other shadows and agendas.
There are serious issues of government corruption in Russia and the
Ukraine but also, as we are discovering, in the U.S. and other
countries;

b. How this entanglement can generate momentum, as each shadow
feeds upon and compounds another's, in what I call the "Negative
Force Multiplier";

c. How can the world find an "offramp" in the Ukraine and other
tragic situations when Shadow forces run amok?;

d. Can values ever be absolute?; is there true evil in the world? Or are all values culturally and time dependent and therefore "relative." (Kate points out that according to Chassidus, the more mystical understandings of Judaism, evil is defined as the illusion of separation from God.);

e. How to find a practical balance in the midst of the Shadow? The following chapters suggest a path through the heart of darkness, which recognizes and accepts that abominable cruelty does exist in the world out of ignorance ("Father, they know not what they do.");

f. That it is possible to discover and to develop an emergent, evolutionary standard or test, namely: will this action reduce misery, enhance joy, peacefulness, and kindness to ourselves, each other, and the living world?; and

g. Where are the acupuncture points to effect a scalable evolutionary shift despite the massive momentum the Shadow already gained? https://www.amazon.com/War-Russia-Putin-Ukraine-Russiagate/dp/1510745815 https://www.counterpunch.org/2014/06/06/washingtons-iron-curtain-in-ukraine-2/

[69] On the same vein, an FCC representative mentioned to one of the plaintiffs in *Environmental Health Trust/Children's Health Defense v. FCC* "We do frequencies not people" (cited in plaintiffs' brief). Ben Levi comment: "For some analysts the Shadow may be thought of the disowned aspects of ourselves, wounds, etc. which lie deep in our subconscious and which we project onto our world. The idea of "negative" is rife with unspoken meaning-making... what's negative to one may be positive to another."

[70] *Normal Accidents: Living with High-Risk Technologies* https://en.wikipedia.org/wiki/Normal_Accidents

[71] two nuclear power plants captured by the Russian Army
https://world-nuclear.org/information-library/country-
profiles/countries-t-z/ukraine-russia-war-and-nuclear-energy.aspx

[72] See 5 *Minutes to Resilience - Going Behind the Mask*
https://drive.google.com/file/d/1objNtojMNooTwa8p6wcEYnkA3Ie
pIvcO/view?usp=sharing

[73] Ben Levi offers this insightful interpretation: "Of the infinite
amount of data that made up your relationship with Omori, you and
your team chose the data which seemed most 'relevant' to the success
of your joint venture. Since he broke his trust with your team, you
simply opened yourself up to seeing what was 'salient' in those new
perceptions of your life conditions. We ALL filter out the data that
comes to us every day and choose what is most salient to us to cope
with our life conditions. You simply chose to allow in different data,
AND a different meaning to the data you chose (i.e. his facial
features). His features didn't change, as much as your meaning-
making salience of them. That is what 'befriending the Shadow' is all
about".

[74] Heraklites https://en.wikipedia.org/wiki/Heraclitus

[75] Healthy Heavens Trust Citizens Petition to the FCC of March 11,
2021
https://drive.google.com/file/d/1GQczihOSqcUuHmRWMOaV9qsH
bcIo-mtD/view

[76] BBILAN http://www.bbilan.org/

[77] *Dragon Guarding the Source*
https://drive.google.com/file/d/1whn835YS5QcD18B8wPIZL95dP69
oxIt6/view?usp=sharing

[78] Robert Aiken https://en.wikipedia.org/wiki/Robert_Baker_Aitken

[79] Great Sitting Buddha https://nippon-touch.com/wp-content/uploads/Kamakura-Daibutsu-1.jpg

[80] The "essential" cannot be described in words. By attempting to do so, we move away from it. See: Yamada Roshi's public talks (*teisho*) on this point, https://terebess.hu/zen/mesterek/KounYamada.html and also John Tarrant's *Bring Me the Rhinoceros* (2008) https://www.amazon.com/Bring-Me-Rhinoceros-Other-Koans/dp/159030618X

[81] Hasegawa Tōhaku (長谷川 等伯, 1539 – March 19, 1610) was a Japanese painter and founder of the Hasegawa school. He is considered one of the great painters of the Azuchi–Momoyama period (1573-1603), and he is best known for his *byōbu* folding screens. This image is based on Tohaku's *byobu*, conceived over 400 years after his death, and is offered in tribute to this great artist. The painting depicts an *enso* clasping the symbol of infinity which, as the Zen master Yamada Koun (山田 耕雲 1907—1989) taught, expresses the essential world of Zen. In this illustration we are witnessing the essential world appearing before a monkey who symbolizes our delusive wandering mind, chasing after this idea, that concern, emotion, or figment of our imagination. The monkey is infused with the color white to suggest the numinous, illusive quality of mind. The background is blue symbolizing the noble moment of realization.

[82] The evidence on this point is mainly anecdotal. Some of it comes from studies of boxing practice and Parkinson's disease. See: *The Neuroscience of Building a Resilient Brain* https://thebestbrainpossible.com/neuroscience-resilient-brain-stress/

[83] For me, Just Click! offers a simple way to by-pass intellect, logic, and causation and to experience, directly, Yamada Roshi's insight.

[84] Here is a link of my practice with a Resilience Ball with the same purpose. https://resiliencemultiplier.com/resilience-and-the-reflex-

ball/ It may have certain beneficial neurological effects. But there may not be anything magical or numinous about snapping or clicking our fingers. The reader may choose another signal to the autonomic nervous system indicating "this is a place of refuge." It will be interesting to explore whether the effect is the result of our own personal meaning making.

[85] On Refuge: Imaginary Garden—Recently, I have begun an interesting practice. I have created an extraordinary garden in my Heart/Mind which I imbue with all the lovely, beautiful, and noble memories I have—great works of music, art, and literature, images from Nature of all kinds—sounds, smells, sights, synesthetic experiences, remarkable people I have met, or from history or literature I would have liked to have met and gotten to know (Leonardo da Vinci and Charles Dickens lead this list), loved ones I have lost, children I might have had. I continuously add to this list with each moment of beauty, idea, or new discovery that come to me each day. I can return to this garden any time I want. It is my sanctuary.

[86] Quieting the Heart is a *qigong* practice based on the work of Grandmaster Li Junfeng. When you Quiet the Heart, naturally the Mind also settles down. This is the opening. See Move # 1: Quieting the Heart – Alliances for Discovery https://alliancesfordiscovery.org/guide/laughing-heart/move-1-quieting-the-heart/ Here is a further commentary on Quieting the Heart from Master Li's daughter, Li Jing, also a qigong master: https://alliancesfordiscovery.org/guide/laughing-heart/move-1-quieting-the-heart/

Although the lineage of Big Heart Intelligence described in later chapters is from qigong grandmaster, Li Junfeng, I pay tribute to the Heart Math Institute which for thirty years has advanced scientific exploration of the potentialities of the human heart. https://www.heartmath.org/

[87] Kokoro (こ ゝ ろ, 心) is the Japanese word which approaches Li Junfeng's and this book's meaning of "Heart." The Japanese word contains shades of meaning—notions of the heart and also of mind. It has been variously translated as "affection", "spirit", "resolve", "courage", "sentiment", or "the heart of things". It is to Li Junfeng's great credit that he has connected the energetic meaning of Heart with Love. Kokoro was also the title of the Japanese author Natsume Sōseki's great novel, which was first published in 1914 and has sold over seven million copies.

[88] Ben Levi makes the interesting observation: "By definition, a "field" has no exterior or interior... it is not a 'noun' as such, but invisible and has no boundaries."

[89] There is a remarkable passage in Beryl Markham's *West with the Night* https://en.wikipedia.org/wiki/West_with_the_Night where she describes the different kinds of silences of her childhood in Africa in the early years of the 20th century. "There are all kinds of silences and each of them means a different thing. There is the silence that comes with morning in a forest, and this is different from the silence of his sleeping city. There is silence after a rainstorm, and before a rainstorm, and these are not the same. There is the silence of emptiness, the silence of fear, the silence of doubt. There is a certain silence that can emanate from a lifeless object as from a chair lately used, or from a piano with old dust upon its keys, or from anything that has answered to the need of man, for pleasure or for work. This kind of silence can speak. Its voice may be melancholy, but it is not always so; for the chair may have been left by laughing child or the last notes of the piano may have been raucous and gay. Whatever the mood or the circumstance, the essence of its quality may linger in the silence that follows. It is a soundless echo." See, also, *Golden: The Power of Silence in a World of Noise.* https://www.dailygood.org/story/3003/golden-the-power-of-silence-in-a-world-of-noise-leigh-marz-justin-talbot-zorn/

[90] I conjecture that one reason it appears to me that the moment responds with Love is that Love, in addition to its other attributes, as suggested is a most powerful form of energy; and what is happening is by opening the Heart energy of Love and connecting it to each random, synchronous moment or happening, an energy field is generated, as the "object" or "moment" responds, and the dialogue proceeds. As noted elsewhere in this book, as the process continues, the distance between "object" and "subject" will close, until they and their respective energy fields merge, and they become one. This interpretation attempts to bypass the explanation of miracle in religious terms, although every moment of life, which the dialogue expresses, is in its own special way a marvel.

[91] I have discovered that remembering this experience and other moments of gratitude counterbalances adversity and interrupts "circuit overload" from too many invading thoughts and ideas. Case 39 Book of Equanimity

[92] I will explore Paying Forward more deeply in later chapters.

[93] As taught by qigong grandmaster, Li Junfeng, the "Heart" is conceived as a dynamic energy field, ever changing, not merely a physical pump. The Heart energy of Love is even more powerful than *Qi* and works in concert with it.

[94] diminishing marginal returns
https://www.investopedia.com/terms/l/lawofdiminishingmarginalret
urn.asp

[95] *The Whole World is Medicine*
https://tarrantworks.com/2009/10/22/1-the-whole-world-is-
medicine/

[96] increasing body of research on placebo effect
https://www.nature.com/subjects/placebo-effect

---

[97] recent Harvard study https://www.nature.com/subjects/placebo-effect

[98] recent study on placebo https://www.medicinenet.com/script/main/art.asp?articlekey=17472 2

[99] oxytocin https://www.medicinenet.com/oxytocin-injectable/article.htm

[100] power of prayer in healing https://www.ncbi.nlm.nih.gov/pmc/articles/PMC2802370/#:~:text=We%20provide%20a%20critical%20analysis,to%20have%20retrospec tive%20healing%20effects

[101] The "jo" in *joriki* can also be written with the character for life (生) pronounced in the same way.

[102] I am deeply grateful to my surgeon, Dr. David Thorardson at Cedars Sinai Hospital in Los Angeles, one of the country's leading specialists on full ankle replacement surgery, which I underwent in August 2022. From the very first day I began a dialogue with my ankle in which I followed the protocol described in the text. I had X-rays taken in September 2022. Dr. Thorardson reported that my progress was "perfect." He suggested I should now try walking, putting aside carefully the wheelchair and the walker. At first, I thought this was impossible. However, with a bit of courage and Heart energy, I attempted it. A few moments later I could walk haltingly. I express deep gratitude to this wonderful surgeon, my wife, and caregivers who are supporting me on this journey.

[103] A deep subject is the interplay of trauma, memory, and Love, and to what extent bringing Love and compassion to memories of trauma transforms trauma in new and surprising ways. I am testing this proposition with my replaced bionic ankle. See:

https://resiliencemultiplier.com/guide/laughing-heart/trauma-and-resilience/, also Chapter 6.

[104] My next challenge is balancing on only the operated leg, with the additional goal if possible with my eyes shut. I am finding this is not so easy. The problem seems to be that the surgery required some of my proprioceptive nerve cells to be destroyed and others, including proprioceptive neuromuscular cells, to be impaired. I choose to imagine them as "asleep." I frame the challenge as gently and patiently awakening them. I do so, again, by inviting a dialogue with the Heart energy field of Love. But this time it is not so easy, as I still face serious challenges of recovering my strength, balance, and agility. These are also amendable to my Heart energy protocol. I am combining this approach by doing some research on medical studies of proprioceptive neuromuscular recovery. https:/www.ncbi.nlm.nih.gov/pmc/articles/PMC3224884

A few weeks later:

What Might Be Just Possible?

I continue to be intrigued by what I am learning from my ankle journey. I have reached the next challenge which is to balance on the operated leg. It seems quite impossible to me, and that is confirmed by the data. I try repeatedly, and I fail. Quite impossible. And then Paul the therapist suggests, "Why not gently touch the table?" And I do so, and lo and behold in an instant, I find my balance." Ok, I say, that little bit provided the balance!" "Only a little bit," Paul, observes. He continues, "Now try holding your hand hovering over the table but not touching, simulating balance." I do so. Suddenly, I am able to balance on the injured leg, and when I start to fall off, I immediately feel (not simply imagine!) my hand supporting me on the table. That's all it takes to recover and hold my balance.

So, which is it? Impossible or just possible? At first, I wouldn't believe it. After all, my narrative is that it is physically impossible.

Somehow this version of limited reality is comfortable. But then I stretch my boundaries, physically, mentally, emotionally. A glimmer of possibility flickers into consciousness, followed by the more general proposition: What if new horizons, evolutionary possibilities, can begin to take form if we just allow, in the most modest ways, that they are in fact, possible. Just allow…

My next challenge is to balance blind, with my eyes closed. I am reminded of Zatoichi—The Blind Swordsman.

https://en.wikipedia.org/wiki/Zatoichi

A final coda, My ankle experiment offers a wonderful example of the power of data. I discover when balancing on one leg, the ankle is continuously providing data in feedback loop with my brain. If I simply pay attention to the unadorned uncensored data—the feedback—I find my balance and my power. This shed some light into why and how data have become under some conditions as valuable as gold.

[105] The lyrics of soran bushi
https://www.mamalisa.com/?t=es&p=5036

[106] Sound of a plucked *samisen*
https://www.youtube.com/watch?v=Znl49rwU4YY

[107] Soran Bushi https://www.youtube.com/watch?v=ETxcPyoSxQg

[108] St. Francis' Simple Prayer has been translated into many languages. Here is the original in Italian and a French translation:

Preghiera Semplice di San Francesco d'Assisi

Oh Signore, fa di me uno strumento della tua pace.
dove è odio, fa ch'io porti amore,
dove è offesa, ch'io porti il perdono,
dove è discordia, ch'io porti la fede,

dove è l'errore, ch'io porti la Verità,
dove è la disperazione, ch'io porti la speranza.
Dove è tristezza, ch'io porti la gioia,
dove sono le tenebre, ch'io porti la luce.
Oh! Maestro, fa che io non cerchi tanto:
Ad essere compreso, quanto a comprendere.
Ad essere amato, quanto ad amare
Poichè:
Se è: Dando, che si riceve:
Perdonando che si è perdonati;
Morendo che si risuscita a Vita Eterna.
Amen

French original:

Seigneur, faites de moi un instrument de votre paix.
Là où il y a de la haine, que je mette l'amour.
Là où il y a l'offense, que je mette le pardon.
Là où il y a la discorde, que je mette l'union.
Là où il y a l'erreur, que je mette la vérité.
Là où il y a le doute, que je mette la foi.
Là où il y a le désespoir, que je mette l'espérance.
Là où il y a les ténèbres, que je mette votre lumière.
Là où il y a la tristesse, que je mette la joie.
Ô Maître, que je ne cherche pas tant
à être consolé qu'à consoler,
à être compris qu'à comprendre,
à être aimé qu'à aimer,
car c'est en donnant qu'on reçoit,
c'est en s'oubliant qu'on trouve,
c'est en pardonnant qu'on est pardonné,
c'est en mourant qu'on ressuscite à l'éternelle vie.

[109] Saint Francis https://en.wikipedia.org/wiki/Francis_of_Assisi

[110] Zenrinkushu https://en.wikipedia.org/wiki/Zenrin-kush%C5%AB

[111] Discovering Beauty https://alliancesfordiscovery.org/guide/laughing-heart/move-3-discovering-beauty/

[112] *Softly Sweet in Lydian Measures* https://www.youtube.com/watch?v=_GDpfahL9b4

[113] *Art Thou Troubled?* https://www.youtube.com/watch?v=Dp7JG7_c3Tk

[114] See James Hillman's work: *Returning Soul to the World: Culture and Community.* https://www.mary-watkins.net/wp-content/uploads/2019/05/Breaking-the-Vessels.pdf

[115] *Connecting with Nature* https://alliancesfordiscovery.org/guide/laughing-heart/move-4-connecting-to-nature/

[116] *Secret Teachings of Plants* Buhner, Stephen Harrod, 2004 https://www.youtube.com/watch?v=P3rSQ8fxMJU

[117] *Plant Intelligence and the Imaginal Realm* Buhner, Stephen Harrod, 2014 https://forthewild.world/listen/stephen-harrod-buhner-on-plant-intelligence-and-the-imaginal-realm

[118] *Stop! Look! Go!* https://gratefulness.org/resource/stop-look-go/

[119] *Compensation* https://archive.vcu.edu/english/engweb/transcendentalism/authors/emerson/essays/compensation.html

[120] I have found both Emerson's dictum and the Swami Vivekananda's key message in *Karma Yoga* to be verifiable. Over the years I have tracked this concept of hoarding and not hoarding in my

Field Notes on many negotiations. I have discovered that Need increases when I am attached, and decreases when I don't hold onto the benefits of what I receive; the more I pass on these benefits, the more goodness seems to flow my way. The reader of course needn't accept any of this on blind faith. You can confirm this principle for yourself. "Need" is a crucial principle in my book, *Piloting Through Chaos–The Explorers Mind.*
https://www.amazon.com/Piloting-Through-Chaos-Julian-Gresser/dp/1626430004

[121] Seamus Heaney on writing *"Postscript"*: a "sidelong glimpse of something flying past" —*The Irish Times*
http://www.irishtimes.com/culture/books/seamus-heaney-on-writing-postscript-a-sidelong-glimpse-of-something-flying-past-1.1517558

[122] *The Lake Isle of Innisfree* read by Yeats
https://www.youtube.com/watch?v=hGoaQ433wnw

[123] "My salad days" is a Shakespearean idiomatic expression that means a youthful time, a period of carefree innocence, idealism and pleasure associated with youth. It comes from the play *Anthony and Cleopatra* (Act I, Scene 4), and the full quote, spoken by Cleopatra, is: "My salad days, / When I was green in judgment, cold in blood / To say as I said then!"

[124] Bob Dylan's *Back Pages*
https://www.youtube.com/watch?v=rGEIMCWob3U

[125] *Finding Your Power*
https://alliancesfordiscovery.org/guide/laughing-heart/move-2-finding-your-power-becoming-a-great-wave/

[126] Master George Xu
https://www.youtube.com/watch?v=Y3UdXVpxfrI

[127] The Bund https://en.wikipedia.org/wiki/The_Bund

[128] *The Many Great Waves of Kanagawa* https://vimeo.com/9932554

[129] *Laughing Heart* https://alliancesfordiscovery.org/

[130] *Harvesting Creative Genius in Music*
https://alliancesfordiscovery.org/guide/laughing-heart/move-5-harvesting-creative-genius-in-music/

[131] Mozart's *Jupiter Symphony*
https://alliancesfordiscovery.org/guide/laughing-heart/move-5-harvesting-creative-genius-in-music/

[132] *Many Great Waves of Kanagawa*
https://alliancesfordiscovery.org/guide/laughing-heart/move-2-finding-your-power-becoming-a-great-wave/

[133] Beethoven's *Kreutzer Sonata*
https://alliancesfordiscovery.org/guide/laughing-heart/move-5-harvesting-creative-genius-in-music/

[134] See Documentary.
https://www.youtube.com/watch?v=x9IHUPamCB4

[135] Mnemosyne https://en.wikipedia.org/wiki/Mnemosyne

[136] Euterpe https://en.wikipedia.org/wiki/Euterpe

[137] Dr. Oliver Sacks https://www.oliversacks.com/

[138] These findings suggest that advanced musical abilities in musicians are reflected in training-induced neuroplastic changes, particularly increased activation of brain areas associated with auditory processing, motor responses, as well as attention while listening to the music. How Musical Training Shapes the Adult

Brain: Predispositions and Neuroplasticity.
https://www.frontiersin.org/articles/10.3389/fnins.2021.630829/full

[139] Hermann Ebbinghaus
https://www.mindtools.com/pages/article/forgetting-curve.htm

[140] On neuroplasticity–*The Brain That Changes Itself (2007)* interview with Dr. Norman Doidge.
https://www.youtube.com/watch?v=sK51nv8mo-o

[141] See, e.g. Engagement in community music classes sparks neuroplasticity and language development in children from disadvantaged backgrounds.
https://www.frontiersin.org/articles/10.3389/fpsyg.2014.01403/full

[142] One study
https://www.frontiersin.org/articles/10.3389/fpsyg.2014.01403/full

[143] *The Explorers Wheel*
https://alliancesfordiscovery.org/guide/laughing-heart/move-6-the-explorers-wheel-connecting-laughing-heart-with-everything/

[144] *The Explorers Mind*
https://www.google.com/books/edition/Piloting_Through_Chaos_The_Explorer_s_Mi/9kGJJwBqCUEC?hl=en&gbpv=1&printsec=frontcover

[145] Concerning the Explorers Wheel, which is essentially a tool to discover connections, there is a medical term for a pathological over-tendency to see intertidal connections. The medical term is called "apophenia," which in its dark form is associated with schizophrenia. The bias against seeing connections may be culturally deeply engrained. After all, in academic circles young scholars are strongly encouraged to specialize and to become experts in narrow silos of knowledge. In fields like medicine a doctor risks a lawsuit for medical malpractice and liability for jumping out of his or her expertise. From a historical perspective, persistent curiosity and the

search for knowledge were deemed a sin by the Church. There was a special place for curiosity seekers in Dante's Circles of Hell in his *Inferno*. I have often wonder if a baby were born with wings and could fly, the first thing a surgeon might be constrained to do would be to amputate the wings. Everything it appears to have its shadow side.
https://www.rxlist.com/apophenia/definition.htm

[146] *Octopus Intelligence Contemplating Eternity* – Octopuses are extraordinarily intelligent creatures with eight separate "mini-brains" at the base of each of their eight tentacles, in addition to a central brain between the eyes. Each mini-brain can function somewhat independently in harmonious dialogue with the central brain. The octopus in this calligraphy is contemplating Eternity presented as Infinity within an *enso*. What might we learn from these octopus-*rishis*?
https://drive.google.com/file/d/1IOwHF2PthnUazui-EyMrVrfn4OotKu1b/view?usp=sharing

[147] octopus intelligence
https://en.wikipedia.org/wiki/Cephalopod_intelligence

[148] Op. cit. endnote [53]

[149] See this Zen story of two monks illustrating this point.
https://medium.com/@soninilucas/two-monks-and-a-woman-zen-story-c15294c394c1

[150] Bassui https://en.wikipedia.org/wiki/Bassui_Tokush%C5%8D

[151] Zhongtian Movement https://www.youtube.com/watch?v=h-VvfeknzCY

[152] *Laughing Heart—10 Essential Moves*
https://alliancesfordiscovery.org/

[153] *A Simple Smile* (pdf)
https://drive.google.com/file/d/1l61VWT690tQhM6AOy-
HgjU6ahqVWVcFd/view?usp=share_link

[154] *Finding Your Power* https://alliancesfordiscovery.org/#move_two

[155] *Connecting to Nature*
https://alliancesfordiscovery.org/#move_four

[156] formal studies by researchers at NASA
https://www.prnewswire.com/news-releases/nasas-landmark-twins-
study-reveals-resilience-of-human-body-in-space-300831287.html

[157] *Adversity's Spiraling and Creative Waveform*
https://alliancesfordiscovery.org/guide/laughing-heart/move-9-
creating-your-own-luck/

[158] *Creating Our Own Luck*
https://alliancesfordiscovery.org/guide/laughing-heart/move-9-
creating-your-own-luck/

[159] Grand Master Li Junfeng *Lost in the Gobi Desert*
https://alliancesfordiscovery.org/guide/laughing-
heart/conversations-with-li-junfeng/

[160] *The Tales of Dr. Harry Brown*
https://alliancesfordiscovery.org/guide/laughing-
heart/conversations-with-harry-s-brown/

[161] SEE International https://www.seeintl.org

[162] *The Heroism of the Nass Family*
https://alliancesfordiscovery.org/guide/957-2/

[163] Hexagram 39
https://en.wikipedia.org/wiki/List_of_hexagrams_of_the_I_Ching#H
exagram_39

[164] Shenguang https://terebess.hu/zen/huike.html

[165] Huike https://terebess.hu/zen/huike.html

[166] The poet, Ikkyu, who was also a great maverick Zen master, expressed this world in a famous poem: "From a well without a source. There is a bubbling spring that doesn't flow. Someone with no shadow or form is drawing water." https://en.wikipedia.org/wiki/Ikky%C5%AB

[167] The *koan* invites going beyond thinking about realizing or non-attachment. I encourage the interested reader to work with this famous line "Not knowing is most intimate." *Book of Equanimity* Case 20. https://www.pacificzen.org/library/koan/not-knowing-is-most-intimate-mk62-bs20/ See also, *Mushin: How The 'No Mind' State Can Help You* - The Minds Journal. https://themindsjournal.com/mushin-the-state-of-no-mind/

[168] Aitken Roshi https://tricycle.org/magazine/remembering-aitken-roshi/

[169] Ben Levi, who is a deep thinker about meaning making, suggested this article about Isak Dinesen's skill as a writer to create meaning. https://www.highteawithelephants.com/people/12-things-didnt-know-karen-blixen/

[170] There is a beautiful passage in Nikos Kazantzakis' *The Odyssey, A Modern Sequel* (translated by Kimon Friar 1958) on the passing of Ulysses that reminds me of Yamada Roshi's passing, although Yamada Roshi's death was quieter and more subtle.

> As a low lantern's flame flicks in its final blaze
> then leaps above its shriveled wick and mounts aloft
> brimming with light, and soars toward death with dazzling
> joy

so did his fierce soul leap before it vanished in air.

[171] "*Teisho*" refers to a commentary or instruction on Zen classics delivered by a recognized Zen master.

[172] Hojo Tokimune https://samurai-world.com/hojo-tokimune/

[173] Bukko https://en.wikipedia.org/wiki/Mugaku_Sogen

[174] "Present this case" means the adept must present his or her understanding of the *koan*, or more deeply a direct experience of the "essential world" which necessitates going beyond words, concepts, or intellectual maps.

[175] Some Zen teachers have challenged this account. However, I am reporting my direct conversations with Aiken Roshi. They assert that Aiken Roshi made this up or imagined it. I have not been able to confirm this point. I do believe, however, that Aiken Roshi was absolutely sincere, and I have first-hand knowledge and a clear memory of the negotiations that we prepared together one evening on the phone, he in Hawaii and I in Sausalito, California, with the assistance of my colleague, a former fighter pilot/master negotiator. Almost thirty years later, a disciple Zen teacher in this lineage, Henry Shukman, has developed a deep new training program, *Original Love*, which is the best antidote to this aberration, if in fact it took place. https://originallove.org/ See also this series of podcasts. https://www.mountaincloud.org/category/original-love/original-love-introduction/

[176] Hakkō ichiu (八紘一宇, "eight crown cords, one roof", i.e. "all the world under one roof") or hakkō iu (Shinjitai: 八紘為宇, 八紘爲宇) was a Japanese political slogan meaning the divine right of the Empire of Japan to "unify the eight corners of the world." The slogan formed the basis of the Empire's ideology. It was prominent from the Second Sino-Japanese War to World War II and was popularized in a speech by Prime Minister Fumimaro Konoe on January 8, 1940.

https://en.wikipedia.org/wiki/Hakk%C5%8D_ichiu

[177] *Zen at War* https://www.amazon.com/Zen-War-Brian-Daizen-Victoria/dp/0742539261

Note on Forgiveness, Redemption, Individual and Collective Responsibility

Just as this book goes to print, the hand of the past reaches out and touches the present through the power of CSS. I take this chance occurrence as a sign that I must probe even more deeply in the book into this matter of evolutionary values.

The Case

On February 3, 2023 I went to my physical therapy for my ankle with Paul who is also a serious Zen student. Paul mildly inquired, "Did you know Yamada Roshi?" "Yes, he was my great teacher," I replied. Paul continued somewhat puzzled, "I read in Wikipedia that he was involved during WWII with a mining company in Manchuria, in fact he was the "labor supervisor." I was surprised. I had not once ever thought to look up Yamada Roshi in Wikipedia. I fancied I knew him intimately from my own close training relationship over many years as his Zen student and friend. After my physical therapy session, Paul and I visited the source on Wikipedia, and indeed it confirms Yamada's involvement with a Manchurian Mining Company in which he rose to become the deputy director of its general affairs department.
https://en.wikipedia.org/wiki/Yamada_Koun

I don't know what occurred in Manchuria; I don't have any data, and I have no easy way to find out. I don't even know whether Wikipedia's write up is accurate. Certainly, all the victims are long dead. I can imagine what might have happened, but it would be pure speculation. My personal experience with Yamada Roshi was that he was a benevolent force in the world. As a lay Zen practitioner, he was an innovator. His modest *zendo* in Kamakura was ecumenical. He welcomed explorers from many faiths; there were many Christians, including nuns training in the Sanun Zendo. Yamada Roshi was particularly interested in finding common ground between Zen and other great spiritual traditions, especially Christianity. He welcomed foreigners, some of them prominent like Jerry Brown. His students and their students in the Sanbo Kyodan lineage number hundreds, possibly thousands around the world, particularly in Europe and the U.S. He was ever warm and kind to me. https://en.wikipedia.org/wiki/Sanbo_Kyodan

This chance event raises for me these additional questions that I believe must be considered in any serious exploration of evolutionary values. Each of these questions could be the subject of entire books. I will only provide a few brief comments.

Question # 1: What is the role of forgiveness? When I look into my Heart and bring up the Wikipedia story, my first sensation is of great sadness, first for the Chinese who must have suffered terribly, have no voice, and are now long dead; but also for Yamada Roshi, who had to carry this memory of their suffering and possibly his hand in it. Never once did he confide in me, and I doubt that he expressed his inner feelings on this matter to any of his other students. I believe he came to personal terms with the past through his benevolent work after WWII.

Question # 2: What is the role of *metanoia*? In Greek the word *metanoia* connotes literally a change of mind or metamorphosis. Such a metamorphosis came to Yamada Roshi, which was reported by Phillip Kapleau, his student, in his book *The Three Pillars of Zen.* The Wikipedia article contains this brief account:

> On 26 November 1953, Koun Yamada, a Japanese business executive in Kamakura, was returning home with his wife on a suburban train. He came across a passage in a Zen text in which the author declared: 'I came to realise clearly that Mind is no other than mountains and rivers and the great

wide earth, the sun and the moon and the stars.' He broke
into tears with the realization that after eight years
of *zazen* he had finally grasped what this statement meant.

Later that night he awoke abruptly from sleep and saw the
same passage flash in his mind, which was followed by
a *kensho* experience. The next day Yasutani (his teacher,
Haku'un Yasutani) confirmed that what Yamada had
experienced was a *kensho*.

The most famous account of *metanoia* is the transformation of Saul
of Tarsus on the road to Damascus to become Saint Paul, who some
Christian theologians suggest was the closest apostle of Jesus. Before
his conversion, the historic Saul of Tarsus is known in history as a
violent persecutor of Christians.

Question # 3: What of redemption? My personal view is that
redemption is not a binary thing but a process. The world is filled
with deep shadows and as well as light. But can we become free of
our *karma*, in other words, the consequences of our deeds and
actions, in this life or future lives? (See:
https://en.wikipedia.org/wiki/Karma) The Buddhist tradition
recognizes that the historic Buddha himself was subject to the law of
karma, even as he pointed the way to ultimate freedom from it. For
me, some important questions are: what can we learn from each
encounter in life, how does it deepen our understanding of the
human condition, and can it enable us to have a larger perspective as
we navigate our own lives? Without distorting or fleeing from the
truth, will this experience take us deeper, help us to learn, become
kinder, more compassionate, and wiser?

**Question # 4: Are planetary stewardship and a collective conscience
important evolutionary values? Do we have collective responsibility
to future generations?** In *The Nutmeg's Curse* (See end note [218])
Amitav Ghosh makes a powerful case that the western world (and
surely also Japan) bears direct responsibility for the consequences of
"extractivist capitalism," which he contends historically depended on

both genocide and omnicide. We who are alive today continue to bear moral, if not legal, responsibility, because we continue to exploit the earth, the skies, and oceans, and oppress the poor and defenseless while doing so. From an evolutionary perspective, it seems to me clear that we have a collective responsibility to future generations. (See film series cited in end note [6] "*While the Rest of Us Die*"). The challenge is how practically to embody these values in useful actions that truly advance our evolutionary path, rather than produce new forms of dissension and conflict?

Question # 5: What actions will increase significantly the chances of our species' and the planet's survival? For me the question itself contains an essential criterion of success. If we are careful that each action, program, or policy we propose or undertake in the name of evolutionary values will tangibly, practically, and measurably answer this question in the affirmative, without engendering new forms of even greater discord and conflict, we will have a good indication that our decisions will contribute toward an evolutionary shift.

For some tribal peoples struggling against gold miners in the Amazon a shift toward evolutionary values is literally a matter of life or death. See: Davi Kopenawa/Bruce Albert, *The Falling Sky—Words of a Yanomami Shaman*, 2013: "The forest is alive…You must hear me. Time is short."

[178] See Joseph Campbell, *The Hero's Journey (1990).*

[179] Ben Levi observes: "Things are getting better and better, worse and worse, faster and faster, all at the same time."

[180] Big Heart Intelligence (BHI)
http://www.alliancesfordiscovery.org/

[181] *Quieting the Heart*
https://alliancesfordiscovery.org/guide/laughing-heart/move-1-quieting-the-heart/

[182] Faten Amal Harby
https://www.youtube.com/watch?v=Ic3PN7DD6XQ

[183] Conscience https://en.wikipedia.org/wiki/Conscience

[184] *Daimon* https://en.wiktionary.org/wiki/daimon

[185] Logos https://en.wikipedia.org/wiki/Logos

[186] Pachelbel *Canon in D*
https://www.youtube.com/watch?v=Ptk_1Dc2iPY

[187] NIR Basics https://en.wikipedia.org/wiki/Non-ionizing_radiation

[188] https://www.saferemr.com/

[189] International Commission on Biological Effects https://icbe-emf.org/

[190] How the FCC Shields Cellphone Companies From Safety Concerns
https://www.propublica.org/article/fcc-5g-wireless-safety-
cellphones-risk?emci=b9ffcace-f160-ed11-ade6-
14cb6534a651&emdi=1953150b-0261-ed11-ade6-
14cb6534a651&ceid=8208367

[191] See: Norman Alster, *Captured Agency* 2014
https://ethics.harvard.edu/files/center-for-
ethics/files/capturedagency_alster.pdf

[192] Some legal scholars have begun to explore the question of whether
government lying is a violation of the First Amendment and various
federal and state statutes. See Helen Norton, *"Government's Lies and
the Constitution"* https://scholar.law.colorado.edu/faculty-
articles/54/

[193] Ionizing and non-ionizing radiation monitoring
https://www.sensaweb.com.au/

[194] Hunter Lundy litigation where evidence that cell phone companies are well aware and are actively suppressing patented protective inventions. http://www.cellphonecancers.com/hunter-lundy-founding-partner/

[195] David Carpenter - Oxidative Stress Slides 6.17.20 https://docs.google.com/presentation/d/1G1XKaoUlIsSd_NKVpwv mdhzUisLoNtIy/edit?usp=sharing&ouid=10971886319680520 5561 &rtpof=true&sd=true

[196] Access Board, NIBS Indoor Environmental Quality, 2005 https://drive.google.com/file/d/1jcA-lmbRFn8-2qQZaC98I1MoZgAhRUJA/view?usp=share_link

[197] Scientific Evidence for Cell Phone Safety | FDA https://www.fda.gov/radiation-emitting-products/cell-phones/scientific-evidence-cell-phone-safety

[198] Citizen's Imminent Hazard Petition to the FDA https://www.propublica.org/article/fcc-5g-wireless-safety-cellphones-risk?emci=b9ffcace-f160-ed11-ade6-14cb6534a651&emdi=1953150b-0261-ed11-ade6-14cb6534a651&ceid=8208367 and https://drive.google.com/file/d/1i3hlvBxGmxMvV3bwTiwEx5xgI6eo IU_N/view?usp=share_link

[199] Senate Report 104-140, pg. 91 https://www.congress.gov/104/crpt/srpt140/CRPT-104srpt140.pdf

[200] *Legal Ethics in the Wireless Age: Time for a Change?* https://www.bbilan.org/blog/2015-09-15-legal-ethics-in-the-wireless-age-time-for-a-change

[201] *Tragic Choices* https://www.amazon.com/Tragic-Choices-Lectures-Public-Analysis/dp/039309085X/

[202] And the war came
https://en.wikipedia.org/wiki/Abraham_Lincoln%27s_second_inaug
ural_address

[203] an estimated 620,000 men, lost their lives in the line of duty
https://www.battlefields.org/learn/articles/civil-war-casualties

[204] As Low As Reasonably Achievable (ALARA)
https://www.cdc.gov/nceh/radiation/alara.html

[205] Broadband Equity, Access, and Deployment (BEAD) Program
https://broadbandusa.ntia.doc.gov/resources/grant-
programs/broadband-equity-access-and-deployment-bead-program

[206] Fiber First Los Angeles https://www.fiberfirstla.org/

[207] Cost Los Angeles County billions of dollars
https://www.amazon.com/DISS-CONNECT-Americas-Telecoms-
Billions-Created/dp/B0BLFR2GNV/

[208] Bruce Kushnick documents the history http://irregulators.org/

[209] Fiber First Los Angeles http://fiberfirstla.org/

[210] Air Force Materiel Command
https://en.wikipedia.org/wiki/Air_Force_Materiel_Command

[211] Nuclear Weapons Center (NWC)
https://en.wikipedia.org/wiki/Nuclear_Weapons_Center

[212] Author's testimony before New Mexico Legislature Committee
https://drive.google.com/file/d/1YvO6Xx-
RLFg8ZWZHSU88b10r1aS5-8_R/view

[213] Havana Syndrome https://www.saferemr.com/2021/11/the-
havana-syndrome.html

[214] documented risks to pilots
https://www.microwavenews.com/short-takes-archive/iceman

[215] *Does Cockpit RF Disorient Pilots?*
https://www.microwavenews.com/short-takes-archive/iceman

[216] Tech Safe Schools https://www.techsafeschools.org/resources

[217] https://www.bbilan.org/blog/2021-dec-21-fda-hhs-citizen-petition

[218] Misleading images https://www.fda.gov/radiation-emitting-products/cell-phones/scientific-evidence-cell-phone-safety

[219] legal advisory
https://www.techsafeschools.org/_files/ugd/2cea04_9edd62aa69d747
5d87fc4ef20d56348a.pdf

[220] In these and many other cases, all levels of government and the wireless purveyors are using false and deceptive claims to cloak the corporate-profit-driven values that actually motivate them. The FDA is relying largely on industry-paid science for guidance and even refuses to accept the findings of its own taxpayer-funded research. https://drive.google.com/file/d/1K6_kMeDLdrktU9_ABwL_jdzPKHf
uFi8l/view?usp=share_link

The telecom industry asserts that the 1996 Telecommunications Act ties the hands of state and local governments with respect to permitting these small cell and macro cell towers, thus preempting local precautionary action—a shibboleth based on false assumptions that is almost universally accepted by local governments and a great part of the general public. In the Fiber First case our legal team has provided a detailed analysis that local officials, such as the Los Angeles Board of Supervisors, have substantial leeway and authority to impose reasonable and balanced limitations on the accelerated installation of small cell and macro cell towers in densely populated residential communities. Notwithstanding, wireless industry proponents of the 1996 Act (which was signed by President Bill

Clinton) have been successful in convincing Congress, as well as state and local governments, that a wireless telecommunications infrastructure is critical for national economic security and infrastructure integrity; and that for this reason it is necessary to strip local communities of ownership and control of their communications and energy/power infrastructure, and deny their citizens the opportunity—indeed the fundamental human right—of informed consent.

[221] The Fund for Global Human Rights https://globalhumanrights.org/what-we-do/childrens-and-youth-rights/?utm_source=google&utm_medium=cpc&utm_campaign=34 2195722&utm_content=24026677922&utm_term=childrens%20laws &campaign_name=issues-worldwide

[222] recognize the principle that children must be consulted https://globalhumanrights.org/what-we-do/childrens-and-youth-rights

[223] COVID protections https://www.guttmacher.org/gpr/2000/08/minors-and-right-consent-health-care

[224] See: Plato *Gorgias* translations, William Hamilton, Chris Emyln-Jones 1960, 2002

[225] Blueprint for Legal Action to Protect Children's Health https://docs.google.com/document/d/1qGzGXABacEMMsXe1Z23R LciG62Ctga9uSBGy5Q29SOI/edit?usp=share_link

[226] *The Nutmeg's Curse: Parables for a Planet in Crisis* Amitav Ghosh, 2022 https://blogs.lse.ac.uk/lsereviewofbooks/2022/05/20/book-review-the-nutmegs-curse-parables-for-a-planet-in-crisis-by-amitav-ghosh/

[227] See *The Nutmeg's Curse*, op.cit.

[228] See: International Rights Advocates law suit, JOHN *DOE1,. Et. al. v. Apple et. Al,* US Court of Appeal DC Circuit (December 8, 2022)

[229] See interview by Joe Rogan of a Harvard researcher, Siddarth Kara, who is discussing his new book, *Cobalt Red—How the Blood of the Congo Powers Our Lives.* https://www.amazon.com/Cobalt-Red-Blood-Congo-Powers-ebook/dp/B09Y462D6Z#:~:text=Cobalt%20Red%20is%20the%20searing,into%20cobalt%20territory%20oto%20document

[230] Net of Indra https://en.wikipedia.org/wiki/Indra%27s_net

[231] Actually, this tragedy has been reported and the industry has known about it for several years, As incremental efforts to end child labour by 2025 persist, Congo's child miners – exhausted and exploited – ask the world to "pray for us" https://www.equaltimes.org/as-incremental-efforts-to-end

For a description of current litigation on behalf of fifteen killed or maimed Congolese children who impressed into forced labor in the cobalt mines, see: https://www.internationalrightsadvocates.org/cases/cobalt

[232] Is your phone tainted by the misery of the 35,000 children in Congo's mines? The case is now being litigated in the DC Circuit Court of Appeals— https://www.internationalrightsadvocates.org/cases/cobalt See, also, press coverage on the case. https://www.cbsnews.com/news/apple-google-microsoft-tesla-dell-sued-over-cobalt-mining-children-in-congo-for-batteries-2019-12 -17/

[233] draw world attention to this atrocity https://www.equaltimes.org/as-incremental-efforts-to-end

²³⁴ *See Cobalt Free Vehicle Batteries Are Here, So Why Are We Still Mining the Mineral?* https://thenextweb.com/news/the-cobalt-free-electric-vehicle-batteries-are-here

²³⁵ On one hand it appears that Elon Musk's company, Tesla, is leading the campaign to replace cobalt mined lithium batteries. Yet, on the other, Elon Musk's company is reported to have signed a major contract with the Chinese company, Glencore, to supply its Tesla factory in Shanghai and seriously contemplated an investment of 10%-20% in Glencore as recently as 2022. https://www.carscoops.com/2022/11/tesla-almost-purchased-stake-in-worlds-largest-cobalt-producer-glencore/

²³⁶ Over the longer term, a leapfrog step will be to accelerate collaborative research and development through government/private sector partnerships of quantum computing, including battery storage by light, which may obviate the present need for many life-destroying technologies altogether. https:/www.scientificamerican.com/article/light-based-quantum-computer-exceeds-fastest-classical-supercomputers

²³⁷ An interesting debate on business axiom of "Move Fast and Break Things" was sponsored by the Action Think Tank, TANDO, with reference to some historic antecedents—Creative Destruction(Schumpeter), Survival of the Fittest (Spencer), Devil Take the Hindmost https://www.youtube.com/watch?v=NV40WbjHW00

²³⁸ Although the Harvard Business Review author, Hermant Taneja opines that *The Era of Move Fast and Break Things is Over*, this does not seem to be the case with the wireless and satellite industries for whom speed to market heedless of the suffering it causes appears to be of highest priority. https://hbr.org/2019/01/the-era-of-move-fast-and-break-things-is-over

[239] Here is an insightful quote on Synchronicity: "Humiliating to human pride as it may be, we must recognize that the advance and even the preservation of civilization are dependent upon a maximum opportunity for accidents to happen."—Fredrich Hayek, Nobel Laureate

[240] Serendipity Society https://theserendipitysociety.wordpress.com/

[241] The Old English *wyrd* meant 'destiny', of Germanic origin. The adjective (late Middle English) originally meant 'having the power to control destiny'.

[242] Cartesian worldview https://ecampusontario.pressbooks.pub/introhps/chapter/chapter-8-cartesian-worldview/

[243] See Dr. Bernard Beitman's book released September 6, 2022 (Simon & Schuster): *Meaningful Coincidences: How and Why Synchronicity and Serendipity Happen.*

[244] The Coincidence Project https://thecoincidenceproject.net/ and Dr. Beitman's website https://www.coincider.com/

My abbreviation to CSS is a bit clunky. Dr. Bernard Beitman suggests the refinement of "CSS" to "Meaningful Coincidences", the title of his 2022 book by this name, implying that all Synchronicities and Serendipities are meaningful, while some Coincidences are and some are not. Dr Beitman is striving to develop a science and practical taxonomy for meaningful coincidences, and for this purpose his protocol may be very helpful. As described in Chapter 9 and elsewhere in this book, I suggest this matter of nomenclature can be problematic. As developed in the pioneering book by Ogden and Richards, *The Meaning of Meaning*, the essays of Oxford don Glanville Williams on *The Language of the Law*, as well as in this book, I question where there is a singular meaning to anything apart from the meaning we ascribe to "things" in the external or internal domains. Personal meaning can transform based on how we ourselves transform and evolve. In one day a coincidence can be sterile and meaningless. A month later upon reflection the same event can become deeply meaningful. The event hasn't changed. We may have changed. I learned this principle over several years in facilitating clients in our brainwave biofeedback sessions described in Chapter 9. In the early years of Discovery Engineering International (DEI), we engaged Dr. Willis Harman, then president of the Noetics Institute in Sausalito, California. Wills' first hypnagogic image (a coincidence) was of peas in a pod. His immediate reaction was that this image was of no possible interest, and he suggested we move on. However, as we facilitated his discovery, he suddenly realized the image was redolent with significant meaning, simply lurking a bit below the surface of his awareness.

[245] *An Introduction to Koan Study in Zen Buddhism*
https://www.learnreligions.com/introduction-to-koans-449928

[246] See: What is Cultural Diffusion? Examples of Every Type | Fiveable; also, Stimulus Diffusion. https://library.fiveable.me/ap-hug/unit-3/types-of-cultural-diffusion/study-guide/DAioJEBluIVWISVGkv6g

[247] Elmer Green in this video
https://www.youtube.com/watch?v=mVTAQoykcMU

[248] *Serialism*
https://en.wikipedia.org/wiki/An_Experiment_with_Time

[249] It is likely that our understanding of time itself is culturally influenced, as this study of the sense of time among Australian aboriginal societies suggests. *Remembrances of Times East: Absolute Spatial Representations of Time in an Australian Aboriginal Community.*
https://www.jstor.org/stable/41062425

[250] Ben Levi comments: "I would note that millions of people have chance meetings with celebrities all the time. I myself met Richard

Burton when I was a kid while browsing a toy store, and he bought me an expensive toy.) So "remarkable" depends on the participants' perspectives... remarkable for you, but likely not for Yoko. Again, meaning-making is always in the mind of the beholder."

[251] Ben Levi comments: "It seems to me that CSS can reach backward in time. In your case with Yoko, both of you had previous experiences that morning that led, in that moment, to your both being in the same place at the same time in the gym. If the past had been different, the meeting may never have happened."

[252] Eric Wargo and his 'time loops' https://www.youtube.com/watch?v=bL-fScHKwf8&t=5s

[253] hypnagogic https://en.wikipedia.org/wiki/Hypnagogia

[254] hypnopompic https://en.wikipedia.org/wiki/Hypnopompic

[255] superconscious mind https://en.wikipedia.org/wiki/Superconscious

[256] CSS graphs https://docs.google.com/document/d/1rPQ1UrS61qjkD67SmmtulM C-a7eABc5az26ZhSk-xfo/edit?usp=sharing

[257] Big Heart Intelligence (BHI)—All the items under the External Line combined can be influenced by BHI and reflect field independence, when Need is not entrained by the External Field. Whether events move "up" or "down", we still maintain our equilibrium and balance, which is another way of speaking of "integral resilience". http://www.resiliencemultiplier.com/ I have developed a metric I call the "BHI Quotient" which disaggregates the critical elements of BHIQ and enables the navigator to track each item individually and to explore their interactions. This is an expanded version of the categories listed in the first edition of

Piloting Through Chaos. https://bighearttechnologies.com/bhi/bhi-in-collaborative-innovation/bhi-certification/

[258] *Paying Forward* https://alliancesfordiscovery.org/guide/laughing-heart/move-8-paying-forward/

[259] *Science of Paying Forward* https://www.nytimes.com/2014/03/16/opinion/sunday/the-science-of-paying-it-forward.html

[260] BK Blog | *Synchronicity in Business* by Joseph Jaworski. https://www.bkconnection.com/bkblog/joseph-jaworski/synchronicity-in-business

[261] As I am writing this book, I have continued to reflect on some important implications of CSS and the law, especially as CSS gains more predictive weight. The following are some observations I conveyed to my late law partner, Jim Turner, by email in 2021. Jim expressed enthusiasm to join our CSS Corps of Discovery, but sadly passed away in January 2022 before adding his reflections. Jim was a true explorer.

Legal Positivism—Law embeds within it a series of assumptions and presumptions about the nature of reality. Legal positivism is the thesis that the existence and content of law depends on social facts and not on its merits. Legal positivism is highly complementary with Realpolitik and the economic theory of Nobel Laureate, Milton Friedman, that places corporate responsibility of boards of directors primarily on creating shareholder value, not societal value. It is a self-enclosed system. CSS, on the other hand, invites inquiry into the basic questions of what is **real**. Every facet of law depends upon one version or interpretation of reality. But what if the subject of what is real is richer and more interesting than conventionally supposed. CSS invites this inquiry. It has especially interesting implications for practicing lawyers.
https://en.wikipedia.org/wiki/Legal_positivism

Public Policy (Eunomia)—CSS opens us to a larger perspective of connection and good order which has direct implications for legislators. https://en.wikipedia.org/wiki/Eunomia

In Greek mythology, **Eunomia** (Ancient Greek: Εὐνομία) was a minor goddess of law and legislation (her name can be translated as "good order", "governance according to good laws"), as well as the spring-time goddess of green pastures. https://en.wikipedia.org/wiki/Greek_mythology https://en.wikipedia.org/wiki/Ancient_Greek_language

CSS and Jurisprudence:

Torts

How might CSS discoveries influence the legal treatment of causation?

How might CSS discoveries influence the legal treatment of foreseeability, and duty of care?

How might CSS discoveries influence the legal treatment of joint and several liability?

How might CSS discoveries influence risk assessment and the allocation of risk and burden of proof?

Contracts

How might CSS discoveries influence the interpretation of the Act of God exemption? In some cultures, CSS may be construed not to relieve liability but rather to mandate action. See L'Aquila case below.

Administrative Law

What implications does CSS have for agency risk assessment? Suppose the most natural events—floods, earthquakes, hurricanes, volcanic eruptions—and human disasters are predictable and foreseeable?

Is a failure to take advantage of CSS knowledge evidence of negligence toward an imminent hazard?

Environmental Law/International Climate Change Law.

Again, suppose CSS offers a viable adjunctive methodology to provide early warnings of catastrophes? Is there an obligation of agency decision makers and policy makers to make practical use of this knowledge in determining and assessing risks in EIS and other required practices?

Criminal Law

Should CSS findings have any bearing on the determination of mental state (*mens rea*) of criminals, levels of responsibility, or sentencing guidelines?

For example, in the L'Aquila case, a district magistrate held consulting Italian scientists criminally liable for their failure to predict the 2009 earthquake in the town of Aquila. The judgment was overturned in 2014.
https://www.theverge.com/2014/11/11/7193391/italy-judges-clear-geologists-manslaughter-laquila-earthquake-fear

New Rights, Enhanced Public Responsibilities

Connectedness. If we are all truly connected in wondrous ways, what new rights does this imply?

Public Trust

What new public responsibilities do CSS findings create for the protection of significant natural resources, when looming catastrophe becomes apparent?

National Security

How can we use our growing knowledge of CSS to help alert us to catastrophic events that might jeopardize national security?

[262] Hummingbird pool party
https://www.youtube.com/watch?v=YAer4rDnA6I

[263] Matthew X: "There is special providence in the fall of a sparrow."

[264] Apophenia https://en.wikipedia.org/wiki/Apophenia

[265] The term (German: Apophänie from the Greek verb ἀποφαίνειν (apophaínein) was coined by psychiatrist Klaus Conrad https://en.wikipedia.org/wiki/Klaus_Conrad in his 1958 publication on the beginning stages of schizophrenia. https://en.wikipedia.org/wiki/Prodrome#In_mental_health https://en.wikipedia.org/wiki/Apophenia#cite_note-Klaus-2 Apophenia demonstrates how close sometimes is the border between creative inspiration and illness. BHI and Love provide one way to maintain mental integrity and health.

[266] Looking to the data and subtracting biases is one powerful analytic and logical tool to combat the Shadow. See Nobel Laureate Daniel Kahneman, *Thinking Fast and Slow* 2013. See, also, Ben Levi's Inference Ladder on how we rapidly, at times instantaneously, transition unconsciously from data to unchecked narrative. The mind habitually can make these transitions in a split second and the process is usually unconscious. As Bill Moulton notes, these steps in the ladder can be seen as organically "nested" with each other within the experiential field. The process of self-delusion can be further checked and transformed by Love, balance, boundaries, and humor.

Ladder of Inference

I take **ACTIONS** based on my beliefs.

I adopt **BELIEFS** about the world.

I draw **CONCLUSIONS**.

I make **ASSUMPTIONS** based on meaning.

I add **MEANING** (cultural and personal).

I select "**DATA**" from what I observe.

Observable "**data**" as a video camera might record it.

Reflexive Loop: our beliefs affect what data we select next time

Based on the work of Chris Argyris

[267] 'Gut' is usually understood in its physical sense in the West. In Japan the concept is far more expanded and nuanced in the concept of "*hara*" (in Chinese martial arts roughly, "*dantian*"). *Hara* includes the physical (*onaka*) but is far more developed to mean the energetic and even mystical gut. In Japanese we speak of reading the stomach ("*hara wo yomu*"), and ultimately, cutting one off from vital energy source, ie. *harakiri* (literally cutting the *hara*, meaning suicide). The formal term is *seppuku*. In Japanese culture *Haragei* (腹芸) refers to a highly developed form of stomach communication based on intuition and culture, that provide deep intelligence on a critical situation. Cultural differences have played a tragic role when in WWII. Notwithstanding that U.S. analysts had deciphered the Japanese military's encrypted messages, they missed entirely the *haragei* signals that Japan was willing to engage in peace talks— See Robert Butow *Japan's Decision to Surrender* 1954. https://www.amazon.com/Japans-Decision-Surrender-Robert-1967-11-01/dp/B01A1M44MQ

[268] Jizo's instruction https://www.pacificzen.org/library/koan/not-knowing-is-most-intimate-mk62-bs20/

[269] Viktor Frankl, in *Man's Search for Meaning*: https://www.themarginalian.org/2019/08/19/viktor-frankl-humor-survival/

[270] 5 Minutes to Resilience https://resiliencemultiplier.com/5m2r-details/

[271] Children Interrupt BBC Newscaster
https://www.youtube.com/watch?v=Mh4f9AYRCZY

[272] Sid Caesar - *This Is Your Life*
https://www.youtube.com/watch?v=BQBlEnsylIo

[273] Sid Caesar Visits a Health Food Restaurant
https://www.youtube.com/watch?v=Kpn4_QeS7w8

[274] Simply Smiling
https://drive.google.com/file/d/1l61VWT690tQhM6AOy-HgjU6ahqVWVcFd/view

[275] *Laugh Lots, Live Longer* – Scientific American
https://www.scientificamerican.com/article/laugh-lots-live-longer/

[276] In Chinese philosophy a community's line to the TAO was believed to be integrity (pronounced in Chinese as "Te"—德) When integrity was compromised, the people perished.

[277] Mandate of Heaven
https://en.wikipedia.org/wiki/Mandate_of_Heaven

[278] https://www.hemmings.com/stories/2019/09/05/fact-check-did-a-gm-president-really-tell-congress-whats-good-for-gm-is-good-for-america

[279] "What is good for General Motors is still good for America." attributed to Charles Wilson and later Lee Iacocca).
https://www.hemmings.com/stories/2019/09/05/fact-check-did-a-gm-president-really-tell-congress-whats-good-for-gm-is-good-for-america

[280] Milton Friedman, NYT, Sept. 13, 1970 *"A Friedman doctrine-- The Social Responsibility Of Business Is to Increase Its Profits"*

[281] Richard E. Neustadt and Ernst R. May describe in their 1986 book, *Thinking in Time* https://www.amazon.com/Thinking-Time-Uses-History-Decision-Makers/dp/0029227917 As this book goes to print, Synchronicity again enters in the lead article in the March-April 2023 issue of the Harvard Magazine—announcing Harvard Business School Professor Geoffrey Jones' recently published book (Harvard University Press), *Deeply Responsible Business: A Global History of Values-Driven Leadership*, 2023

[282] For a good review of the debate see: Michael J. Vargas

[283] The field of Welfare Economics
https://www.investopedia.com/terms/w/welfare_economics.asp#:~:te
xt=Welfare%20economics%20is%20the%20study,of%20people%20in
%20the%20economy

[284] Polluter Pays Principle
https://legalinstruments.oecd.org/en/instruments/OECD-LEGAL-
0102

[285] Public goods
https://en.wikipedia.org/wiki/Public_good_(economics)

[286] An important June 2020 report by the University of Oxford confirms a significant positive correlation between average ESG scores at companies and their native countries' macroeconomic performance.
https://www.greenbiz.com/article/companies-esg-scores-improve-
countries-macroeconomic-growth-report-finds
The data align high ESG performance with an improvement in GDP per capita and a reduction in unemployment. An interesting question is whether the same results will correlate positively with the Gross National Happiness Index. If so, this will point to a pathway that practically balances and reconciles economic growth with (possibly other) Evolutionary Values.
https://en.wikipedia.org/wiki/Gross_National_Happiness

[287] Salvator Mundi
https://en.wikipedia.org/wiki/Salvator_Mundi_(Leonardo)

[288] wisdom as more precious than rubies
https://www.bible.com/bible/116/PRO.3.14-18.NLT

[289] An important reference is the wrongful death case currently being tried by our colleague, Hunter Lundy. His client, a rising star attorney, died of a brain cancer which his estate is claiming was caused by exposure to NIR emanating from cells phones. In his magnificent brief, Hunter Lundy documents in detail the suppression of protective technologies and patents by the major cell phone manufacturers.
https://drive.google.com/file/d/16ugkIbZAKyyyEghWg9_xoXdo_nH9CIeT/view?usp=sharing

[290] *Cultural Creatives*
https://en.wikipedia.org/wiki/The_Cultural_Creatives

[291] The military is, of course, a primary source for researching and developing technologies of all kinds. National defense is a primary public goods application. A problematic imbalance arises when powerful commercial and military interests align without any regard for other public goods interests, such as public health, the environment, scientific research, as in the current race to exploit Outer Space.

[292] *Walker et. al.. v. Motorola et. al.*
https://drive.google.com/file/d/16ugkIbZAKyyyEghWg9_xoXdo_nH9CIeT/view?usp=sharing

[293] Lundy Complaint
https://drive.google.com/file/d/16ugkIbZAKyyyEghWg9_xoXdo_nH9CIeT/view?usp=sharing

[294] As result, the highest potential and best use of these new frontier technologies from the perspective of society is minimized and, in

some cases, their most harmful uses (market manipulation, for example) are financed to optimize profits for investors, managers, and shareholders.

295 See: Rubert Sheldrake, *The Rebirth of Nature—The Greening of Science and God* 1994

296 Ben Ehrenreich, *Desert Notebooks-A Roadmap for the End of Time*, 2020

297 *The National Parks—America's Best Idea* https://www.pbs.org/kenburns/the-national-parks/

298 March 11, 2021 Citizen's Petition for Rulemaking https://drive.google.com/file/d/1i3hlvBxGmxMvV3bwTiwEx5xgI6eoIU_N/view?usp=sharing

299 FCC's current position on US liability https://drive.google.com/file/d/1NJi4vQdFQ7WoefPZMQpTP-SauAZcUVDe/view?usp=share_link

300 Ben Levi points out: The margin for a near miss in October could have been as little as a few hundred meters if the astronauts onboard the Space Station hadn't shifted to a different orbit. SpaceX satellite narrowly missed Chinese lab. Los Angeles Times. https://www.latimes.com/business/technology/story/2021-12-28/spacex-satellite-narrowly-missed-chinese-lab-before-complaint

301 Bruce Kusnick, founder of the *Irregulators* http://irregulators.org/

302 There were enough votes in the Republican-controlled Congress to override a presidential veto.

303 Mark Zuckerberg Called People Who Handed Over Their Data "Dumb F****" https://www.esquire.com/uk/latest-news/a19490586/mark-zuckerberg-called-people-who-handed-over-their-data-dumb-f/

[304] Cell phone addiction rates as of 2022: 44 Smartphone Addiction Statistics for 2022.
https://www.slicktext.com/blog/2019/10/smartphone-addiction-statistics/#:~:text=Over%2050%25%20of%20smartphone%20owners,they're%20using%20the%20bathroom
In behavioral science, addictive behavior narrows our capacity to identify error and thereby resiliently correct our course.

[305] See: James Engell, *"Humanists All"* Harvard Magazine January-February 2023

[306] https://emraustralia.com.au/blogs/news/5g-will-use-the-same-frequencies-as-pain-inflicting-military-weapon

[307] The pendulum of legal academic writing is starting to move away from this ostensibly radically conservative and arguably heartless position toward a more balanced perspective.
https://corpgov.law.harvard.edu/2018/07/20/the-boards-role-in-corporate-social-purpose/.

[308] Sir, I canna, wi' my little learning an' my common way, tell the genelman what will better aw this—though some working men o' this town could, above my powers—but I can tell him what I know will never do 't. The strong hand will never do 't. Vict'ry and triumph will never do 't. Agreeing fur to mak one side unnat'rally awlus and forever right, and toother side unnat'rally awlus and forever wrong, will never, never do 't. Nor yet lettin alone will never do 't. Let thousands upon thousands alone, aw leading the like lives and aw faw'en into the like muddle, and they wille as one, and yo will be as anoother, wi' a black unpassable world betwixt yo, just as long or short a time as sich-like misery can last. Not drawin nigh to fok, wi' kindness and patience an' cheery ways, that so draws nigh to one another in their monny troubles, and so cherishes one another in their distresses wi' what they need themseln—like, I humbly believe, as no people the genelman ha seen in aw his travels can beat—will never do 't till th' Sun turns t' ice. Most o' aw, rating 'em as so much

Power, and reg'latin 'em as if they was figures in a soom, or machines: wi'out loves and likens, wi'out memories and inclinations, wi'out souls to weary and souls to hope—when aw goes quiet, draggin on wi' 'em as if they'd nowt o' th' kind, and when aw goes onquiet, reproachin 'em for their want o' sitch humanly feelins in their dealins wi' yo—this will never do 't, sir, till God's work is onmade.'
—Charles Dickens, *Hard Times* (1854) (in the dialect of Manchester, Northern England. (The word "soom" in the above text refers to a hem or seam, hidden but present on the periphery.)

309 Portrait of Leonardo https://www.rct.uk/collection/912726/a-portrait-of-leonardo

310 Neuroscience the "connectome" https://en.wikipedia.org/wiki/Connectome

311 Ben Levi points out that in some way every brain is "wired" differently. Thus the metaphor of a "wiring diagram" is a bit misleading, simply because it generally refers to a mechanical device (whose wiring diagram doesn't change) to a living system, which really doesn't have a wiring diagram, given the uniqueness of each individual and the neuroplasticity of the brain to modify itself.

312 Michael Porter and Mark Kramer, *Creating Shared Value* https://hbr.org/2011/01/the-big-idea-creating-shared-value

313 Julian Gresser, *Beyond Shared Value: Character as Corporate Destiny* https://ssir.org/articles/entry/beyond_shared_value_character_as_corporate_destiny

314 East India Company https://en.wikipedia.org/wiki/East_India_Company

315 However, there is strong historical precedent that exploitation is the tragic pattern. See: Amitav Ghosh, *The Nutmeg's Curse* (2021);

But, see also: Colleen Reilly–*Does Unconditional Love Have A Place At Work? https://www.forbes.com/sites/colleenreilly/2021/03/24/does-unconditional-love-have-a-place-at-work/*

[316] BHI combines two classic forms of Wisdom known in Ancient Greece as "sophrosyne"—soundness of mind, temperance, and balance https://en.wiktionary.org/wiki/sophrosyne; and "phronesis"—practical virtue and wisdom. https://en.wikipedia.org/wiki/Phronesis

[317] There is a German word for this: *Freudenfreude,* the opposite of *Schadenfreude,* taking joy or relief by the misfortune of others.

[318] An important background reference is Charles Eisenstein's "*Sacred Economics*" which explores related themes. Sacred Economics with Charles Eisenstein (2019 Remix). https://www.youtube.com/watch?v=-GoFzU3cRE4

[319] Just as this book opportunity, a former participant in a class I taught on Japanese environmental law at HLS in 1976-77, Sheridan Tatsuno, a visionary city planner and author, now a Fellow of TANDO, introduces me to his vision of Gaiapolis, which aspires a create a global online platform to support a network of 10,000 green cities by 2030, guided by Evolutionary Values. One focal point will be international Partners in Prosperity beginning between the U.S. and Japan ,which was the title of my 1985 book. See Sheridan Tatsuno, *The Gaiapolis Strategy: Designing Bionic Cities For Pandemic, Energy and Climate Resilience in the Coming Bio Renaissance* https://www.amazon.com/Gaiapolis-Strategy-Designing-Resilience-Renaissance/dp/B0B4XBHV9S

[320] BHCs can draw upon other wonderful models for inspiration, in particular the Gupta, Maurya Empire, and early Mughal periods in India, and Islamic Cordoba in 10th and 11th century Spain, which were characterized by religious tolerance and an accompanying flourishing of science, technological achievements, and the arts See:

The Story of India 10th and 11th century Cordoba
https://www.pbs.org/thestoryofindia/

[321] The term "cultural creatives" is the title of Paul Ray's and Shery Ruth Anderson's book published in 2000 which contains an expanded discussion.
https://en.wikipedia.org/wiki/The_Cultural_Creatives

[322] Picasso's *Guernica* https://en.wikipedia.org/wiki/Guernica

[323] *Battle for Los Angeles—People's Tsunami*: The Wireless Juggernaut appears invincible. But then, suddenly, out of the Shadows, a tsunami of grievance, indignation, and power-- the People's Tsunami. The image is the Japanese character for waterfall, which contains the radical for "water" in combination with "dragon"—here, a powerful red dragon, dwelling in and emerging from the mists. Water, infinitely adaptable, in the end prevails over the Juggernaut. The blood stains are metaphorical. They depict the defeat of ignorance, contrivance, corruption, and delusion. The power of light dwells inside the darkness. © Copyright 2022, Julian Gresser. See the image on the website JustClick.Earth Endnotes.

[324] Peter Gloor, describes this phenomenon as *Swarm Creativity* https://www.amazon.com/Swarm-Creativity-Competitive-Collaborative-Innovation/dp/0195304128

[325] latency in networks https://frontier.com/resources/what-is-network-latency

[326] See Tim Schoechle's *Reinventing Wires*. https://drive.google.com/file/d/1zJaVgJmtfSOcU7f6EsMUnJem_TVobS-w/view?usp=share_link

[327] social returns from investing in human capital https://www.nber.org/reporter/spring-2005/social-returns-human-capital

[328] Gross National Happiness
https://en.wikipedia.org/wiki/Gross_National_Happiness

[329] analytic tools to measure a community's human capital
https://www.hcmi.co/human-capital-roi

[330] https://resiliencemultiplier.com/the-resilient-negotiator-2/ and
https://resiliencemultiplier.com/guide/laughing-heart/measuring-integral-resilience/

[331] Tim Schoechle writes in *Re-Inventing Wires: The Future of Landlines and Networks*
https://gettingsmarteraboutthesmartgrid.org/wires.html

[332] The NTIA wrote (pg. 14): (r) Priority Broadband Project—The term "Priority Broadband Project" means a project that will provision service via end-to-end fiber-optic facilities to each end-user premises. An Eligible Entity may disqualify any project that might otherwise qualify as a Priority Broadband Project from Priority Broadband Project status, with the approval of the Assistant Secretary, on the basis that the location surpasses the Eligible Entity's Extremely High Cost Per Location Threshold (as described in Section IV.B.7 below), or for other valid reasons subject to approval by the Assistant Secretary.

[333] This is an active case. The Los Angeles County Regional Planning Department (LACRPD), under the influence of the wireless industry, has recommended to the County Board of Supervisors the accelerated adoption of these two ordinances which would replace the present Conditional Use Permit framework with non-discretionary ministerial site review. Fiber First Los Angeles and other grassroots organizations are challenging the LACRPD on the grounds that its proposal will violate the U.S. and California state constitutions, federal and state environmental and historic site

protection laws. The Fiber First Los Angeles Coalition will file suit in the Los Angeles Superior Court by the end of early March, 2023.

[334] Deckers Outdoor Corporation https://www.deckers.com/

[335] Santa Barbara Foundation's website and in its annual report. https://www.sbfoundation.org/

[336] Organic Soup Kitchen https://www.organicsoupkitchen.org/

[337] The term "bid and ask" (also known as "bid and offer") refers to a two-way price quotation that indicates the best potential price at which a security (in this case, a product or service) can be sold and bought at a given point in time. The bid price represents the maximum price that a buyer is willing to pay for a share of stock or other security. The ask price represents the minimum price that a seller is willing to accept for that same security. A trade or transaction occurs when a buyer and seller agree on a price acceptable to both.
https://www.investopedia.com/terms/b/bidprice.asp
https://www.investopedia.com/terms/a/ask.asp
https://www.investopedia.com/terms/s/seller.asp

[338] For an introduction to Intelligent Solar Microgrids, see: Tim Schoechle's 2018 article.
https://drive.google.com/file/d/1_Wvioaio YYUmVMz6qUOWdgEB 7tvjo1Bo/view?usp=sharing

[339] There is considerable evidence that these "strategic" innovation clusters can rapidly become catalysts for economic growth and job creation. See Austin Technology Incubator https://ati.utexas.edu/ and https://bighearttechnologies.com/the-trigger-method-3/

[340] Clean Coalition https://clean-coalition.org

[341] Arts & Lectures Program https://artsandlectures.ucsb.edu/

[342] introNetworks https://intronetworks.com/

[343] A beautiful, although contrived portrayal of a community's paying forward, is what happened in this small town in Spain on the 130th anniversary of the Sabadell Bank. A little girl gives a coin to a street cellist in the town square; other players begin to drift in, and soon the entire town comes together around the full orchestra in singing Schiller's *Ode to Joy* in Beethoven's Ninth Symphony. https://www.youtube.com/watch?v=87qT5BOl2XU.

[344] Power, For All https://www.youtube.com/watch?v=NrNHbfxryqo

[345] A mega-patent is a legal instrument that allows inventors to pool their ideas in one powerful patent, rather than disaggregating their inventions and competing with each other by filing and asserting rivalrous individual patents.

[346] *The Resilient Negotiator* https://resiliencemultiplier.com/the-resilient-negotiator-2/

[347] Public Banking Institute https://publicbankinginstitute.org/

[348] National Infrastructure Bank Act of 2021 https://www.congress.gov/bill/117th-congress/house-bill/3339

[349] *Solar Dollars: A Complementary Currency that Incentivizes Renewable Energy* https://www.frontiersin.org/articles/10.3389/fbuil.2021.785145/full

[350] Integral City, Compassionate Cities, Mayors for Peace https://integralcity.com/ http://compassionstaugustine.org/compassionate-cities.html https://www.mayorsforpeace.org/en/

[351] There are other mega-satellite constellations in orbit besides Starlink. See e.g. Large Satellite Constellations and their Impact on

Astronomy. https://www.eso.org/~ohainaut/satellites/ and http://astria.tacc.utexas.edu/AstriaGraph/

[352] March 11, 2021 FCC Petition for Rulemaking filed by the Healthy Heavens Trust Initiative (HHTI) https://drive.google.com/file/d/1GQczihOSqcUuHmRWMOaV9qsH bcIo-mtD/view

[353] FCC is reported in *Scientific American* to be updating its agency review of satellite debris https://www.scientificamerican.com/article/the-fcc-is-finally-taking-space-junk-seriously/

[354] See FCC cancels Starlink's $886 million grant from Ajit Pai's mismanaged auction. https://arstechnica.com/tech-policy/2022/08/fcc-rejects-starlinks-886-million-grant-says-spacex-proposal-too-risky/

[355] Congress's Government Accountability Office (GAO) has just issued a report: Large Constellations of Satellites: Mitigating Environmental and Other Effects https://www.gao.gov/products/gao-22-105166

The restoration of scientific integrity and evidence-based policy making has also recently been reaffirmed by the White House as cornerstone national priorities. See:

Scientific Integrity Task Force | OSTP | The White House https://www.whitehouse.gov/ostp/ostps-teams/nstc/scientific-integrity-task-force/

PROTECTING THE INTEGRITY OF GOVERNMENT SCIENCE | The White House https://www.whitehouse.gov/wp-content/uploads/2022/01/01-22-

Protecting_the_Integrity_of_Government_Science.pdf

Memorandum for the Heads of Executive Departments and
Agencies 3-9-09
https://obamawhitehouse.archives.gov/the-press-
office/memorandum-heads-executive-departments-and-agencies-3-
9-09

[356] HHTI Declaration
https://www.bbilan.org/blog/5d8bl37h7h4hsbhaq9cymz9ceaj5d4

[357] FCC persists in granting blanket licenses for millions of satellite
base stations https://satellitemap.space/

[358] Based on private discussions with cybersecurity experts who are
working, or have worked on this issue within the U.S. government.
Amid escalating cyber activity, two separate cybersecurity
frameworks are targeting the satellite arena, highlighting the ease in
attacking the infrastructure and the difficulty in defending it. See:
*Space Race: Defenses Emerge as Satellite-Focused Cyberattacks Ramp
Up* https://www.darkreading.com/ics-ot/space-race-defenses-
satellite-cyberattacks?s=09

[359] "Mosaic Warfare"—putting various weapons systems together in
new and unpredictable ways so an enemy doesn't understand what's
happening and gets overwhelmed… not exactly a comforting
strategy when the enemy has nuclear weapons. One questions the
sanity of such strategies when errors in judgment or confusion can
lead to catastrophic consequences for the planet.
https://www.nationaldefensemagazine.org/articles/2018/11/16/darpa
-pushes-mosaic-warfare-concept https://www.bbilan.org/blog/2022-
06-30-commentary-china-analysis-starlink-military.

[360] U.S. Military experts are proposing a limited war strategy, but
what about an unlimited peace strategy? CNAS's Elbridge Colby to
Serve as DASD for Strategy and Force Development | Center for a
New American Security (en-US). Weapons testing in Space risk
shutting down ATMs and grounding commercial flights.

https://www.cnas.org/press/press-release/cnas-congratulates-robert-m-gates-senior-fellow-elbridge-colby-on-appointment-to-serve-as-deputy-assistant-secretary-of-defense-for-strategy-and-force-development, and
https://arstechnica.com/science/2023/02/enter-the-hunter-satellites-preparing-for-space-war/

[361] Gen 2 satellite is considerably larger
https://www.cnet.com/science/space/elon-musks-new-second-gen-starlink-satellites-are-too-big-for-current-rockets/

[362] The FCC's blanket licenses to a few satellite companies is generating a plethora of high level national security risks that directly involve the risk management programs of other federal agencies that already have in place best practice guidelines and regulations. For example, NOAA has in place recommended best practices on risk management relating to weather forecasting which, as explained below, may be directly affected and interfered with by satellites. There is a special Risk Management Agency within the Department of Agriculture to address risks and calamities for farmers.
https://www.performance.noaa.gov/wp-content/uploads/Risk-Communication-and-Behavior-Best-Practices-and-Research-Findings-July-2016.pdf
https://www.rma.usda.gov/en/Topics/Manage-Your-Farm-Risk

[363] As I write this chapter on the uncontrolled Space grab, I come upon this singular report of a peer reviewed article appearing in Nature on July 13, 2022. I am struck by the convergence of science with poetic metaphor. A team of astronomers, at MIT's Kavli Institute for Astrophysics and Space Research recently detected fast radio bursts (FRB) a billion light-years away from Earth. FRBs are intense radio waves that typically last for a few milliseconds. However, the FRB in this report persists for up to three seconds – about 1,000 times longer than the average. Moreover, it also repeats every 0.2 seconds in a clear periodic pattern, similar to that of a beating heart. The signal, labeled FRB 20191221A, is currently the

longest-lasting FRB, with the clearest periodic pattern detected to date.
https://www.usatoday.com/story/news/nation/2022/07/14/space-radio-waves-fast-radio-burst-space-heartbeat-pattern/10056469002/

[364] Cybersecurity risks. https://www.darkreading.com/ics-ot/space-race-defenses-satellite-cyberattacks?s=09

[365] Conflicts in Space.
https://www.technologyreview.com/2019/06/26/725/satellite-space-wars/

[366] Order 23-1 https://docs.fcc.gov/public/attachments/FCC-23-1A1.pdf

[367] FCC Agrees to Form Space Bureau to Keep Up With Growing Satellite Industry https://gizmodo.com/fcc-form-space-bureau-satellite-industry-1849971227   Just as this book goes into print bipartisan bills have been introduced aiming to promote competition, innovation, security and leadership in the commercial satellite industry by modifying FCC licensing rules and authority.
https://www.nextgov.com/policy/2023/03/bipartisan-space-and-satellite-bills-reintroduced-secure-americas-interests/383655/

[368] FCC establishes space bureau to meet growing demands (2023-01-10) https://www.telecomstechnews.com/news/2023/jan/10/fcc-establishes-space-bureau-meet-growing-demands/

[369] https://www.space.com/spacex-falcon-heavy-ussf-67-mission-success

[370] 1337 USCA Case #22-1337 Document #1979555 Filed: 12/29/2022 Page 1 of 87

[371] Dark-Sky Association Appeal https://www.darksky.org/wp-content/uploads/bsk-pdf-manager/2023/01/IDA-FCC-Notice-of-Appeal-Dec-2022.pdf

[372] The Kessler Syndrome
https://en.wikipedia.org/wiki/Kessler_syndrome

[373] On January 27, 2023 there was an orbital near miss with the two large pieces of space junk, both from the Soviet era, missing each other by an estimated 20 feet. LeoLabs describes this type of potential collision between "two massive derelict objects" as a "worst-case scenario," saying it would be "largely out of our control and would likely result in a ripple effect of dangerous collisional encounters." At present there are approximately 5,000 low orbit satellites in orbit. One can easily imagine how the risks of a worst case scenario catastrophe will increase, possibility exponentially, when the number climbs to 40,000 within the decade. https://gizmodo.com/near-miss-orbit-collision-satellite-rocket-soviet-1850048253

[374] Starlink which are 5 times bigger than the first generation https://www.teslarati.com/wp-content/uploads/2021/11/Starlink-V1.5-renders-Oct-2021-SpaceX-V1.0-vs-V1.5-c.jpg

[375] The FCC Fact Sheet (pg. 24)
https://docs.fcc.gov/public/attachments/DOC-358437A1.pdf

[376] FCC Rule 22-91 (released 2022-12-1)
https://docs.fcc.gov/public/attachments/FCC-22-91A1.pdf

[377] Starlink and other low Earth orbit (LEO) satellites will not affect weather forecasting (disputed here: https://nltimes.nl/2023/01/27/dutch-meteorologists-say-musks-starlink-network-disrupts-weather-forecasting

[378] Increasing rocket launches of satellites will have no negative impacts on the environment and climate change, disputed here: https://www.space.com/rocket-launches-damage-ozone-climate

[379] Military use of mega-satellite constellations will not result in increased threats of "war in space" disputed here:

https://lieber.westpoint.edu/can-starlink-satellites-be-lawfully-targeted/

[380] The threat of cybersecurity attacks on mega-satellite constellations will not be significant enough to affect increasing deployments, disputed here: https://link.springer.com/article/10.1007/s10207-020-00503-w

[381] LA case/cite March 11, 2021 HHTI Petition https://drive.google.com/file/d/1GQczihOSqcUuHmRWMOaV9qsHbcIo-mtD/view

[382] Christopher Stone, *Should Trees Have Standing: Law, Morality, and the Environment*, 2010; also, Marth C. Nussbaum, *Justice for Animals: Our Collective Responsibility* January, 2023 https://www.environmentandsociety.org/mml/should-trees-have-standing-law-morality-and-environment

[383] Cybersecurity Experts Push President Biden To Protect GPS Satellites And The Connected Car. https://www.forbes.com/sites/stevetengler/2021/05/18/cybersecurity-experts-push-president-biden-to-protect-gps-satellites-and-the-connected-car/?sh=1b193b9e7628å

[384] 2023 Doomsday Clock Announcement, January 24, 2023, This year, the Science and Security Board of the Bulletin of the Atomic Scientists moves the hands of the Doomsday Clock forward, largely (though not exclusively) because of the mounting dangers of the war in Ukraine. The Clock now stands at 90 seconds to midnight—the closest to global catastrophe it has ever been. https://thebulletin.org/doomsday-clock/

[385] series of complex vortices https://en.wikipedia.org/wiki/K%C3%A1rm%C3%A1n_vortex_street

[386] https://twitter.com/zelc88/status/1600777319232131074

---

387 And then this startling coda: "Since all of the energy is supplied by the vortices, it doesn't matter at all whether the fish is alive or dead, if the timing happens to be right." Even dead fish can swim upstream!

388 Dee Hock https://en.wikipedia.org/wiki/Dee_Hock

389 Epigenetics https://en.wikipedia.org/wiki/Epigenetics

390 A review of epigenetics in human consciousness https://www.tandfonline.com/doi/pdf/10.1080/23311908.2019.16682 22?needAccess=true

391 A wide range of environmental factors can trigger epigenetic modifications https://www.ncbi.nlm.nih.gov/pmc/articles/PMC3752894/

392 *Epigenetics and Lifestyle* https://www.ncbi.nlm.nih.gov/pmc/articles/PMC3752894/

393 *Molecules of Silence: Effects of Meditation on Gene Expression and Epigenetics* https://www.ncbi.nlm.nih.gov/pmc/articles/PMC7431950/

394 The study concludes with this qualification and conjecture: "However, it is unclear whether stress and meditation act antagonistically on shared epigenetic mechanisms and, because of the relative novelty of the field, molecular and epigenetic evidence of the effects of mindful activities is still not sufficient to demonstrate a cause–effect relationship. It is conceivable that, by improving the immune system, metabolism, and stress–response pathways, and by promoting neuroplasticity, meditations of several kinds could affect mechanisms of energy saving, promote homeostasis, and potentiate the reciprocal mind and body's relaxation abilities, with a positive impact on psychology."

[395] See: Malcom Gladwell, *The Tipping Point* (2006); See, Julian Gresser, Inventing for Humanity: A Collaborative Strategy for Global Survival 2000 op.cit. fn.6.

[396] fifth-century Patriarch Bodhidharma https://en.wikipedia.org/wiki/Bodhidharma

[397] Ashoka, founded by my Harvard '65 classmate Bill Drayton https://www.ashoka.org/en-nrd/about-ashoka

[398] I am continuously amazed—I perhaps shouldn't be—how Synchronicity appears to have accompanied the writing of this book. Just as I am completing the final prepublication draft, I come upon by chance last night the Netflix series, "*Shamwari Untamed.*" There at the beginning of the very first episode one of the Shamwari Game Park managers, John O'Brien, presents us, the viewers, with living proof of what his wife describes as a "one in a million" chance of his deep personal twelve year relationship with a female leopard. We see Obrien sitting on a rock and suddenly there appears out of the bush a large leopard who approaches him carefully, then settles right by him and gently caresses him with her long tail, greeting her old friend. They pass these moments of timeless time together. "The leopard sought out John, not the other way round," his wife observes. https://www.netflix.com/title/81635357

[399] Sean Rowe https://www.youtube.com/watch?v=6c5BMg78mh8

List of Author's Images

Chapter 2
- o *Dragon Guarding the Source*
- o *Essentials—Moonbeams (as falling rose petals)* "The Moon sets at midnight. I walk alone through the town." Case 76 *The Book of Serenity*

Chapter 3
- o *Octopus Intelligence Contemplating Eternity*

- *Monkey Mind Contemplating the Source—In Homage to Hasegawa Tohaku and Yamada Koun Roshi*

  Hasegawa Tōhaku (長谷川 等伯, 1539–1610) was a Japanese painter and founder of the Hasegawa school. He is considered one of the great painters of the Azuchi-Momoyama period (1573-1603), and he is best known for his byōbu folding screens. This image is based on Tohaku's byobu, conceived over 400 years after his death, and is offered in tribute to this great artist. The painting depicts an *enso* clasping the symbol of infinity which, as the Zen master Yamada Koun (山田 耕雲 1907—1989) taught, expresses the essential world of Zen. In this illustration we are witnessing the essential world appearing before a monkey who symbolizes our delusive wandering mind, chasing after this idea, that concern, emotion, or figment of our imagination. The monkey is infused with the color white to suggest the numinous, illusive quality of mind. The background is blue symbolizing the noble moment of realization.

Chapter 6

- *Explorers Wheel*

Chapter 10

- *Happy Fish*

Chapter 12

- *Enso and Flower*

Chapter 13

- *Battle for Los Angeles County—People's Tsunami*—The Wireless Juggernaut appears invincible. But then, suddenly, out of the Shadows, a tsunami of grievance, indignation, and power—the People's Tsunami.

- *Water Dragons at Play*—The image is the Japanese character for waterfall, which contains the radical for "water" in combination with "dragon"—here, a powerful red dragon, dwelling in and emerging from the mists. Water, infinitely adaptable, in the end prevails over monoliths. The blood stains are metaphorical. They depict the defeat of ignorance, contrivance, corruption, and delusion. The power of light dwells inside the darkness.

Acknowledgement

I am deeply grateful to my colleagues Ben Levi and Bill Moulton, who are like brothers to me, for their ideas and creative suggestions, and critique that has caused me at different times to stretch and to ground this chronicle. I look forward to continuing the conversation with them and many others, and to connecting the basic theme of Evolutionary Values to new horizons and applications. I pay homage to my teachers, all grandmasters in their arts—Professor Jerome A. Cohen (law), Koun Yamada (Zen), Elmer Green (psychology/ physicist/ shaman), and Li Junfeng (qigong) who entered and shaped my life in pivotal times. I am also deeply indebted to our benefactors and many others known and unknown who are supporting the work of the Broadband International Legal Action Network (BBILAN). I also express my appreciation to Ann Kathleen Bradley and Alexandra Haynal for their skillful editorial suggestions on early drafts of this book. Lastly, I am indebted to Angela, my soul's joy, dear friend and wife, who has greatly supported my labors in writing this book and who brightens each day with tender love kindness and great peals of laughter.

Author's Bio

Julian Gresser is an international attorney, professional negotiator, inventor, and recognized expert on Japan. He has been twice Visiting Mitsubishi Professor of Japanese law at the Harvard Law School (1976, 1981), a visiting professor at MIT, Doshisha University (Kyoto), and Beijing University, and as well as a senior consultant to the U.S. State Department, World Bank, Prime Minister's Office of Japan, People's Republic of China, and European Commission (where he trained the Commission's Japanese negotiating teams). He is the author of eight books in English and Japanese, including: *Environmental Law in Japan* (MIT Press, 1981), *Partners in Prosperity: Strategic Industries for the U.S. and Japan* (McGraw Hill, 1984;(in Japanese, *Cho Hanei Sengen*), *Piloting Through Chaos: Wise Leadership/Effective Negotiation for the 21st Century*, (in Japanese, *Ishi Kettei Isutsu no Hosoku–Koshodo no Gokui*), *Piloting Through Chaos—The Explorer's Mind* (2013), *Laughing Heart—A Field Guide to Exuberant Vitality for All Ages—10 Essential Moves*; *Integral Resilience—Helping Communities Thrive*, and *5 Minutes to Resilience*, in addition to numerous articles on technology, economics and law. In 2019 Julian Gresser returned to the practice of international, environmental, and public interest law, and is today among a few attorneys in the world who are challenging the onslaught of radiation emitting wireless devices and the invasion of the Heavens by hundreds of low orbiting non-geostationary satellites. With hope of restoring balance and sanity, he co-founded the Broadband International Legal Action Network to accelerate practical solutions to these complex problems based on a new field of Big Heart Intelligence that he helped to originate.

tent.com/pod-product-compliance
e LLC
'A
30626
004B/1414